Butterfly Song

D1571291

A Battered Woman's Journey Back Into Life

Evelyn Dahlke

Plain View Press
P. O. 42255
Austin, TX 78704

plainviewpress.net
sb@plainviewpress.net
512-441-2452 (phone/fax)

ISBN: 978-1-891386-60-2
Library of Congress Number: 2007931788

Cover Art by Evelyn Dahlke, 2006.

Contents

With Gratitude

To all who helped bring this book from memory to memoir, I offer my heartfelt thanks:

To my writing class instructor, Mary Caroll Moore, and to my personal writing instructor and coach, Elizabeth Andrew of the Loft Literary Center. To Rochelle Melander, writing coach, who offered additional coaching expertise.

To those who read manuscripts as I wrote and for their critique and reviews—staff at the Domestic Abuse Project, particularly Dave Mathews, to Jan Bucher, my spiritual director, to Dianne Lockman and Dr. Janice Nadeau, therapists.

To Sandy Bauer for taking her time to proof read.

To members of my family and of my congregations for their praise and encouragement.

And, to my daughters, whose pain and stuggle is also given voice through this writing, for their patience and encouragement.

God bless you all!

for my daughters . . .

One: **Incinerating Shirley**

Shirley, a three foot tall walking doll, was made of a creamy-pink vinyl, which smelled sweetly scented when I held her. She had a powdery, rose-pink lipstick smile, and what looked like a touch of rouge on her cheeks just below her eyes. Her blue, glass eyes opened and closed as she stood or lay, the curling, life-like eyelashes sweeping up and back as she awoke or slept. Her silky, golden hair was tied up in a ponytail with a white ribbon. And her bangs were curled at her forehead in a stiffly permed sort of way. When I first saw her, she had on a light pink, linen dress with a white eye-let yoke and sleeves. She also wore white nylon stockings inside her shiny, black, vinyl shoes. A gold metal bow sat atop the front of the each shoe, making every step I took with her noticeable.

The really wonderful part about Shirley for me at the time was that she was so large. She actually fit into much of the "real people" clothes we girls had worn as toddlers. It was fun to dress her in the dresses and bib over-alls we had seen ourselves wear in the pictures my mother had pasted into one of the family albums. And, although my mother would only allow us to use the more washed-out articles of the clothing, Shirley had many changes of clothes and seemed as real to me as any doll could ever be.

When the times I took Shirley out for a walk were behind me, I dressed her again in the special, pink, Sunday dress and black, vinyl shoes with the gold, metal bow she had come in on that unforgettable Christmas Eve when I looked at her as an eight year old. I carefully laid her in the yel-lowed tissue paper of her box. I placed her on the top shelf of my bedroom closet. There she slept until I married in July, 1974, after I graduated from college. I then lifted her off the shelf and brought her, along with my other treasures and belongings, to the farmhouse which would be my new home. One special day a year and a half later, I carefully pulled her out of the box and left her gently nestled among the pillows on our bed.

Steady rain all day. It was May of 1976, and this day was like most of the others—dreary and wet. The farmyard, always a smeary mess in the spring, had gotten steadily worse. It was a challenge to get in and out of the house without leaving tracks or slipping and falling into the soup of dirt and water the rain left in its wake.

My husband and I had dairy cattle. Mud and dairy cattle definitely don't mix as the cows get infections from the mud, which cause both sickness, and milk that cannot be shipped to provide income and pay expenses. As I drove up to the house following my day at work, the car squished around in the smeary mud. If I sighted a straight line from the drive up to the yard, I faced the east barn door directly. That was the door from which the cows would pass as they entered the barn or left it to go out to the cow yard, the area in which cattle exercised and ate hay and fodder.

Although we were already a year and a half into our marriage, the cow yard was still as completely run down as it had been the day we moved onto the farm. Because of the rain, this spring the cow yard was an especially huge, sloppy mess. For decades manure from the cattle had been removed from the dirt of the yard. Along with the manure, much of the original soil had also been hauled away. This left the yard a large soup hole, basically unusable for cattle. Once I had to wade with bare feet and shorts through the muddy manure slop, thigh-high deep in the greenish-black slosh, to get an unwilling new mother cow so we could milk her.

On the day of the incident I found it strange as I proceeded up the drive that the east barn door stood wide open with our milking cattle wandering into and out of the door. This would make a huge cleanup necessary before Bob and I would be able to get to the evening milking. Since I was the one who had to do most of the cleaning, this scene concerned me immediately. I also remembered that we were planning to take part in a birthday party for my husband's aunt and uncle that evening, which also made me nervous.

Our dairy barn had reached a state of disrepair by the time we took over the farm. And although Bob had hope of restoring and improving it, we had not yet found a way to obtain the many thousands of dollars that such a project would require. Dairy cattle usually have small, drinking cups, which they can operate themselves when needed. Most of the drinking cups in this old barn were not in working order.

Earlier in spring, Bob and I had been hosing water into a pail from which each cow could individually drink. We would go down the two rows of stanchions holding twenty-some head of milking cattle. This was a tedious and time-consuming task, especially since each milking cow drinks several gallons of water a day. It was especially cumbersome for me since this was a chore above and beyond my full-time job in the small town some five miles away from where we lived.

Later, when the yard seemed to have dried out to a somewhat tolerable state for cattle, Bob and I placed a large, galvanized tank outside on a high area of land near the east door of the barn. We then allowed a few cows at a time to go out to drink until they were full, following this pattern so that each of the cows from the herd had a number of turns at the outside tank each day. We would then only pail the water to the cows after they had eaten their evening hay before bedtime. But we had only used the tank on good days, not on days such as this.

I quickly drove up to the house, changed into my chore clothes, and went outside to see what was up. I walked through the barn and milk room where the milking equipment and cooling tank were kept. I couldn't see my husband. I quickly scanned the calf barn and a few other areas where he might be. I checked if he was forking corn silage out of the silo for the cow's evening meal. I called several times as loud as I could. No answer. Although I felt some concern about where Bob was, I also knew that often he was working at something somewhere on the farm. He had always reappeared sooner or later.

Drenched from the rain and muddy from my trip from the farm yard, it was obvious to me that the cows were, at this point in time, doing nothing but making a mess. I began my feeding chores, putting the allotted amount of feed in front of each stall for the cow's evening meal. This I knew would bring them back into their stalls where I would tie them. Since dairy cattle are very set in their routine returning to the same stall each time they come into the barn, my plan worked. One by one the cows settled into their barn homes. I tied each into its place. I scraped the mud and manure out of the aisle. I then prepared the milking equipment for the evening milking chores. Returning to the house, I felt satisfied that I had done what was needed.

Once in the house, I took off my soaked clothing, throwing it in the laundry basket, and hung up my barn jacket to dry. I put on clean duds and began to figure out what I would make for supper.

I was searching through the freezer section of the refrigerator when I heard the door bang shut. Before I knew it, the freezer door had slammed into the side of my head, and I was being shoved fiercely along the cupboard, past the stove, and into the cupboard of the adjoining wall. I managed to keep my balance only to be pushed again to the side and through the dining room doorway. Everything was a blur. The stove and the cupboards were sliding by. The picture of the red, coffee pot surrounded by fruit, which I had painted in art class in college and had hung on my kitchen wall, was a smear of color. The circular, fluorescent light in the middle of the kitchen ceiling flashed intermittently as I opened and closed my eyelids.

I fell through the dining room door and felt myself hit the plastic runner that protected the carpeting between the china cupboard on the north wall and the sofa to my left hand side, a three-foot wide path that absorbed the bulk of travel from the kitchen to our downstairs bedroom and the bathroom up the stairway steps. For a time the pushing stopped, and I struggled for a gasp of air. My husband, the one who had so violently attacked me, had gone up the steps, I assumed to the bathroom. I was on my stomach as I lay there gasping. My clothing was wet from the wetness of his clothing and muddy from his wet, muddy hands and arms forcing me ahead and down.

When I caught my breath, I rolled to the side. Opening my eyes, the bottom drawer of the china cupboard was ahead of my face. I reached my hand up to grab one of the silver drawer handles in order to pull myself up.

Once again the force came upon me. Down I went on my back this time, just seeing enough to catch the outline of my husband's wet, dark, matted hair above me. He had an intense look of anger in his grayish-blue eyes, and his beard-covered jaw was set tight as he gritted his teeth. He had something in his hand—something large. I closed my eyes with the next blow.

Before I knew it, something—an object—was striking me. It was hard as it struck me, as was the force behind it. It struck me in the stomach once and then again! I curled up, trying to protect myself from what I knew was coming. Doing so exposed my right shoulder and hip. Again and again he thrust the object at me! Curling my face into the hole made by my arms, stomach, and legs, I tried to protect what parts of me I could. I could both hear and feel pieces of whatever my husband was hitting me with flying and landing. I felt a sharp edge hit my upper arm. Then came a blow to the side of my head. Then another. It seemed like the blows came for an eternity.

When I became aware of myself again, it was quiet. I lay there for a few minutes, eyes shut, hurting coming from my shoulder, my hip, my chest, my back. I was feeling a little wetness on the shirt covering my upper, right arm. I breathed slowly and quietly trying to decide if I was still alive or if this was some dark hell I had been transported to. I wiggled my finger, moving my hand at the wrist. It hurt when I moved it, but it did move when my mind told it to.

I gradually straightened a leg, hearing and feeling my socked foot swish the plastic runner under me. My left arm, the one on which I was lying, was asleep. I lifted my left shoulder slightly, feeling the circulation coming back into it. It had been stuck to the plastic surface of the runner. I moved it, and it freed itself, feeling a little moist.

I opened my eyes just a crack, fearing that doing more might bring on one big, final attack. Nothing. Quiet. I opened them further, enough to begin to see light. Time had elapsed. The room had darkened. The light of the day was dwindling behind the drapes. Still nothing. Opening my eyes I noticed first that the space in which I was lying and the area I could see from it were empty. I moved my right arm to begin to push myself up. It ached in the shoulder, and there was a burning along with the wet feeling of my shirt against my skin. I brought one leg around and then the other to get on my hands and knees in a crawling position. I was definitely sore around all the edges. But, relieved, I found myself still intact, all body parts moving and accounted for.

I inched myself to the end of the sofa, sliding on my hands and knees silently along the plastic runner. I could tell there were pieces of something on the floor around me, but I didn't try to identify them. I wanted to make sure my assailant—my husband—had left the room or the house.

When I reached the corner of the sofa, I peered around it into the space of the room as it was continuing to darken with evening setting in. The furniture stood silently in its formation. The curtains hung neatly in their positions. The newspaper was on the dining room table where it had been earlier when I had innocently come in from work and changed my clothes. A plant quietly cascaded from its etched, brown pot, suspended by macraméd cord in the bay window on the dining room's south wall. The phone, which hung on the wall, poised in its place beside the east window's curtain, had not rung in the span of time between my coming home and my crawling around the sofa corner. The sturdy, dark, oak frame, which surrounded the broad door between the living room and dining room, stood as gallantly as ever. The greenish-brown screen of the television reflected light from the kitchen. In its reflection I could see that there was no one in this room. Neither was there anyone in the kitchen, where the refrigerator was humming away. A quick analysis told me that the house was empty, and I was alone.

I gradually moved my sore and aching body into a standing position only to become aware that the pieces lying around me on the floor seemed to be a hard, pink vinyl of some sort. As I looked further, I noticed more than just pieces of vinyl. Beside where I had been lying, there was a pink, vinyl foot and part of a leg. Further over were some fingers and part of a shattered arm. Nearly five feet away lay an entire arm, a large arm—a doll arm! Dreading what I would see next, I turned toward the sofa to see, lying in front of it on the floor, the torso and head of the victim of the onslaught. Shirley! Shirley had been the weapon of choice that day as I unsuspectingly had searched through the freezer for supper.

Shirley's body, broken and mangled, lay beside the length of the sofa cushions. The foot was off of her right leg. The left leg shattered off above the knee. One arm was completely missing. The other hung from the socket, some chunks of vinyl broken off of it, fingerless. I took Shirley's body, or what was left of it, in my arms. I brought her head to my face and smoothed back the mess of hair that had once been her neat, blonde ponytail. Wiping mud, dirt, and blood from her face, I noticed her right eye no longer blinked when I lifted her. Her left eye was gone! It rolled around inside her hollow head like a marble. I closed my eyes and opened them slowly, looking again. Shirley had been destroyed bit by bit as he beat me. She had been both weapon and victim! How could I forgive myself for whatever I had done to make this beating happen! I held her tight, and I cried with a pain so deep the inside of my body hurt.

Soon becoming alert to the reality of the situation, that supper must soon be on the table, I laid what was left of Shirley on the couch cushions. I put supper on the stove. While it was cooking, I went upstairs to the storeroom closet, pulled out Shirley's box, and brought it down to the dining room. With the open box lying on the carpet, I carefully placed all the pieces of Shirley on the tissue paper of the box bottom. I then, ever so carefully, wrapped the remaining tissue up around the pieces. In a last silent motion, I tucked the box flaps up and into each other to secure the package and I carried the box up to the storeroom closet and placed it between the other boxes that were nestled there. I closed the closet door, walked out of the room, and down the stairs. I washed up at the sink, changed shirts, set the table, and finished preparing supper. As I did so, I felt nothing, absolutely nothing, except a stinging and soreness in the areas of my body which took the brunt of the beating.

When Bob came in to eat, he and I had supper together, went out to milk the cows, and went to the birthday party as planned. I wore a long-sleeved blouse that would not reveal my wounds. Not a word was said about Shirley or the episode. Not an "I'm sorry," not an explanation, nothing. As far as we were concerned, nothing out of the ordinary had occurred. Nothing had happened! Shirley was merely asleep in her box in the closet—just as she had always been. I made myself believe that. And my husband and I just kept on living—as we had always been as the days and weeks turned into years.

Several years later an inquisitive preschooler, our first born, was beginning to investigate throughout the house. I was determined that she should never know her father had beaten me breaking the doll in pieces.

On a warm spring day, I tiptoed past the room in which my sleeping toddler lay and moved slowly down the stairs. I carried Shirley's box through the kitchen doorway, across the farmyard, passing pieces of recently refurbished, greased, and readied machinery. "The grass is getting long," I thought to myself. "Soon I will need to mow it."

I followed the path that led past the woods and around the barbed wire of the calf yard fence my father-in-law and I had erected a few years before. Leaving the path behind, I began crossing the black, lumpy dirt of the field, which was adjacent to the burning fire. The plowed ground had a springtime moistness to it, which left V-shaped prints in the dirt and stuck to my green, rubber boots. But it held me up so as the trek to the designated area was not too difficult. With the tractor roaring in the distance, I could see my husband working some of the land behind the ditch bank, which ran diagonally through our farmland. In the light breeze, which brushed my cheeks, was the smell of freshly cultivated soil.

I crossed from one hump, which the plow had overturned the autumn before, to the next, not really thinking about the effort of it. Rather, I focused on the task at hand in a mechanical way.

Reaching the burning brush, I analyzed the best place to position the box without spilling its contents. I wanted a spot in which the entire box, along with every piece in it, would burn completely. There must be nothing left! Nothing! This job must be complete, and I would make sure of it.

Selecting just the right area, which I could reach without getting myself too close to the fire, I laid the box down on some paper sacks and dried leaves near the flames. Soon the flames were dancing through it. Gradually, the cardboard was disintegrating into a blackened armor. As the ashes of the box fell away, I could see that the pink vinyl had already begun to melt and was weeping into the burning branches. The flames turned bluish as it did so. The hair went up in one great, golden-black flash. I stood silently, seeing what was left of Shirley burn, but feeling absolutely nothing but an extreme emptiness inside. In time, all that was left to see was a piece of shiny, black vinyl with a gold, metal bow on top of it. Soon the black vinyl disappeared, and the gold bow fell into the flames.

I turned back towards the farmyard, walking the plow mounds to the calf yard, then followed the path along the calf yard fence past the woods. The birds were singing and cackling with each other in a playful manner. Yellow dandelions brightly marked the edge of the path. The fragrance of the blooming, lilac bush which stood gallantly in the cornered-edge of the lawn wafted into my nostrils. The sun, shining on my back, warmed me through my shirt. Otherwise, I felt and noticed nothing. Nothing at all!

I crossed the farmyard and followed the aged-gray sidewalk, which paraded up the three, broad, cement steps and old, red-painted, wooden porch leading to my kitchen door. I opened the door turning the round, golden knob, which I had patched into place with wood filler after Bob had blasted through it in anger one time earlier. I proceeded into the kitchen. Going in, I knew my young, sleeping child would soon be waking.

I took off my boots and sat them on the rug carefully, not wanting any of the fresh, black soil to drop on the linoleum floor. I washed my hands, arms, and face at the stainless steel, kitchen sink, barely glancing at my reflection in the mirror above it. I rinsed the soap bar of the gray grime, which had come off my hands, before setting it back in its gold, plastic holder. I wiped myself dry with the faded, gold, terry towel, which hung on the towel bar to the left of the sink. I threw a load of diapers into the washing machine in the pantry. Then I sat down on one of the padded, embossed-vinyl, chrome-legged chairs sitting beside the old, Formica, kitchen table. I studied the yellow gingham print of the tablecloth briefly, and then looked up. "This is a pretty kitchen," I thought as I admired the curtains I had made to match the mixer and toaster covers. The yellow in the print of the curtains matched perfectly the fresh coat of yellow I had painted on the walls shortly after my marriage. The curtains' red-trimmed borders with their eyelet accents looked perfect. "This is a pretty kitchen indeed," I thought as I waited for my precious little one to make her stirring noises.

As I reflect back through what seems like eons of time since the day of Shirley's incineration, I again see myself sitting calmly, placidly in my sunlight-filled kitchen. As if in sudden flight, I am flung back to the Christmas when Shirley came into my life, now nearly a half century ago. I remember holding her cheeks up to my face for the very first time and smelling that sweet fragrance, a combination of new, soft vinyl, combined with the fresh, wispy tissue and cardboard box she had been packed in. I suddenly see around me the sight of my sisters opening their boxes of life-size dolls, the smell of newness through the living room of the old farmhouse in which we grew up. Flames peeked up into the window of the great brown oil burner, which threw warmth throughout the room on that cold December Christmas Eve. I see my dad, sitting in his favorite rocking chair, clean-shaven, ready to attend the children's program at church, the smell of soap and deodorant still hanging in the air. My mother watching in the doorway leading to the kitchen. The giggles, and excitement, and glee of us girls, sitting in our flowered, flannel nightgowns in the middle of the old, maroon rug. The memory of dad's laughter. The flash of the old, black Kodak in my mother's hands. The lighted angel with real angel hair looking down from the top of the tree. The many-colored, bubble lights on the tree reflecting mystical beauty on the thin, long strands of tinsel we girls had hung so carefully on the many branches. There is childhood innocence in the room, and the feeling of being loved and cared for. The careless safety of being a child on that magical Christmas Eve. I remember Shirley's face once more.

Suddenly, into my memory comes such a feeling of deep pain, an aching in the very core of my being. I bring my hands to my chest to press it back to a distance at which I can bear it. I again feel the wetness of my bloodied shirt against my arm following the beating, which destroyed Shirley. Not only was Shirley taken from me that day. Part of my own life was also stolen—ripped away in a few moments time—that early, gray, spring afternoon as the fresh, green grass was poking its spindles through the wet, winter-pressed earth. A tear squeezes from my eye and passes slowly, meanderingly down my cheek—a tear of terrible sadness, of grief, of mourning. The tear turns to a flood of salty wetness I can smell and taste as it spills into my nostrils and lips. And then there comes, at last, relief

Two: **Pretty In Pink**

Lying flat, atop a dark, mahogany-wood shelf is a book to which I am drawn by a magnetism I can't deny. It is small and thick, and the edges and binding of its brown, cloth cover are grayed and worn. Grasping it gently between my fingertips, I lift it from the shelf, blowing the years of dusty mustiness from its cover, and carefully turn open its cover to find the pages yellow-edged and somewhat brittle. It suddenly becomes apparent why this particular book among the shelves and shelves of colored bindings has drawn me. It contains the beginning, the beginning of a story—my story—woven and tangled through time and memory, horror and pain. It is within these pages of living that I become ensnarled in chapters of life that plunge me into the core of my being and later lift me to a ethereal freedom that transcends the cares and worries of this life. In pages of this book I both lose and find myself. A certain smell wafts from the pages to my nostrils—not of dust, or even mustiness but the scent of springtime showers steaming from winter-weary pavement, a smell of birthing grasses and leaf buds warmed by springtime sunshine ready to burst. I am taken back, as if through a time tunnel, to a springtime so many years ago. It is to a springtime and an April evening in 1969.

That spring I was nearing the end of my sixteenth year, and life was opening up for me like a big, picture window full of opportunity. I was a junior in high school and was enjoying school that year like never before. I was in charge of my schedule and was participating in many extracurricular activities, both in school and outside of school. I was a straight A student, and the prospects for the next year and beyond were endless. Life was bliss.

Along with several of my classmates, I had recently earned my driver's license. Those being the days of the great, wide automobiles, on a nice, balmy, spring afternoon, several of us would pile into someone's hardtop Chevy, roll down the windows, turn up the radio, and enjoy life as only a teenager can do. The worries of life were minimal. The confines of childhood had lessened. In the '60's, if you had a few dollars, you could not only buy a few gallons of gasoline, but also a hamburger and malt at the local hangout.

My older sister, Lorraine, was away at college. This fact took much of the pressure of her bossing me around or getting her way with my mother, whose life seemed to revolve around Lorraine's talents and accomplishments, out of the picture. It was not that I didn't like her. I did, of course. She had been my lifeline in getting many of my basic needs met as a young child. She would speak up for me when it seemed I was not getting a fair shake at home or elsewhere. In some ways, since she was also a good student, she paved the way for me in getting on the good side of teachers in school, even though they did often call me by her name. She was outgoing and talented, in music especially! Her voice was like an angel, and her fingers whisked across the piano's keyboard to play tunes that I loved in an extraordinary way. Maybe I was jealous of that. Maybe I was jealous of her for claiming the attention of my mother. And then, maybe it was her ability to be outgoing and excellently articulate in every situation that bothered me. I was extremely introverted and always seemed to be following in her shadow.

But in 1969 with Lorraine away at college, in some small way I had finally come into my own. I was using my artistic talents at school, at church, and through my involvement in 4-H. Without Lorraine to speak for me, I was learning to take the initiative to speak for myself. I had discovered an ability to write and give speeches in high school declamation. I had won local contests and had gone on to regional and state competitions. I was continuing to be an excellent student and totally enjoyed my studies. The possibility of post-secondary education was before me, still safely in the distance, but still before me, as I was told I would be able to qualify for scholarship money if I kept up the good work.

As the spring of 1969 was nearing, we high school juniors were not only responsible for organizing the prom, but also were eligible to attend. As we moved into March, we were busy deciding how we would decorate and ordering crepe paper, balloons, and such. Because of my artistic abilities, I was selected to chair the prom decorating committee. I was thrilled!

Of course, at the same time, there was a buzzing among my classmates of who would go with whom to prom. There were some established couples by that time of our junior year, so there was no doubt that these pairs would be going with each other. Then there was the rest of us, with either endless or no possibilities of getting a date for the prom. I had been asked out a time or two before and had spent time with groups of gals and guys, but my dad hadn't been too eager for "us girls" to start dating too early. The magic number was "sixteen," and the dates had to meet dad's approval. The person could not be Roman Catholic (heaven forbid!), and had to come from a respected family in the community. Yet I was a quiet introvert, often left out of popular circles because of both my shyness and my intellect. So I was not holding out too many possibilities for a prom date—only dreaming that it might be so, as all young girls dream.

By early April matchmaking was in full swing. As the artist in the group, I think I actually was so busy planning the decorating, I wasn't thinking too seriously about a real date for me. But into my adolescent unconsciousness would come just that opportunity.

It came, as a complete surprise to me, between chemistry and English classes on April 1, 1969. A boy classmate of mine, a shy and quiet kind of guy, not at all popular nor particularly admired by his male classmates, asked me to the prom. We were hurrying between classes. The hallway was a rush of teenagers making their way from one class to another. Lockers were squeaking their way open and banging shut. Out of nowhere, I felt a poke on the shoulder, and in response, I looked around. Curly, blonde hair and a long narrow face met my glance. "Will you go with me to the prom?" was the question.

I stammered on the words, "I—I don't know."

It was an honest answer. He had caught me by such surprise, I really didn't know. Besides, classmates had told me that someone else had wanted to ask me, someone I had met in our Latin class. I had no idea that this person, nice as he seemed to be, was wanting to ask me as his date for the prom!

Needing to get from one end of the long hallway to the other, down a flight of stairs, and to my next classroom, and also feeling the pressure my classmates were putting on me to respond to this other date possibility, after what seemed an eternity, I finally blurted out, "I'll think about it." I hurried on my way, not looking back.

I was flustered, and the day passed slowly. Another guy friend convinced me not to respond to the first offer, to wait for the other person. So I gave the first suitor no reply during the rest of that school day.

That evening my school's chapter of the Future Homemakers of America was holding a fashion show in which we modeled garments we had made during the year either in Home Economics class or on our own. I was not a Home Economics student that year, but I had been sewing almost all of my own clothing by the time I was sixteen. I was anxious to show my work because of my involvement in the sewing project in 4-H.

By evening the tension was high. I was aware of my not giving an answer to my first suitor, who was watching in the audience. As well, I knew the guy, who I had been told wanted to ask me to the prom, was there along with a group of guys, who hung around together in my class. Into this tension and anticipation, the fashion show commenced.

It was raining as we girls arrived at school to get ready, that wonderful kind of refreshing spring rain which sends the smell of winter away and makes the world shiny with wonder. The sun was turning golden-orange as it was gently setting along the western horizon. The smell of the rain was warm and welcoming, not at all a rain one would rather hide from inside some building. The cars made cushing sounds as they drove up to the school doorway to let out girls who would be participating in the show.

It was the spring of Tiny Tim, and "Tiptoe Through The Tulips" was the theme selected for the evening extravaganza. The stage was set. Red-orange clay pots filled with artificial, plastic tulips and other spring flowers formed a garden in which we would stroll. Risers had been put up to form a runway going out perpendicular from center stage. "TIPTOE THROUGH THE TULIPS" was pinned in large, silver-glittered, light blue, construction paper letters across the tan, weighted, back curtain of the stage. A few lawn chairs and a garden swing had been brought in to add to the realism of the scene. The sound system was set up to play popular musical tunes in the background. Teenage girls were dressed in their special outfits, ready to model.

The crowd was gathering in the auditorium as the rows of beige, metal, folding chairs began filling up. People were chattering as they waited for start time, so there was a dull, humming sound, made up of their many voices blending together, within the massive, open space. Dressed in our modeling attire, the girls waited in the narrow, ceramic-block hallway off to stage left.

Of course, this particular fashion show had somehow become a big event for the junior and senior boys as well. Large groups of gangly, blue jean and tan panted, slightly whiskered, young guys congregated in sections of the audience. Perhaps this was their chance to choose the perfect girls as their prom dates.

I was ready, a bit nervous, and certainly excited, as the music began to play in the high-pitched, vibrato voice of Tiny Tim. The fashion show commenced, and we girls, well over one hundred in number, paraded in turn as we modeled dresses, aprons, skirts, tote bags, or whatever it was that our nimble fingers had produced. One of the guys in the senior class dressed with a long, dark-haired wig, held a cardboard guitar in hand. With the help of the sound system back stage, this "would be" Tiny Tim strummed out the infamous tune. We strutted among the tulip-lined paths, turning and stopping as we had been cued. For some girls, the groups of guys whistled or cheered or made some sound that said they were pleased with what they were seeing. The crowd clapped attentively. And once off stage with our turn behind us, we girls chatted with each other, and giggled, and had a wonderfully happy time.

It was afterwards in the crowded hallways as the audience disbursed into the showery, blue-black night, that this person, whom I had been cued would ask me to prom, actually did. I don't really know if he was cuter or nicer than the first person who had asked me. I know the peer pressure was high to say yes to the second suitor's invitation. So I did. I would have been laughed at for choosing the other guy. And heaven knows I was trying as hard as could be not to be just the artistic, intelligent nerd in the junior class! I gave in to the peer pressure. And to tell you the truth, I don't think I ever even had the decency to respond to my first admirer, who was waiting for an answer. He found out silently from afar. I glanced the direction of the first suitor at almost the same moment I said yes to the second. He silently shuffled through the back, orange, steel doors of the auditorium's wide hallway and disappeared into the night. I visited briefly with Bob, and soon we were joined by a crowd of friends chatting, carefree and cocky. Little did I know on this most innocent evening that this person, this Bob to whom I had just said yes, would become my husband.

The weeks leading up to prom were filled with excitement. Not only was there class work to keep up with, but there was decorating to be done. I also had to make decisions about my prom dress. I fell in love with a white-dotted, sheer-over-taffeta, full-skirted, flowing gown, which was accented with a wide band of pink just above my small waistline. The pink, leather shoes I ordered from the Montgomery Ward catalog, my older sister's above-the-elbow length gloves, and a pink bow in my brown hair completed my outfit. I was ready, anxious, and more than a bit nervous since this was my first real date.

I waited expectantly for Bob to find his way the fifteen miles from the farm where he lived with his parents to my family's farm. I peered periodically through the wide, dining room window, which gave me a clear view down the stretch of gravel-covered driveway leading from the main road to our farm. Butterflies fluttering in my stomach gave me a gleeful feeling of anticipation.

It was not the usual, bronze-colored '59 Olds that Bob drove daily to school that brought him to pick me up that night. He arrived in his dad's new '68 celery-green Impala with a black, vinyl roof. He was wearing a blue suit and dark tie. His hair was slicked back, almost glued into place with hair cream, and he smelled of fresh cologne.

After introductions inside the house and the pinning on of flowers at which time my mother embarrassingly took pictures, he escorted me to the car, opening and closing the wide passenger side door for me like the prince out of my Cinderella dreams. His elegant formality and his attentiveness to my enjoyment of the evening tore at my heartstrings.

Our prom date grew into a regular dating relationship. Summer came with vacation from the normal, day-to-day interaction we shared between classes or at lunch at school. Bob and I continued to go out on a regular basis. On long, balmy, summer evenings, we would go to the show, on a picnic with friends, or to a teen dance at the local community center, usually ending the evening with a long walk around the squared-out blocks of the small town where we shared our high school years.

Gradually, evening by evening, we learned more about one another—parents and family, likes and dislikes, whether or not we had enjoyed a movie or event we had just shared—the regular stuff young people talk about when they are just getting to know each other. Throughout this summer of young love and into and through the next school year, our senior year, I would watch for Bob's familiar, wide-seated, bronzed-colored sedan as it came over the hill on the paved, black highway near the gravel drive that led to my parent's farm place.

Sitting close to each other, we drove to our destination. I remember that the car was so wide, two other young lovers could have ridden in the front seat as well. Besides the car's extreme width, what I remember most about our driving together in this car was that, as the speedometer indicated we were speeding up, there was a bar of colored lights above it that would gradually change hue. I no longer remember the sequence of the color change, but I had learned that out on the open, county road without another car in sight, the light indicator would turn a bright purple as we sped swiftly along above 100 miles an hour. A hint of fear would crawl over me from head to toe as my date accelerated, but I wouldn't let my fear show. I didn't want to be considered a coward. Besides, I did like the change of colors as the acceleration increased. And the color of the purple speed indicator light was beautifully bright indeed!

Somewhere between the balm of the summer of 1969, the sharing of exciting experiences in our senior year in high school, and the sheer feeling of freedom as the speedometer light in that old Oldsmobile went through its spectrum of rainbow colors, I fell in love like only a seventeen-year-old can—the kind of love that is in love with itself, regardless of outside indicators that sounded a siren of concern. I had landed a boyfriend and a long-term relationship all in one. Our relationship soon became a thing in the eyes of our high school classmates. Little did I know my thoughts of us and our relationship were filled with childlike simplicity.

Our high school dates gave me no indication of what was to come. My future husband was polite and attentive, always arrived showered and smelling of English Leather or Old Spice. I would say, if anything, with me he was a bit shy, especially initially. He was courteous to my parents, sometimes nodding his head toward them in what seemed to me at times to be an overly attentive fashion.

There were a few things, however, that did seem odd to me. At school our lockers stood like narrow, tan, tin soldiers along both sides of the hallways, upstairs and downstairs, as far as the eyes could see. These lockers were assigned in alphabetical order by year in high school. As classmates shared lockers in proximity to one another, friendships among these small clusters of classmates were made. That was the case among those who found their locker near mine as well as among other clusters of lockers. Since Bob has a last name beginning with the letter D, his locker was far up the row but not out of sight of my W locker. On either side of his locker were two girls' lockers, so, of course, he initiated interactions with these two female classmates. I could say that these interactions bothered me because of natural, teenage jealousy. Maybe this is partly true. I think what bothered me more, however, was the way he interacted with them. The verbal comments seemed inappropriate to me. He teased these two girls terribly, about their hair, the way they walked, their interactions with other guys, and even the size of their breasts. I couldn't stand to watch this! I felt embarrassed for them. I felt embarrassed for him. I felt embarrassed for others who would see or hear this. And I felt embarrassed for me! At the time, I thought the problem was with me. "This is just jealousy," I thought. My lockermates did not have such interchanges with me.

As our senior year progressed, such interchanges not only increased, but they became more sexually inappropriate in nature. The girls responded in a teasing sort of way, but I know they didn't appreciate his words or actions because they would say so. When I mentioned to him how I felt about this he blew me off, saying I was a jealous bitch. I didn't bring up the subject again. Bob continued to ask me to go places, not them, so I figured it was just me, the over-jealous girlfriend. Never did I consider not going out with him anymore. Oh, no, I would never consider that! In the late '60's, a girl was nobody without a boyfriend—or so I thought. I was absolutely certain no other boy would want to ask me—a thin, gangly, practically breast-less, studious girl—out or so I thought. Besides, I had become Bob's gal, and was untouchable. I never thought that, if I did break up with him, someone might want to ask me out, that maybe I did have some special or endearing qualities, that maybe someone might find me attractive in some way, that not everyone ran the other way when a person who got good grades entered the room. I was smart enough to keep my mouth shut if I wanted this relationship to continue! And, believe me, I wanted this relationship to continue!

There had been a rough spot at Christmas that year as well. Always enjoying my family's Christmas celebration, I invited Bob to share Christmas Eve with us. After church services, as a family, we exchanged and opened gifts. We then enjoyed hot chili and Christmas goodies together. It was a time I really looked forward to. Although Bob couldn't make it to the church service, he did come over for the family celebration. He did seem unusually moody however. When I questioned him if something was wrong, he answered in an unpleasant tone, "Nothing!" As we began passing out and sharing gifts, he became even more sour. My attempts to find out what was the matter were to no avail as he completely shut me out of his emotional problem with rude comments. My family tried to ignore it, but soon he had me in tears. I went upstairs to regroup. My family scattered into the kitchen to serve up the chili and goodies. He sat sulking on the couch, not choosing to be part of the group and also not choosing to share with me what his problem was. He took his gift from me home with him without saying much of a goodbye.

The next day, when Bob picked me up to share Christmas with his family, he seemed to be his usual self and said nothing of the evening before. After the Christmas Day celebration with his family came to a close, I tried again to find out from him what had been wrong the evening before. He didn't want to talk about it. I assumed I had somehow ignored him in favor of celebrating with my family, or that there was something inherently wrong with the way my family celebrated Christmas Eve. Anyway, once Christmas was over, the problem seemed to go away. So I let it pass. I assumed that it must have been something I had done. After all, I was Bob's gal.

Another incident occurred in February of our senior year in high school. All students taking speech class were required to write an essay for the Voice of Democracy contest sponsored by the local veteran's group. Bob was not a speech student, but I was. The chosen winners were announced in front of the student body at a pep rally at the end of the school day. I won second place in that contest. Bob had been there to see the announcement. He went out of the gymnasium ahead of me and without speaking to me. Hearing me call him numerous times, he turned around and retorted angrily saying I had acted like I was going to win first place. Totally satisfied with my placement among several dozen contestants, I couldn't figure out what he meant. Certainly I hadn't acted in any superior way nor had I acted disappointed when I had placed second instead of first—or had I? I must have done something to make him think this. Certainly I had shown off in some way about getting the award that made him displeased with me. He went to his car in a huff, leaving me standing, bewildered, on the sidewalk by the school bus. It took a few days for him to act normally towards me again.

There was one aspect of our budding relationship during high school that, for me at least, cemented us together like glue. Bob clung to me many times as desperately as I clung to him. If he needed help with some aspect of schoolwork, I would help him out. This was particularly true in English and writing skills. He seemed unable to organize his thoughts and research notes into a coherent body to support the theme he was trying to defend. I was especially gifted in the use of words to portray thoughts and images so I would help him out. He also needed help organizing matching or appropriate clothing, and I could help him with that. He sometimes needed me to provide insight into a topic that seemed most obvious to me but eluded him, for example, to think and follow through with taking care of a real life problem. He needed me to help him organize his thoughts and figure out how to solve the problem. Organizational skills seemed to elude him. Bob especially needed to be reinforced and complimented on his thoughts and opinions. Often he would ask me to do so in almost a repetitive fashion. Although I cognitively perceived this repetitious parroting need, it was easy to comply, so I did it. In short Bob needed me. At that time of my life and in so many times since, I needed to be needed.

From the time I was a very young child, I never felt loved or accepted for who I was. I was an unplanned child, and although my mother stated that that fact did not make her not want me, her continual praise and adoration of my older sister clearly conveyed the message that I was just not good enough. I think my mother was dismayed by my shy personality. I clearly got the message that there was something wrong with me because I was older when I began to talk and definitely a more introverted child than my older sister.

After my younger sister was born, I was the middle daughter, sandwiched between an older sister, who seemed to do everything right, and a younger sister, who was loved for being the baby of the family. Also my mother suffered a severe post-partum depression after the birth of my younger sister. With my older sister away at school, I often was the target of her inability to cope or her being wrapped up in her own world. When she was hospitalized, I was dismayed at being stuck at Grandma's house with my older sister and separated from the baby, who stayed with a family friend.

I cannot remember being hugged, or held, or rocked—ever—by my mother. By the time I was five I had developed my own little world inside my mind. To escape the situation in the house, I would walk the long driveway from our farmyard to the mailbox and sit in the road ditch to wait for my older sister to come home with all of the exciting worksheets and art projects from her day at school. It was while I sat in the road ditch waiting for the school bus that I first intimately met God. Feeling rejected and abandoned at home, somewhere in the rays of sun touching the water trickling into the tile that passed under the driveway, a part of me felt the angelic presence of a God who loved me in spite of myself. God was sparkling and iridescent—like a beautiful and loving angel. We carried on conversations together in my mind.

Yet this God did not have the loving arms and face of a real person. So when Bob seemed to really love me *and* really need me, for the first time I felt that I was really wanted for who I was. His neediness, which I interpreted as love, and my need-to-be-needed fit together like a key in a lock. He and I, like key and lock, were made for each other. So certainly I had no need for concern.

Innocence Lost

When is innocence lost?
When a first word of unfriendliness is spoken?
When a hug is not given?
When criticism hangs heavily on your heart?
When is innocence lost?

When is innocence lost?
When youth meets youth
and blind love falls in love with need?
When disaster waits to make its visitation
on your heart, and soul, and body?
When need turns sour
and you become the target of someone lost in time?
When is innocence lost?

When is innocence lost?
When you let one disaster turn into two or three or more
without rebuking, retreating—fleeing?
When you join your heart
with clinging insecurity
and bear the brunt of
unleashed, unbridled brutality?
When unfairness reigns over reality?
When is innocence lost?

Or has innocence been lost so long before
you cannot even remember
there ever being a better, different way of being
because there never was one?
Because from the beginning you had to fight
for breath, for life, for love
in the midst of chaos and uncertainty.
Perhaps it is there, where "innocence"
was never allowed its own space of reality,
that it is lost—lost for all eternity.

April, 1999

Three: **Crossing A Line**

"Congratulations!" some of my classmates greeted me with early one warm May day as the cold days of winter passed into another spring filled with another prom and an upcoming graduation.

"What for?" I queried them as I took my assigned seat in study hall.

"You've been named co-salutatorian! Haven't you heard?"

As more classmates greeted me with the same congratulatory honor, I found the news to be true. Along with another classmate, I was to hold the academic honor among the one hundred and three graduates in the class of 1970 from our small, rural Minnesota town. This meant that we would wear the stoles of honor as well as speak at the graduation ceremonies to be held early in June.

Upon hearing the news, Bob told me that I, with my concentration in the social sciences, had taken easier courses than the other girl, who was more focused in the physical sciences. Thus, I had really won the honor unfairly and did not deserve it.

When my mother heard the news, her response was, "Well, your sister would have won that honor if there hadn't been more students in her class with higher academic scores than in yours." There was no "Congratulations!" or "You did a good job!" even though my GPA was higher than my older sister's had been. That fact did not really surprise me as it seemed I had always taken second place to Lorraine. In fact, by the time the day the honor was announced had come to an end, I believed deep in my heart that I did not deserve it. But the decision had been made, and, regardless of what I thought by day's end, I could not reverse it. I wrote my speech and gave it at graduation knowing that I didn't deserve the honor and that I shouldn't have been on stage at the podium that night.

With graduation ceremonies behind me, the summer days flowed into one another as warmth and work became the norm. I worked in a sewing factory that summer, sewing pile-lined, brown, corduroy coats, earning money for college in the fall. Bob worked for an agricultural plant, driving a spraying machine which applied herbicide to row crops, making twice as much as I did in my factory job. This didn't seem unusual. In 1970 most women were paid much less than men, even if they did the same work.

Bob and I worked long, hard hours and dated in between. Often he would be one or even two hours late for a date, saying that he needed to work until he had finished a particular spraying assignment and was not near a phone to call. I could accept that. I knew that jobs could be demanding. I had learned the importance of work, having grown up in a hard-working family of German ancestry, which prided itself on hard work, and also which was never financially very well off. And certainly there was no such thing as a cell phone in the summer of 1970! It never occurred to me that Bob might have called me when he did get off work to tell me he was still planning to come.

I assumed, because Bob had been accepted by a college, that he wanted to go. He would be going to the University of Minnesota/Morris in the fall. But although he didn't say so until later, Bob didn't really want to go to college. He wanted to be a farmer, taking over the family farm since his father was nearing retirement. College for Bob was his mother's dream. She said he was the smart one in the family and that going to college was important. Bob finally conceded to go when his father promised to run the farm until he graduated. Of course, I didn't know all these secrets until much later.

I was accepted as a member of the freshman class at Augsburg College in Minneapolis. It wasn't really by my choosing but rather by default. When I mentioned to my mother that I wanted to go to the Minneapolis School of Art and become a graphic designer, I could both hear and feel her disdain. "You have to go to school and learn something that you can earn money doing. After all, you never know, something might happen, and you might have to earn a living some day!" She was right about the earning a living part. I've been working all of my adult life. But the un-stated part of the comment was that there was no way I could earn a living doing graphic art. And, truthfully, that may have seemed true in rural Minnesota, which was the only source of information my mother had. I went to Augsburg because my sister went there, which was what my mother expected of me.

Why Bob chose the University of Minnesota/Morris out in mid-western, rural Minnesota, I don't know. We didn't talk about it. What I did know was that the coming of autumn would separate us in a way that both frightened me and seemed unimaginable. I had the distinct feeling inside that life would actually somehow end on Labor Day weekend. I could tolerate Bob's moods. I could tolerate his put-downs. I could tolerate him showing up late, or not showing up, for a date. What I could not tolerate was being separated from him. I needed him. Even if he wasn't consistent in his moods, I needed whatever positive reinforcement and feeling of being wanted I received from him. I had lost my innocent belief in the Cinderella tale, but I clung to Bob in my neediness.

When September came and I was required to start college three weeks earlier than Bob, it didn't occur to him that I would be lonely. Each day I would go to the mailboxes in the student union and check for a letter. Each day no letter would arrive. Of course, he didn't have time to write! I knew that! By this time in the autumn of 1970, he was working long hours and late nights at the canning company in our local town during its sweet corn pack. And, of course, he wouldn't call. He'd never been one to use the phone much. I found excuses for his failure to make contact with me to reassure me that we were still together even if we were, at the time, far apart.

The first letter from Bob came after he had started college. The whole letter was about a few girls he had met during orientation and what he, his new roommates, and these girls had done during breaks in the usual orientation routine. I was as devastated as any young woman would be when it appears that her steady boyfriend is wandering.

We saw each other once every few weeks throughout the year. I wrote almost daily. He wrote almost not at all. Infrequent telephone calls often ended in quarreling over his partying, drinking too much, not finishing waiting projects, and failing calculus, which led to the demise of his hopes of a mathematics major. I knew this situation could not go on, so I decided to transfer to his college after my freshman year. Never did we consider that Bob might be the one to transfer. No, I would be the one to follow him. And I did.

Actually, the transfer went smoothly and was a wonderful, new opportunity for me. I loved the campus and the atmosphere of the new school. I had a wonderful roommate, Mary, with whom I shared living space for the three years I was there. And, since the tuition was less than the college I had been attending, I didn't have to put in as much work/study time. I, too, had time to party. And I did. I partied right along with Bob—at least partly. My classes in English and art, the two fields I had chosen as my majors, required more study, writing, and lab time than Bob's political science and sociology majors. Sometimes I needed to stay home to get my required work done. I was receiving academic scholarships so my work needed to show academic excellence. And it did. I had a 3.999 grade point average throughout my college career.

Of course, Bob continued to deny my academic abilities, although never when anyone else could hear. In fact, around other people he sometimes even bragged about me. In private he called me a spoil sport. Peer pressure did influence me, so more than once I was among the crowd celebrating with kegs of beer at the dam near the college campus. And whether or not

I initially wanted to take part, I joined in with the crowd and went out there anyway. This pleased Bob and kept our relationship intact.

By the time Bob and I reached our junior year in college, we seemed to settle into a routine of normalcy with each other and with our required course work. Bob continued with his major in political science and sociology. I gave up an English major in favor of elementary education. Bob made no secret of the fact that after college he wanted to go back to the farm. By then there wasn't really a question of whether or not we would be together after college. If we were going to be tied to his parents' farm, I would need to prepare for a teaching position. Elementary education would broaden the scope as schools hire many more elementary teachers than English or art teachers.

In the 1970's the schools near the farm had dropped art education in an effort to balance their budgets. I enjoyed teaching, so all was not lost. I did tutorial teaching in the second grade at St. Margaret's, a private Catholic elementary school and in the Headstart program in the county where the college was located. I later did my student teaching in the public elementary school in that town. I loved teaching the kids. I had so many opportunities to be creative and artistic, the job seemed suited to me perfectly. It had been a good decision after all!

Bob, I, and several other college friends lived on a co-ed floor in one of the dormitories on the university's campus. Several of the people had been living on that floor ever since coming as freshmen and knew each other well. We liked our fellow living-mates and often attended activities on campus as a group.

On one winter evening in February, I walked alone back to the dorm, having finished a work/study session, which consisted of typing a book for a sociology professor. The task was tedious to say the least, typing on one of those old-style, electric typewriters about some human settlement thousands of years ago. Going outside into the fresh, crisp air was a welcomed relief to my bogged-down mind. The weather outside was warm for February, probably in the high 20's. The campus was quiet with an occasional student passing from one hall to another or down to Louie's, the campus' hamburger joint. Large snowflakes drifted slowly through the black sky around me. They flittered past the large, white-globed streetlamps, which lined the paths from cement and brick instruction halls to the residence halls along the way. They were like dancing spotlights in an ice show. The flakes sparkled many colors in the rays of artificial, evening light. I enjoyed the silence of the snowflakes, silently, gracefully finding their way to a bank of snow, a frozen sidewalk, a tree branch, or a street lamp. I took my time, enjoying the freshness coming into my head.

When I arrived on the dorm floor, several dormmates were in the lounge clearing their heads from the heaviness of the daily grind. The lounge was often an evening or weekend gathering place, and Bob was already among the lounge group since his classes took up less hours of his time, and he didn't have a work/study assignment. The group was shooting the breeze in a way only college kids can do. After I arrived at my room and put down my book bag, which held the required textbooks and notes from the day's lectures, I too joined the group in the lounge. By then it was after nine o'clock.

One of the girls on the floor, Cathy, was very shy and sophisticated in a way that often separated her from the rest of the crowd. I had grown to know her through private conversations. She talked of a boyfriend she had at another college, that she was studying to become a nurse, and planned to marry this boyfriend after they each had finished their college careers. She seemed like a very nice person, and I enjoyed our in-depth conversations. The interactions between us were not the usual, more superficial, joking kinds of conversations most common in the lounge. In fact, she rarely spent time in the lounge, at times giving the guys on the floor the impression that maybe she thought she was too good for them. When I got to know her more deeply, I found this wasn't true. She was introverted, studious, and focused on her purpose for being in school—to get her education. She was not unfriendly, just directed, and didn't enjoy the larger group interactions. Bob had occasionally met her in the hallway, lounge, or kitchen area and had had some verbal interactions with her at those times. But his conversation often turned to teasing, not just a little, but sometimes quite a bit as he got carried away and made some rather crude comments. Considering Cathy was the type of person she was and liking her as I did, the inappropriate assertions troubled me, but I had remained silent about them.

On this particular evening as she passed through the lounge, the guys tried to pull her into the group by making some comment that would get her to respond. She stopped briefly before going on her way. But it was when she tried to walk away and Bob moved in on her that I got upset. He continued the teasing, "What's the matter, Cathy, you think you're too good for us? What's so great about that boyfriend of yours anyway? Come and sit down on the couch with us. There are lots of guys out here for you. Come on. You look like you could use a hug. Come on. Let me give you a hug," as he reached out to grab her. I could feel how flustered and irritated Cathy was becoming as she was trying to get past him to escape into her room. He continued as he followed her into the hallway towards her dorm room. "Who is this guy anyway, that he's so special. You could at least have a little fun with the rest of the guys on the floor. Still thinking about the great sex you had this weekend? What do you think you are—a queen or something?" Cathy ducked to avoid his outstretched arms before slipping into her room and closing the door. He would have followed her had she not locked the door behind her. The people in the lounge were quiet. I was embarrassed for Bob, feeling what he should have been feeling—ashamed of his actions! Yet he seemed totally oblivious to Cathy's feelings or to the reactions of the rest of us in the lounge. He came back and kept on joking and laughing as if he had done nothing wrong.

I left the lounge area and went back to my room. Bob followed me there and closed the door behind him. We were in the room alone since Mary had gone to the gym. He tried to make sexual advances towards me, and believe me, I was not in any kind of mood to be near him. He criticized me for leaving the lounge. When I tried to open a book to read an assignment, he criticized me for studying too much. He told me to lighten up and have fun. I then pointed out to him how hurt I knew Cathy was by what he had said and done to her. We stood facing each other in front of two desks with the long, fluorescent tube lights above them. I turned away from him to the side to get out one of my books. "You jealous bitch--!" was all I remember hearing as the power of his fists in my ribs whipped me onto the bed. He continued striking me in the stomach and ribs and over the right shoulder. There was a fierceness in his eyes I had seldom seen before, but which would grow to be the most familiar of sights as years went by. His jaw was set tight.

When the outbreak of physical violence was over, he just stood over me, looking down at me like he didn't know what had just happened to bring me down. Moving slowly, I tried to lift myself up from the bed. I definitely hurt, and as I moved, there was a jabbing pain in my lower left rib area. I was having trouble breathing, as well as moving, because of the pain. As I half lay and half sat on the edge of the bed gasping for air, I didn't feel anything emotionally except perhaps confusion. I wasn't surprised. I wasn't angry. I wasn't sad. I didn't question his motives or shout at him to get out of my life. I didn't even think he was wrong to do such a thing. I remember thinking that I was wrong to have pushed him so on the subject. Like always, I was to blame. I was stubborn, thick-headed, and certainly second rate. I knew it. I deserved the beating.

After what seemed a long time, Bob started talking to me calmly and quietly as if nothing had happened. I moved slowly from the bed's edge and tried to sit down at my desk to study, but the pain in my rib was too great. It hurt when I sat. It hurt when I lay down on my bed. I took two aspirin, and it still hurt. It seemed like the hurting was getting worse. Finally, I told Bob that I thought I needed to go to the doctor.

Since by then it was about eleven at night, the campus health service was closed. I would have to go to the emergency room at the hospital downtown. I didn't have a car. Bob did. Slowly and cautiously so as not to disturb the hurting rib, I got into the car with Bob's help. He drove me to the emergency room for the X-ray. The rib was separated the doctor reported. "How did this happen?" he asked.

I lied, "One of the guys came down with his elbow into my rib while we were playing basketball tonight." I was too ashamed to tell him the truth.

The doctor looked at me for what seemed to be an eternity not saying anything. I felt like he was reading my mind, and that he knew I was lying through my teeth. But he said nothing. He gave me an elastic bandage to wear around my mid-section, which really made the terrible aching not quite so bad. Bob, who was waiting just outside the doctor's office and had heard what I had told the doctor, took me back home to my room not saying a word.

The next noon when I returned to my dorm room following my morning classes, there was a bouquet of red, pink, and white carnations with some fine, white babies breath sitting on the shelf above my desk. I remember the fuzzy, red, heart-shaped, pipe cleaner that stuck in among the small cluster of flowers. It was from Bob with love. "Yes, it's February eleventh and almost Valentine's Day," I thought as I observed the Valentine arrangement.

When my dad received the bill from the hospital and the insurance statement, I told him the same story I had told the doctor. He believed me. Bob, who was standing next to me and knew the truth, said nothing. And by that time I believed the story to be true myself.

The rib-breaking incident was the first serious physical offense Bob inflicted on me in the four years that we had been dating. Yes, he had at times given a push here or there, or he had taken my jaw in his large hand and squeezed it hard when I had inadvertently said something that Bob deemed wrong. And there had been an occasional twist of the wrist when I gave him "that look"—that look that he hated from me, which said that I didn't agree with what he was doing or saying, or with his actions in some way.

The second painfully physical offense at that time came when we were college seniors. It was winter quarter, Bob's last quarter in college. He was happy-go-lucky that quarter as all the really hard studying was behind him.

He was looking forward to being out of school and back at the farm in time for spring planting. I, on the other hand, was in the middle of student teaching. I was not only busy creating lesson plans, but I was also spending my days in classrooms filled with active and noisy children and having a constant flow of evaluations by supervising teachers and college professors. I also had much preparatory work to do each evening.

In addition to all this, I had also been writing and typing Bob's papers throughout our college time together in exchange for him giving me rides for home trips. "You owe me," he repeatedly said. Paying back my debt for the rides and trying to keep up with my own required assignments and duties as a student teacher was difficult. And although Bob was kind enough to give me rides to the school each morning in the freezing, winter weather of my required student teaching, he continued to expect his papers done as usual in return. He also expected me to go with him at times when a group of peers were going out to party. And he expected me to have a good time.

One wintry evening, I refused to go to the bar when he told me we were going. I had work to do, and tomorrow morning would come early! He shoved me into the wall hard enough for me to know that, yes indeed, I would be accompanying him to the bar. He grabbed my coat and shoved it into my face. As we got out onto the frosty sidewalk, he took hold of my hand to drag me along because I wasn't walking fast enough. He was getting behind the group! As he did so, he twisted the little finger of my right hand. The twisting grasp was so hard and so tight that he broke the finger. It ached dully all evening and through the night. When I really looked closely at it the next morning as I readied myself for another day in kindergarten, the finger bent inwards at the top knuckle. It was black, green, and blue, swollen, and extremely sore. I bandaged it so it wouldn't show, and, throughout the day, told questioners that I had fallen on the frosty sidewalk the evening before. I was ashamed that I had once again made Bob angry with me. By this time I didn't question my own fault. I had gradually and completely been brainwashed into believing what Bob told me about the incidents. And, because I had not developed a strong self-image as a child, I could not fight against his strong assertions. It had been made clear to me that I was not to come home to live after college. I needed a husband to provide a home for me. Bob would be that person. These messages from my parents and within my own thought system kept me captive both to Bob and to the abuse.

As I played the three cords on the piano to draw the kindergarten children's attention to sharing time, I could hardly strike the third key. I nearly choked with pain. It took months for the pain to disappear. The finger is bent and the knuckle enlarged today. It is a constant reminder of that night and that incident.

Neither Bob nor I ever said another word to each other or anyone else about the broken finger. Our relationship continued as it had for nearly five years. After all, I was wearing a diamond ring by this time, and certainly the truth would have humiliated me. Besides, wedding plans were in progress. We were to be married in July following college graduation. What would people think if I changed my mind now? No, I couldn't even consider the possibility! It never occurred to me that I should be afraid of Bob. After all, I thought, after we are married I will show him how to love by my love for him. Didn't I grow up to believe in the Cinderella fairytale? But even as Bob's behavior confused me, and as I pushed it into my subconscious, I can remember feeling the shame of it. In fact, sometimes shame ate me alive! No one must ever know the truth, I thought! Besides, who would I be without a man? Bob and I were married in July as planned.

As I write this, I look at the crooked finger. It is now a permanent part of me. Once in a while I feel a twinge of the lower, left rib as well. The finger and the rib are just two among many painful, crooked remembrances I have of the time I spent with Bob. But I am no longer held captive by him or my own self-denigrating thoughts. And I know now many things that I didn't know then: I can live by myself and provide for myself. I am doing both. I also know that a woman can survive without a man. I know that no violence or abuse, either verbal or physical, is acceptable, that I did not deserve to be hurt, and that a person can become so brainwashed that reason and judgment fall away. I know now that one person cannot love another person into responsible, acceptable, and loving behavior. But it is, as Helen Reddy asserts in one of her '70's songs, "wisdom born of pain."

Loneliness

Loneliness is
the place you find yourself
when the walls scream of fresh paint
instead of telling family tales,
the pictures hang silent
as if stopped by time and space,
disconnected,
the floors, all scrubbed and waxed,
contain no friendly footsteps
to tell you that you belong.
And instead of inviting you in,
the rooms ooze thick
of emptiness
and silent echo.
When no loving hug
comes walking through the door,
and the garden plants
in all their rows of neatness
blow empty in the prairie wind.
Loneliness is
when terror and fear
along with drudgery
come to sleep
in your bed,
creeping under your covers
with chilly detachment.
Loneliness is
when crows in the distance
crowd out the singing of songbirds
in your heart.
Uncaring, unloving,
unfriendly, unoccupied space—
that is where loneliness
comes to make her home.

July 1996

Psalm 121
Assurance of God's Protection

A Song of Ascents

I lift my eyes to the hills,
   from where will my help come,
My help comes from the LORD,
   who made heaven and earth.

He will not let your foot be moved;
   he who keeps you will not slumber.
He who keeps Israel
   will neither slumber nor sleep.

The LORD is your keeper,
   the LORD is your shade at your right
hand.
The sun shall not strike you by day,
   nor the moon by night.

The LORD will keep you from all evil;
   he will keep your life.
The LORD will keep
   your going out and your coming in
   from this time on and forevermore.

Four: For Better Or Worse

Lonely is the word I would use to describe the first few months of married life. After having lived with a family and then with college friends, I now found myself alone in the farmhouse that Bob's parents had vacated the week before our wedding.

Summer of 1974 came with a vengeance. The spring had been cold and wet which had delayed Bob getting the crops planted for his first season of total responsibility in farming his father's land. The summer was extremely hot, windy, and dry. Our wedding day boasted 105 degrees. And the brief thunderstorm which came through the area in the early evening was a most welcome relief.

The havoc caused by turbulent weather resulted in Bob being overwhelmed by farm work. We didn't have a honeymoon because we couldn't afford it. Bob no longer needed to go out with me because we were married. I didn't see much of Bob or anyone else unless he needed help fixing a piece of machinery. The reason he gave after the marriage ceremony for bothering to show up at the wedding was to have sex. Driving into town to see other people or have some companionship was a waste of gas and unnecessary wear-and-tear on the car. Besides, within a few weeks of the wedding, I was entrenched in the farm's unforgiving schedule—morning milking, walking the fields to remove weeds, feeding cattle, and making sure the cattle's water tank was filled regularly.

When I began my teaching job in September, my outside chore schedule didn't change. I was just adding a workday off the farm to the hours I was already putting in on the farm. "It's okay," I thought. After all, I had grown up on a farm so the style of life was not entirely new to me, although my mother and we sisters had never played a large part in the actual farming operation and no role in the cattle regimen. Although the farm environment was familiar to me, I was not prepared for the demands Bob continuously put on me. When I baulked at the load of work, he pointed out to me all of the neighbor women, who were doing the same kinds of tasks he was requiring me to do. He even cited a neighbor's wife, whom he claimed gave birth to one of the couple's children in the morning and was out feeding the cattle silage that evening. His father had told him that story over and over again.

So I followed Bob's demands without much more fuss. After all, I did know that if we were going to make a go of this farming business and get financially established, it would require devotion to the task.

Yet I thought, "These other farm women don't have jobs off the farm as well!"

And I did point out to Bob that the woman who fed the silage the same day she gave birth had a good-for-nothing, alcoholic husband!

"Who knows," I added, "it might have just been a tale." He denied that possibility emphatically. In order to avoid further confrontation, I didn't say anymore about it. I will never really know the truth. Regardless, that kind of expectation is not one a loving spouse would demand of his partner.

In the meantime, Bob took most of our wedding gift money to the farm implement dealership to make a payment on the tractor he had purchased in the spring. It did seem a little unfair I thought. But after all, he needed the tractor to run the farm. And there would be money later for household needs.

In time the demanding schedule became so routine that one day when a co-worker asked me how I could possibly keep up with the demands at both work and home, I simply responded that, "It's like there's a frame on each side of my teaching day. I don't think about it anymore." And I didn't think about it.

Following the wet, cold spring, and the hot, dry summer, frost came to the crops on the fourth of September that first year of our marriage. The corn and beans were not nearly mature. The frost forced an early filling of the silo. The amount of feed, which could be preserved over winter for the cattle, was reduced. Bob was devastated, and I didn't feel too good about the entire situation either. Our first year of farming, even with all the hard work, was basically a failure. Oh, it was not a failure on our part! We had done our part in taking care of the farm and raising the crops. But the weather hadn't done its part! Little did I know that the weather would continue to wreak havoc with Bob's farming occupation and, in turn, with our relationship. In the final picture the weather along with the farm's ever-demanding schedule would be a contributing factor to the abusive nature of our marriage.

When the weather was foul, Bob was foul. He broke out in angry fits on many occasions: when it rained too much or too little, when the sun didn't shine when he needed to make hay, when it rained when he had cut alfalfa and was waiting for it to dry in order to bale it for fodder for the cows. He cursed when storms would come up and hail on the crops or flatten them to the ground by furious winds. Finally, he decided that I was a witch. There had never been such storms over this farm until I had moved onto it! I had brought all the bad weather my family had experienced on my dad's farm to this farm! I listened to him, and I believed him.

Bob was easily and extraordinarily angered by broken machinery as well. Since most of our machinery was "well-used", he was angered at the machinery quite often. He was angered by cattle when they continuously broke through the dilapidated fences of the cow yard and pasture, which, by the way, he told me soon after our marriage, he didn't do meaning that he didn't build, repair or otherwise maintain fences even though fences are necessary if one is going to have cattle. He was angered by milking cows, which became ill, failed to get bred, didn't eat as they should, or didn't produce as much milk as he thought they should. He was also angered by calves that were either stillborn, born weak, or born too early to survive or thrive. Since I was given all calf chore duties (even though I had never raised a calf in my life), it was my fault when the calves had problems. I was not taking care of them properly. I was a calf killer. "Calf killer! Calf killer!" Bob would holler at me over and over again. I killed the calves that died. In fact, I was responsible for all the misfortunes we experienced while we farmed together. Bob told me so. And I believed him.

Why did I believe such incredulous nonsense? After all, one of my therapists asked me, "Do you hold power over life and death?" All I can say is that feeling dependent on Bob (since he told me constantly that I could not live on my own), and being in love with Bob, who also on the other hand abused me verbally, emotionally, and physically, took all rationality out of my thinking. I was unable to think beyond trying to stay out of the way of a swinging fist, a flying wrench, or an onslaught of verbal put-downs. By constantly deriding and discrediting my abilities, Bob ate away at both my self-esteem and my personhood. Gradually, he brainwashed me into believing against all rationality that what he said and did was always right. Like a prisoner of war or a person in a concentration camp, I did what I was told, I believed what I was told, and the I part of me simply ceased to exist.

The situation of abuse was further exacerbated by my work schedule, which often didn't suit Bob's moods either. He broke out in fits often: when I came home too late from work, when I was at work when he needed a helping hand fixing machinery, when I could not get out of work when he wanted me to come home to help him bale hay, when I worked overtime for special meetings or workshops, when I needed to get to work on time and he wanted me to stay home a little longer in the morning to help with an errand, run to the implement dealer for a machinery part, or just to have sex after breakfast.

There were other situations that aroused Bob's anger as well. He became angry when supper was not ready at the time he deemed he was ready to eat it, when supper was accidentally overcooked or undercooked because I had been out helping him instead of in the kitchen when I needed to be. He became angry when I called him to come home for supper and he didn't feel like quitting what he was in the middle of doing. "Don't you know it's going to rain over night, and I need to finish cultivating those last rows of corn!"

I didn't do the actual milking of the dairy cows those first years of our marriage, so he always became angry when he had to either quit what he was doing on the field to milk the cows or milk the cows late, which he constantly reminded me would ruin them. He never gave up thinking that I should do the milking chores when he was otherwise occupied. The cows usually wouldn't cooperate for me to milk them. And I was afraid of their kicking me. Although through the years I did become comfortable around the cows, I never did get over my fear of being kicked, especially in the milking process when my head and face were so near their feet and hooves. And I know they didn't get over their tendency to want to kick me as I would apprehensively put on a milking machine now and then. The cows were accustomed to being milked by Bob, and although it might have been a simple but time-consuming task for him, to me it was extremely frightful.

When Bob became angry, he became mean. Anything could fly, and it did! The first object to fly through my kitchen soon after our wedding was a drinking glass. It passed violently right out of his hand, against the south wall of the kitchen, and landed in pieces on the floor. Not long after, the flying object was a pork chop with barbeque sauce on it. It hit the kitchen wall near the ceiling above the doorway going into the dining room. Later, I would be the one on a kitchen chair removing the barbeque sauce that had splattered on my newly painted, yellow wall and freshly whitened ceiling. When I questioned him, he told me, "My mother always threw things!" Although I thought it strange since I had never experienced this while I was growing up, I said nothing. In fact, I did more than say nothing. I thought my dad to be a strange person for not having fits of anger like Bob had. I thought my family strange for not throwing things in anger. Why did I believe Bob to be right and my family strange? I can't explain it except to say that Bob had such a tight hold on me by that time I was irrational.

Not long after the glass and pork chop incidents, when Bob was angry at a broken piece of machinery and at me for not noticing that he needed help outside, he hurled a wrench into the door of the new, harvest-gold refrigerator my parents had given us as a wedding present. It both made a dent and scratched off the paint of the smooth, shiny door. Some time later at the hardware store, I bought a small bottle of appliance paint to fix the problem. Later when my parents and others asked how the refrigerator door got dented, I told them that I had accidentally struck it with a wrench I was carrying when I turned around too quickly. Once everyone who ever came to our house (which wasn't very many people) had received an answer to the query, the dent was just a dent year after year. There were no more questions. Twenty-nine years later, it is still there.

One day Bob was angry because by accident I had over-fried his breakfast eggs. In order to save time, I had put the eggs in the frying pan on the stove and gone into the bedroom to get ready for work. I must have set the heat of the burner a little high or else it took me too long to figure out what I wanted to wear because the butter that I fried the eggs in had formed a crisp, black edge around the white circles the eggs made in the pan. When Bob came in after finishing the morning milking chores, he threw the eggs, the plate, and the fork across the room. He threw the fork with such force that it cut an indention in the chrome trim around the oven window of the stove.

There was another incident that involved a broken cultivator during those early years, Bob was trying to get a bolt loose. He tried. And he hollered. And he swore. And although I had come out of the house at the sound of his bellowing, I really couldn't be of much help. Before I knew it, he whipped a large, steel wrench at me. It hit me in the left knee, taking some of the skin with it. He made no apology. Later I iced and tenderly babied my scabbed, swollen, black, green, and blue knee. But since I usually wore slacks to work, aside from my limping, the injury didn't show. I never told anyone the truth of why I was fairly one-legged through that week.

Another time I wanted to go to a ladies' circle meeting at church. We were in the middle of some farm-related work at the time that I needed to get going. It angered Bob that I had to leave when I did. While I was in the house washing up and changing clothes, he was feeding cattle using our bucket tractor. When I had readied myself for the meeting, I started down the driveway in the car, the car Bob had received from his parents when he started college. He had driven it proudly throughout our college days since he was among just a few college students who could brag of having such a vehicle. We now shared it as a couple. He said I came to him with nothing but debt, not even a car.

As I was coming around the curve by the garage to leave the farmyard, Bob was just coming up the field road along the cow yard fence. Since he was still furious that I was determined to go even though he didn't want me to, he rushed towards the car with the tractor and lowered the bucket, denting the smooth, velvety, black-vinyl top. Of course, I never attended the ladies' circle meeting that evening. I also didn't repair the dent in the top of the car. This time he did the clean up work.

Finally, of course, there was the incident with Shirley. Although I didn't cognitively realize her importance to me until she was destroyed, she represented love from my parents for me. She was a reminder of a warm, childhood Christmas. She also represented some level of equality with my sister in my mother's eyes since Lorraine and I both received the same kind of doll. It is little wonder that the Shirley incident was, among the many episodes, the most lethal for me!

Throughout the early years of our marriage, I heard often about how inept I was, how stupid I was, how I wasn't making enough money at my job, how I needed Bob because I would never be able to support myself, and how "tight" my parents were for not giving us some money or doing more tasks around our farm without pay. If I ever felt like arguing, I don't remember it. I believed him and even agreed with him when he required me to respond to his comments in an agreeable manner, although at first there were times when I would seem to burn inside as I did so. But I knew if I said a word of protest I would be severely punished and our day would be ruined. Soon I no longer even felt the protest from within. I began to believe that what Bob said was right, and his cruel actions no longer seemed strange to me. They were just a part of ordinary, everyday life.

If there was any part of my life on the farm in which I found release, it was in the farm's inherent beauty when it had been mowed and cared for. A quiet walk along the ditchbank that ran through our land, a walk through the young trees of the windbreak we had planted, or time in my large garden with the vegetables sleeping silently in their neat rows with clean, black dirt surrounding them on either side—the tiny little plants growing against the prairie breezes—lifted my soul. To go out and pick fresh, juicy, green peas to go along with a few early, red potatoes for supper was heavenly. As I would work the quiet hours in the garden all these thoughts of the difficulty of my life with Bob on the farm would churn alongside the songs of the Psalmist: "To you, O Lord, I lift up my soul . . .turn to me for I am lonely and afflicted" (Psalm 25). The sunlight would glisten from the wet, leathery leaves of the cucumbers and squash, and I knew God must surely be hearing me.

One would think that it would have been impossible to live in these circumstances for weeks or months, much less years. I shoved all thinking away when shame, or guilt, or disagreement, or maybe even anger would creep in. And I could do so because we also had many good times in between the situations of abuse. We were both very hard workers and very directed in our goals—I thinking at the time that one of my goals was the future success of the farm. What loving wife wouldn't want her husband to succeed?

We also enjoyed some fun times together. Bob had a nephew, David, who was just five years younger than we were. He would often come over, not only to help with farm work, but just to shoot the breeze, laugh and joke. He was like a brother to my husband since Bob's mother had been his babysitter when the two boys were growing up.

The first few summers after we were married, Bob played softball at a local ball field with a group of guys whose team was sponsored by his brother-in law's business. David was a player on that team, as were many other male friends. Although I wasn't much of a sports fan, I enjoyed being out in the park where the ball field was located. I enjoyed conversing with the other young wives whose husbands played on the same or opposing teams. I enjoyed the picnics and parties that went along with participation on the team. And I enjoyed David's presence at our place. The relationship was life-giving for Bob and also provided enjoyable company for me.

Both Bob and I were devastated when David was killed in a forklift accident at the age of eighteen, just ten days after his high school graduation. I know that this reality hit Bob very hard. The summer of 1975, we both missed David terribly. I even sometimes felt his spiritual presence with me as I mowed the lawn under the trees on an evening when he would have probably been visiting had he still been alive. David's death soured Bob's emotions in a way that affected him for many years afterwards.

The demands of the farm were never-ending, and, in over twenty years of marriage, Bob and I never did take that missed honeymoon or any other vacation for that matter. We were able to get away one weekend the autumn following our wedding to attend the homecoming celebration at our alma mater. Bob's dad, though aging, agreed to do the cattle chores that weekend. Because of his help, we were able to spend some final time with college buddies in celebration together. We went to the football game, the dance, partied with friends, and had a most enjoyable time.

Bob's mood was uplifted by our getting away as well as was mine. He was appropriate and enjoyable to be with. We shared conversation and spoke of the sights we saw along the way as we drove the three-hour distance each direction to and from the town in which the college was located. The trip cost us very little because we stayed with college mates who still had rooms or apartments on campus. The weekend was both stimulating and exciting. It bonded Bob and I together in a way that cemented the marriage vows, which, although I wasn't really aware at the time, had unraveled a bit under the pressure of life. I went back to work on Monday morning feeling refreshed and revived.

As unbelievable as it may seem because of the abuse, often also in the early years of our marriage, we were very satisfied just being together. Once in a while we would go to a nearby town for a root beer float or a shake and drive around a nearby lake. The crickets singing in the tall grass around the lake just as the sun was shining in orange-yellow hues over the silent, glassy surface of the water filled me in a way that work on the farm could not. Bob talked of farmers and fields and straight rows of crops, and of how far so-and-so was with making hay while I enjoyed the sheer delight of the evening breeze filtering into the open windows as the car sped along. Crows would fly like dark shadows above the water and over the trees that outlined the edge of the lake. Wood ducks would be sleeping with their young families, nestled with heads tucked in under their wings. Fireflies would light up the air just above and before the car lights as we headed back home after dark.

The farmhouse, though run down and in need of repair and roofing, was a pleasant place to be. Two open porches lay on both the north and east sides of the house, with a large bay window facing south, shaded by an aged elm tree. I'd open the doors and windows and let the calm, summer breeze drift through the house. It was one of those large, wood-framed houses surrounded by many trees that would remain inherently cool through many days of hot weather without any artificial, air conditioning. Nothing would feel more wonderful after a long, hot day of baling hay and doing cattle chores than coming into the cool house, taking a shower, and lying down in dry, comfortable pajamas in front of the television with a fan blowing in one's face, and sipping a soda or beer from the refrigerator.

Although we didn't have the money to make any major improvements in the house those first few years, I did paint the rooms and decorate artistically. I placed pictures that I had painted in college on the wall and added a portrait, plaque, doily, or placemat here and there to accent the lines of the turn-of-the-century structure. I hung a plant in the bay window and stood another one on an old, plant stand I had found in the attic.

We didn't have much in the way of furniture those first years—a stove, a refrigerator, a bedroom set, wedding gifts from my parents; a tan, Formica kitchen table and four turquoise-green, vinyl-padded chairs my mother-in-law had left behind when Bob's parents moved to town. We had an old brown sofa which sank deeply in the middle when we sat on it. We found it in the basement of a furniture store in town and paid twenty-five dollars for it. We had a small wooden table I found in the wood grove of the farm-yard, cleaned up, and refinished with a brown, wood-grain paint. There was a bow-back, wooden chair from my grandparents' house from which I had stripped eight coats of paint and finished to match the table. I fitted a lamp from my husband's former bedroom with a new, green shade. There were various odds and ends we had received as gifts for our wedding. I made new curtains for the kitchen. Otherwise, throughout the house hung the drapes and curtains my mother-in-law had hung in the windows. What small amount of furniture we had sat in the kitchen, dining room and bedroom. The living room and upstairs bedrooms stood empty for those first months and even years of marriage. But, it didn't matter. Bob and I were in love! I didn't have high expectations. I knew we had many needs outside on the farm which had to be addressed first. Household needs would come later.

I didn't think much about the intensification of Bob's abusive behavior during those first years of our marriage. For one thing I was a bit relieved at having him out of the uncomfortable dormitory situations that embarrassed me so. For another thing, once away from the college atmosphere, he drank a lot less. Drinking had been part of an attempt to show off and be part of the college crowd. Yes, he might have a few drinks at a wedding dance or special party, or he would have a beer or two after a hard, long, hot day baling hay. So might I. Bob was never an alcoholic. That could never be an excuse for his outbursts.

One might wonder how I could continue to carry on as Bob's wife. Some very positive things were true about him. He was a hard worker and tried to be a good provider. He often recognized my mother's favoritism of my older sister and pointed it out to me and complained about her doing that. He always pointed out good things about me to other people—my work, my artistic abilities, my gift for writing or teaching, or taking a situation by the reins and handling it appropriately.

Also Bob and I shared church, which was an important part of our lives. While we dated, we had often attended together. Either Bob would come with me to my small, country church, or I would accompany him to his church in town near the farm. When we married, I joined Bob's church without a question. We were both Lutheran, so religion was not an issue. Both of us were and had always been active in our church lives. In fact, in high school my youth league would sometimes hold events in conjunction with Bob's youth league, and sometimes we found ourselves sharing an event together.

Bob was the church treasurer for years and served on the church council. I taught Sunday school, attended the Ladies' Circle and the Women's Auxiliary meetings, served on committees, made banners, and assisted with artwork. Later I served on the parish board of education, worked with confirmation students and youth, and was elected to the church council myself.

I have to say that it did amaze me how Bob could be cranky, complaining, hollering, or swearing all the way to an event at church and then be perfect while we were there. It was as if he was two different people, one evil one at times when we were on the farm and one wonderful one at times when we were away. As church goers would be admiring a new banner I had designed for the worship space, he would say to others, "Yah, the wife made it just this last week. She even made up the pattern herself—drew it out on newspaper." As soon as we would be in the car on our way home I heard, "You sure can waste time doing that stuff for church. You can't make any money doing that kind of stuff! How stupid can you be?" He saved the put-downs, the hitting, the slapping, the punching for times when we were in the car or at home and alone, especially in those early years of our marriage.

One time on the way home from church, Bob was terrifically angry at me. I had designed two large murals for the church, which were being painted by me and other church women in the fellowship hall of the church. After I finished teaching Sunday School and while he was still talking with some other men, I busied myself with adding another color to the design. When the other men had left and he was ready to leave also, he was angered that he had to wait for me to finish the area I was working on, close the paint can, and wash up the brush. On the way home the girls and I heard, "What did you think you were doing? You just started painting because you wanted to show off! You always think you're better than everyone else!" he hollered as he drove the car on the wrong side of the highway barely swerving out of the way of an on-coming truck. Why didn't I protest or do anything about it. Again, I was used to it. I didn't even think to be afraid for my children or me. And, after all, I did take him, according to my marriage vows, for better or worse.

Because church attendance and activities seemed so important to both of us, I thought Bob and I shared the same faith. For me, God was central to my life. God was a source of strength for every day. God was the source of the love I could show my students, and family, including Bob's family, whom I loved dearly. Later I would love my own children in a Godly way, although I was not demonstratively affectionate with them, not having been held or hugged much as a child myself. God was a central part of my daily prayer time, which often consisted of a prayer to help Bob be more patient with my mistakes and to help me be a better wife.

How could I lay Bob's abuse alongside my deep faith and come to terms with it? For one thing, Bob told me again and again that I had promised in my marriage vows to "obey" him. Therefore, it was easy to reason that his angry behavior was a result of my disobedience. It wasn't until much later that it was pointed out to me by a pastoral counselor that the word obey was not in my marriage vows.

Also, I somehow saw my tolerance of the abuse as a means for me to get closer to God. Each time I survived an abusive episode it was like climbing another rung on the ladder to eternity and the bliss that would be waiting for me there. After all, hadn't I learned that Jesus said if someone strikes you on one cheek, you are to turn the other cheek to him as well. This theory worked well until it was pointed out to me that Christ had already won redemption for me once and for all. I did not need to go to the cross again and again to be crucified. Christ had done that for me!

Truthfully, I didn't spend much time trying to reconcile Bob's behavior with my own faith. For the most part, it took all the energy I had just to get through each day in one piece. And often I would pray as I crossed the muddy farm yard to save myself from yet another beating, "I lift my eyes to the hills, from where does my help come? My help comes from the Lord" (Psalm 121). God was my protector, my shield, my consolation, and my hope. I knew that whatever happened, I would be held by the hands of God.

Why didn't I question Bob's behavior? Why didn't I object when I was mistreated? And, most importantly, why didn't I leave him? In the years before my children were born, never did I think of leaving. I thought of doing what I needed to do in order to survive. And surely I pondered all of it, the good, the bad, the atrocity and unfairness with what seemed normal from my childhood reference. But because of my own ability to dissociate, a survival technique I had learned as a young child—the ability to pack the most difficult incidences of abuse into separate recesses of the brain where they become mute and out of memory—I was able to survive. I know amid the chaos, there was a constant sense of loneliness. Because of the abuse there was also an ever-widening crevice in my marital relationship, even if I did not recognize it at the time. What I thought of was what I needed to do in order to avoid feeling the shame of the community. But never did I think of leaving the marriage. I now know that this is a natural survival instinct—and that this kind of thinking can change!

Yes, certainly those first years of marriage were both for better and for worse. But I never gave any of it much thought. I needed Bob. That was simply the way it was. And Bob's brainwashing of me coupled with my own disassociative abilities made for an almost lethal, if yet livable, lonely situation.

Time

Time goes by,
and you forget
what it's like
to be held in loving arms,
love's first sweet kiss,
a tender embrace
an uplifting word . . .

You just go on . . .

Day marches forward after day,
and you follow the way
that seems prescribed.

I think that's how
I slowly died
inside.

November 2004

Five: Have You Told Me Lately

Our first daughter was born in March of 1978, almost three weeks early. I gazed down at the perfect, tiny body that lay sleeping, cuddled in a flannel blanket specked with tiny, pink, blue, and yellow butterflies. I will never forget how those tiny fingers with fragile pink fingernails curled themselves into little fists. I would take a little fist, uncurl it for a second and then watch the fingers retreat back to their sleeping positions. The exquisite little head that stuck out of the blanket was covered with a light, brown, downy-film of hair. Every once in a while, her little eyelashes would flutter, or the mouth would turn into a smile or a frown, and sometimes even into a crooked S. When I held her up to my breast, I could hear the faint, but solid thumping of a heartbeat, the slow but steady rise and fall of breathing lungs. Such joy I felt when I had a few moments away from the hubbub of a busy schedule to hold my new, little Bonnie in my arms and rock her.

Though early, Bonnie was fully-formed, strong, and healthy, and a source of much joy and pleasure, I think, for both of us. Initially, Bob had not wanted a baby when, over three years into our marriage, I thought it was time to start a family. He had wanted the barn renovated first. However as time went on, and it was uncertain as to when the barn project would become a reality, I convinced him that starting a family would not be such a bad thing. And although he did not pay much attention to her those first weeks when she slept much of the time with me taking care of her feeding, bathing, and other needs, he did allow her to sleep on his warm, broad chest when he took a rest from the day's activities.

The morning Bonnie had arrived was sunny and bright. The sunrays were shining through my hospital room window. I was still shaking a bit from the intense labor as I ate lunch within an hour of her arrival. This new, little bundle, which to me seemed not quite real, slept silently in her glass-enclosed bassinet, a little pink sign attached to its upper end. "Baby Girl Dahlke" it read along with all those other important pieces of information, date and time of arrival, weight and length, and mother's name. A tiny, tiny wristband wound its way around her wrist, which matched mine to the letter. "This little one is indeed mine." I thought, "all mine."

I think God must have known that this new mom would need an infant who was easy to take care of because Bonnie was that from the beginning. She slept soundly. She ate well and quickly began to grow. And she was healthy. I think even Bob enjoyed having her around once he had become used to her presence in our household.

I had a bit of a break from chores following her birth as Bob's dad came out for a few weeks to help us. I also had taken plenty of time off from work to enjoy my little one. Yes, there were later some times when necessities of her care would interfere with when Bob wanted me to help outside. But those first weeks were Bonnie's and mine together.

As Bonnie grew older, she sometimes was awake at the moment when Bob would need me outside. I was no longer totally at his disposal, not at least without some adjustments. There were times that first summer of Bonnie's life when I would set her in her baby walker near the area where we needed to work. She was never satisfied to sit still with no one paying attention to her for very long, so she would scream and cry, which made Bob holler and yell all the more. At those times he would curse the fact that we now had this baby on our necks!

After those episodes of hollering and yelling, or following other problem times with cattle or machinery, or my being called names because of my ineptness in performing some farm-related task, I would come back in the house and rock my sleeping, little one, who smelled of baby powder and Ivory soap, and I would feel so much better. Sometimes, following a day of Bob's moods which made me feel like the world was coming to an end, in the dark of the night when Bonnie woke for a feeding, I would play an eight-track of Helen Reddy's songs and listen to her gently sing, "You and me against the world. Sometimes I feel its you and me against the world . . ." Bonnie's quiet, steady breathing, her faces and smiles as she was off in dreamland somewhere away from this awful farm and its problems and Bob and his moods, lifted me out of the sourness left by the day.

By 1979 we had saved half of the cost of the renovation of our dairy barn, mostly by skimping on household and personal needs. We decided together that, when half of the money was saved, we would borrow the other half. I thought it was my long-awaited miracle finally coming true. Soon I would be set free of part of the burdensomeness of the cattle's unforgiving schedule, or so I thought. And since by then I had a child to tend, that was a particularly appealing factor to me.

It was an exciting spring to think of the raising of the upper level and roof of the dairy barn, tearing out the old foundation and stanchions, and replacing all of the worn out equipment with modern, top-of-the-line milking units, pipeline, a modern bulk tank to cool the milk, sinks for washing and—what do you know!—drinking cups for each cow that actually worked! Bob was on a euphoric high that summer as the new barn took shape. While it was a bit harder keeping up with the cattle chores with our milking cattle at his uncle's barn, which we rented while our own barn was being built, the prospect of the ease of housing and milking our dairy cattle lightened the weight of any inconvenience that the traveling back and forth from farm yard to farm yard entailed.

One really serious hitch in the process arose. When we secured the contract with the plumbing and pipeline company, we thought it included assembling and plumbing the drinking cups. We signed the contract only to learn shortly later that the quoted price included the water pipes but not the actual assembly and connection of the cups. Because Bob considered it to be my fault that this was not included in the contracted price, I would need to solve the problem without spending any more money! I did. I talked the plumbing and pipeline company into connecting the cups to the pipes if they were assembled and ready. For several weeks that summer, each time I would lay my young toddler down for her afternoon nap, I would go out to the building site and assemble what drinking cups I could until I thought her nap time would be coming to an end. I became quite adept at using wrenches and plumbing tools, and each drinking cup seemed to go together a little quicker than the last. Bob would often be around the building site talking and joking with the construction crew. But never did he offer to lift a wrench for the drinking cup assembly project. I didn't think this strange. After all, it had been my fault that this particular aspect of the project had inadvertently been omitted from the contract for the plumbing. It had been my fault—or so I believed.

Another incident occurred during the building of the barn which I still remember and feel ashamed of when I think of it. Bob's sixteen-year-old niece stayed with us much of the time the barn was under construction to keep an eye on our active and curious little daughter. Late one evening, long after Bonnie had been put down for bed and evening milking chores had been completed, Bob and his niece were joking and fooling around in the dining room. I was in the kitchen cleaning up some mess before going to bed. It wasn't long before Bob got carried away. He exposed himself inappropriately to his niece. I was shocked when I looked towards the two of them through the dining room doorway only to see my husband's penis, full and erect, as a silhouette in the lighted screen of the television. I remember that his niece didn't seem particularly upset by this. But shame crept over me. I cried out to Bob, "What in the world are you doing?" And the episode ended. I never told anyone until much, much later when I was in therapy. I have always felt guilty for not at least telling Bob's sister. But I didn't tell. Shame and fear of what Bob would do to me if I did kept me quiet. Fortunately, as far as I know, he never did such a thing again to her or anyone else.

I have learned two important things since the barn building and this episode with Bob's niece. The first is that no material thing a person can buy or attain will stop the abusive behavior of a person who is an abuser. The second is that Bob's action with his niece that dark evening was sexual abuse of a vulnerable, minor child and severely punishable by the law. I would now take the necessary action so as not to be an accomplice to it.

It was a joyous day in September of 1979 when we moved our dairy cattle to our newly renovated dairy barn. Bob entered the new decade of the 1980's with an uplifted spirit, at least briefly. I on the other hand was exhausted most of the time, trying to figure out how the new barn was actually helping us save labor. Yes, the pipeline, milking system, the automatic, milking-unit washers, and the large sinks with both cold *and* hot water faucets were bliss. I was saved the job of carrying by pail the milk from each cow to strain it into the milk cans, which a trucker from the creamery would then pick up. I was even liberated from the task of hand-washing the milking units. Even the bulk cooling tank, which was emptied when the milk was shipped to the creamery, had an automatic washer. Both Bob and I were freed from the task of manually forking the manure out of the gutters behind the cows each day. That task now, too, was automated.

There was still a huge amount of work to do. We had to take care of the calves and young stock. We had to carry feed pail by pail or bushel basket by bushel basket to each cow's stall, haul hay bales into the barn one by one by hand since we did not have a cow yard or feeding system. And I don't think either of us anticipated the amount of upkeep the automated systems would require to keep them in working order.

Yes, the new barn was nice, but I was waiting for the day when I would not even have to leave the house to do cattle chores altogether. I thought that day was coming with the building of the barn. Little did I know that that day would never come until I flatly refused to help, some fifteen years later.

For the most part I did not think about the intensity of labor on the farm coupled with taking care of an infant. I simply tried to get through each day striving for as much peace as possible, juggling a demanding, often angry husband, machinery and weather that was uncooperative, and the changes in one's life a child engendered. Bob's explosions were buffered by my joy in being a new mother and my striving to figure out how to be a good mother.

We entered January of 1980 with high hopes, a remodeled barn, and an empty bank account with the intended promise of making it big on our now-expanding dairy operation. What we didn't count on was the increase in interest rates from nine-and-one-half percent in March of 1979, when we originally talked to the lender and the actual sixteen to seventeen percent we ended up signing on for when the project was completed in the fall. And the year saw more raising rates. Since the bank would only put the building of the barn on a flexible interest plan, I think the bank was the only entity that actually made a gain by our building it. This is not to say that we made no income on the cattle. However, the way I saw it, we never made enough income to make the bothersome tasks of all that needed to be done with the cattle worthwhile. And also, since Bob was unwilling to allow anyone else to milk the cows because he felt they wouldn't do it right or good enough, our new barn marked the establishment of continued monotony of daily farm labor.

The amount of daily labor actually increased as Bob moved closer to his dream of having all the stalls in the barn full. In order to have more cows milking there needed to be more calves born, more feed ground, more hay baled, more fences fixed—more of everything. Also, in order to ship milk, the barn had to be inspected by the state and, thus, cleaned regularly. Since I was in charge of the calves, Bob didn't do fences, and Bob's involvement in cleaning and polishing the barn and its equipment for the inspector's visits was minimal, guess who was busier than ever! I was still working full time and had a two-year-old to look after. The load was too heavy for me! Yet, I was committed to the marriage relationship and Bob's dream, so I gave it all the time and energy I could.

As I look back on the situation, I can see how the farm was definitely a contributing factor to the abusive nature of our marriage. There was the constant grind coupled with cattle illnesses, inclement weather, well-worn machinery, and a failing farm economy to exacerbate Bob's violent moods. The fact that it was a twenty-four-hour-a-day job for seven days a week didn't help either. Often both Bob and I were at the point of physical and mental exhaustion.

After building the barn and then paying such high interest rates, we hardly had enough cash available to buy necessities and pay monthly bills. As a result Bob and I agreed that I would go off of my birth control pills. After all we had no health insurance and the pills were costing us twenty-four dollars every three months. Since my monthly cycle was very regular, and I always could tell when I ovulated, discontinuing the pill was a wise way to reduce costs—or so I thought.

Work worn and finding that the new barn had only improved Bob's mood for a brief time, I was extremely unhappy. Not long after the cows moved home, Bob's erratic pattern of ups and downs returned. By the time I saw a cold, snowy January pass by, I was both exhausted and battle weary. It wasn't that I was really withholding sex from Bob. I was simply too worn out to want to have it.

On a Friday in late February, I finished a day at work. (I was supervising a pre-school program for socially, economically, and physically disadvantaged young children at the time.) I picked up my two-year-old Bonnie from daycare. I changed both of our clothes on arriving home and brought Bonnie out to the barn with me to feed the cattle. When Bonnie and I returned to the house, I prepared and cleaned up supper and helped Bonnie get ready for bed. With Bonnie tucked in for the night, I went out to help Bob with evening milking and nighttime chores. By the time we finished the chores, I was out of energy and just wanted to wash up and go to bed.

Bob came in wanting sex. I knew I had ovulated just a little over two days before, and I thought it was just too soon to take a chance on having unprotected intercourse. Of course, Bob was never willing to use any protection. I refused. He complained. I said it was too soon to have sex, and besides I was tired. I was tired!—tired of it all, the farm , the cattle, the daily routine with both work away from home, work outside on the farm, and work in the house keeping up with household duties and my family's needs. And I was sick and tired of Bob's moods and insults. I was so tired of his hollering that I remember wishing he would turn into a bug so I could squish him and shut him up once and for all!

As I backed away and wouldn't give in to Bob's sexual advances, he continued pressing. "After all," he yelled, "you are my wife!" I maybe would have given in at this point since I had been taught by my mother and the culture in which I grew up that sex on demand was a husband's right. But I was truly afraid that it *was* too soon.. I wanted to be extra careful knowing that we could not afford to have another baby at this time.

Before I realized what was happening, Bob pushed me down onto the dining room carpet. The more I refused, the more determined Bob became. I had on a shirt with buttons that evening, and he ripped the front open sending the buttons flying. I quit struggling at this point. To do so was only making him more angry and violent. I gave in to my wifely responsibility. Soon he was satisfied and left me lying on the floor next to the end of the orange and brown, floral couch. I got up, straightened myself, put on my pajamas and went to bed. I had done my wifely duty, even though it had been forced upon me. I would not learn until years later that Bob raped me that night.

By early May when I leaned against the bulk tank to connect the
pipe which would deliver the milk from the milking units on the cows
to the bulk tank to be cooled, I had a distinctly hard lump in my abdomen. Denying the reality that I hadn't had a regular period for a couple of
months, just a little light bleeding. I instantly thought of a woman in our
neighborhood, who had recently had an emergency hysterectomy because
of a tumor.. I was sure I had a problem that needed to be checked out by a
physician. And I needed to get that done pronto!

I went to the doctor's office as soon as I could get an appointment, doing so during my workday. "I have this hard lump in my abdominal area,
and I am worried about it." I explained to the nurse in the examining
room. I showed her the area just slightly to the right and below my naval. I
could feel the lump as I pressed my hand against it. So could the nurse.

"I think first we should take a urine sample," she responded.

After complying, I went back to my examining room to wait. Soon the
nurse came in smiling. "You do have a lump that needs some attention,"
she laughed. "And quite assuredly that lump will have a heartbeat by now
if we listen!" It wasn't a joyful moment for me. In fact at that moment I
hated Bob immensely. I was also scared to death to tell him because I knew
that we could not afford a baby in addition to all our other bills. And I
knew I couldn't take maternity leave. Paid maternity leave wasn't available where I worked. We needed my income to pay the bills!

Was abortion ever a consideration? The thought did pass through my
mind, but I never considered it seriously. I had heard about abortions on
the news, but I did not know anyone who had had one. I did not know
where a person could get one, but assumed I would need to go to the city
to have such a procedure done. I was afraid to drive there. Also, our car
was not dependable enough to make the trip. Besides, an abortion also cost
money, and money was what we didn't have! Besides, I was already almost
three months pregnant. There was no way out but to go home and break
the news to Bob, whom I hoped would not break me when he found out.

At first when I told him, he denied having fathered it. He said, "How
could you get pregnant having sex just once in two months?!" He accused
me of having an affair with someone else in town. "No wonder you've
been coming home late from work!" he accused. "Besides, we don't have
money to pay for a baby now! Don't you know how much that will cost?"

Even though he continued to accuse me that the baby was not his
throughout the entire pregnancy, I remember him sometimes acting glad
because the whole, unexpected, pregnancy business displeased me so. In
between accusing me of having sex with someone else, he would say that
it was time for an addition to the family since Bonnie was now over two

years old. And I know he wanted to have a son. But he also didn't go out of his way to make life any easier for me. He expected me to do everything I had been doing and carry another baby as well.

Although I hadn't been sick at all with my first pregnancy, I was often either nauseous or sick to my stomach with this one. This continued, not only during the first months of pregnancy, but into the summer as well. The smell of corn silage freshly thrown out of the silo made me especially ill, as well as did the smell of calf manure. I would often go out of the calf barn to vomit before returning to finish my feeding chores.

After my marriage I saw very little of my parents even though they lived only fifteen miles from our farm. And it was only a rare occasion when some family event intruded on our lives. Between work off the farm, work on the farm, and a toddler to take care of, there simply wasn't time. Bob discouraged visits as well. He criticized my parents to me, at times severely, and it seemed he always had something else that I needed to help him with which kept me at home on the farm even when I was not working at my job. Sometimes three or four months would pass between visits with my parents, and these were usually initiated on their part. Then I would get criticized because they came when he needed to be outside working or when he needed me to be outside working. The visits ended up being very stressful times. My older sister was teaching some one hundred miles from our farm, and my younger sister, who had just recently graduated from college, lived even farther away, so I saw them even less. Since I was seldom free to stay away from home during chores time, there was no way we sisters could visit unless they came to me.

In the spring of 1980 we were influenced by one of these intrusions of my family. My younger sister was getting married that May. It happened that, because of my unplanned pregnancy, I was at the peak of my sick time. We drove the many miles to her wedding, having completed morning chores. We had not had time to eat either before leaving home or on the way. By the time I reached the reception, I was starved. I ate some nuts and mints off the tray by the wedding cake while we waited for the meal to be served.

On the way home I was immensely ill. Bonnie, who was sitting in the back seat of the car, had not had her usual afternoon nap that day and was tremendously cranky. I was too sick to deal with her, which made Bob angry because he was trying to get home as fast as he could in order to milk the cows. He hollered at me to do something with her. At about that moment, I opened the window and lost my dinner. He stopped the car suddenly, getting out and slamming the door behind him. He opened the door to the back seat, picked Bonnie up out of the seat, and gave her a few hard spanks. He sat her back down hard as she screamed her head off. I was upset that he did that but too sick to do anything to comfort her. Luckily, soon the crying ceased. She had finally drifted off to sleep. We drove the last twenty-five miles home in silence.

Once at home, I put my sleeping child to bed, changed clothes, and went out to do the evening chores with Bob. We did not speak to each other. We did everything that needed to be done in a rudimentary manner, as we had hundreds of times before. When we had finished the outside work, we went to bed in silence. I turned my back to Bob and closed my eyes. It had been too long a day for a vulnerable, pregnant wife! And, I knew that Bob had not been pleased with me for much of it. I soon fell peacefully asleep, which is sometimes the most soothing balm God can give to one who has just had a little too much of waking life.

As we moved into the summer of 1980, I continued to work. I continued helping with the cattle chores in addition to unloading hay bales and carrying corn silage by the bushel basket to feed the dairy cows. I continued to not feel hungry, fighting at times to keep food down. And I continued to lose, instead of gain, weight. But, even if the doctor was dismayed by the weight loss at each check up, he said the heartbeat was strong and everything seemed all right with the pregnancy.

That summer I was very depressed. I experienced quite a crying jag one evening when my parents were visiting. After some piece of machinery broke, Bob had been particularly mean. No, there hadn't been much physical contact, but the name-calling, the belittling, the swearing, and the hurtful comments came as regularly as machinery broke down, cattle got sick, or bills, which we couldn't afford to pay, came in the mail. My grandfather had come that evening. He was uncomfortable around me and didn't know what to do so he made conversation with my dad, who also didn't know how to comfort me. I kept my mother company by showing her my vegetable garden and the growth of the lilac bushes my father had planted along the lawn's edge for me that spring. It was a sunny, summer evening, but I found no enjoyment in it.

I silently hated Bob that night more than I had ever hated anyone or anything ever in my life. Although my childhood life had not been perfect, there was not the chaos of Bob's violent outbursts. And my own family's farm life was nothing like the drudgery I experienced with Bob on our own farm. Although I could not have put these two realities into words that night, I did know that I hated Bob. I hated him! Yet never did I think of leaving. After all, I was pregnant and had a toddler, and heaven knows I could not support myself! Bob continually reminded me of what a burden Bonnie, my unborn baby, and I were to him. I blamed myself for getting pregnant. Since Bob and I were married, never did I consider that I had been raped—that this child within me was the product of rape! And, although I thought God was giving me perhaps more of a test of patience and faith than anyone should have to bear, I believed that part of my faith also involved being a patient, caring, and loving wife—to keep life peaceful at all costs! Never did I question God as to Bob's behavior. Never did I curse God for putting me in this difficult situation. I simply believed that God knew what God was doing. After all, God never gives one more than she can bear, I believed. That night as I lay my wearied head on the cool softness of the bed sheets, I prayed to God to take care of my babies and me, and to help keep Bob from getting upset.

By October Bob's patience with me and my condition was wearing thin. I was refusing to have sex with him at all. We had sex two times that entire year, and I was pregnant. I told God that it simply wasn't fair! But fair or not, the baby was growing within me. And when Bob kicked me in the stomach in late October after becoming angry at something I did or didn't do, my abdomen ached and I felt some cramping in my stomach. I called my parents that day. My dad scolded Bob. "After all," he said, "she is carrying your child." That's the first and only time I think I ever heard my dad scold Bob. But we were treading in dangerous waters. A little one's life was on the line. This was serious. After my parents left, Bob's response was, "My child—like heck it is!"

Krista was born on the twenty-second of November, five days early. She was healthy.. There was no question that she was Bob's daughter as she had an indented line high on her cheekbones just like his and his round face. We had hoped for a son, as we had the first time. A farmer always wants a son to be an heir. But, when I looked at my chubby, little, blue-eyed girl with long, sweeping eyelashes, I immediately fell in love with her. Bob didn't complain much either. He could no longer say that she wasn't his. And I think that he was just glad it was over so the life could get back to normal again.

But life was anything but normal with a toddler, a newborn, no paycheck from outside work because of my being on unpaid, maternity leave, winter coming on, and the Christmas season soon upon us. I was weak and often dizzy after Krista's birth, and I didn't seem to have much energy. I walked along the electric, cattle fence eight days after her birth trying to figure out where the trouble spot was that was causing it not to work. I felt very weak and often had to lean against a fence post for fear of blacking out. But the cattle chores went on as usual. And Bonnie, bless her heart, by that time was able to stay in the house and watch cartoons while we did chores, which made my tasks easier. God watched my babies when I was out doing the work that I had to do so that I would not be punished for not doing my share. God was my babysitter. I thanked God everyday for being there for me.

Krista was a beautiful, little baby who smiled a big, broad smile at two-and-a-half weeks of age. Who couldn't fall in love with that? But, if that was her good quality, her unsatisfactory one was the fact that she never (and I mean never!) slept during the day, even as a newborn. To make matters worse, she woke up four times a night for a feeding. I tried to get her to eat more at each feeding, but she simply refused. So she never remained full enough for an extended sleep at any one time. You can imagine what this did to Bob's temper! Every time she woke and cried at night, he yelled at me. "Would you keep that damned kid quiet!" I would hear until I started feeding her. It was hard enough dealing with a baby who didn't sleep well at night. The hollering from one, who was also her parent, was just another added burden to not getting a good night's rest. And, since I needed to go back to work at least two to three days a week when Krista was just six weeks old, the extra stress from his complaining several times each night was not helpful at all.

Bob did take care of Krista the first two months after I was back at work. He had no choice. She was too young for daycare, and we needed a paycheck. It was January, and I certainly didn't want to take a six-week-old baby out in the cold every day and drive the country roads, which were often snow or ice covered. As long as I had the bottles ready, disposable diapers for him to use, and the wind-up swing where he could put her so that he could go outside and feed the cattle during the day, he managed. Yet, as Krista grew older and had other problems and behaviors that irritated him, his verbal abuse of her destroyed whatever bond had grown between them in those early months.

As for me, I don't know how I made it through those months. I think I was often too worn out and tired to feel anything at all. I was glad that it seemed to be working to leave Krista home with Bob when I needed to be at my job. It was hard enough taking one small child to daycare in the middle of winter. Yet, if he had done something around the house to help out when he was home with her during the day, it would have taken some of the burden off of me. Instead, when he was not out feeding cattle, he was either watching television or sleeping on the couch while Krista was in the swing. So he got rest during the day while I did not. It was no surprise that the stress caught up with me by early summer. By June I had walking pneumonia. By the next winter I had mouth and throat ulcers. When these had seemed to clear up, I started having asthma problems, which continued to wear me down for a couple of years. One night when Krista was two, I thought I would choke to death in the bathroom, I developed such a coughing fit during the night. Bob never even bothered to get up to see what was the matter. I also started grinding my teeth at night and had the beginnings of TMJ. The joint in the right side of my jaw would often ache and at times would even lock up. All of the stress, which could not come out in any other way, came out as physical problems, which only cost us more money, making matters worse than they already were.

As the children were growing, the tensions around the house continued to rise. I could no longer devote all of my spare time to the farming operation because the children had needs that required my attention too. I will be the first to admit that, in order to keep peace in the household, peace with Bob that is, I was often forced to leave the girls alone in the house while I went outside to tend to one of his problems.

Bonnie was extremely mature for her young age so she was a good watch-keeper over Krista. She could keep her entertained on the floor or in the playpen, or wind the swing for Krista to keep her occupied in my absence. But anyone who has had young children in the household knows that all is not peaceful all the time. Bob complained when I decided that I needed to tend the girls instead of tend to one of his matters. He complained when the girls were sick and up during the night. This became somewhat often when Krista was two and had terrible, nighttime, coughing spells. He complained when I had to take the girls to the doctor because "it cost money." He complained when I had them outside with me, and they whined and complained at how long the task would take me, and when could we go back in the house. He complained when they spilled milk at the table or didn't finish their food. "Do you know how much those groceries cost! Gees, these kids are wasting us a lot of money!" I tried as best I could to keep peace. But children are children after all, and I was working a full time job as well as helping on the farm and trying to tend to the needs of young children. I didn't realize at the time how God gave me stamina to both endure my daily schedule and endure Bob's abuse. Looking back on it, it's a surprise I made it through that time at all.

One instance in particular when I had to leave the girls alone in the house for a longer period of time than I had wanted to still haunts me today, not because the girls were necessarily endangered by it. Bonnie always kept Krista and herself safe. No, I remember it because I broke my children's hearts that night in a way I don't think I will ever be able to make up for.

It was the night before Halloween, and since it was late October, Bob was trying to get the corn harvested. After I arrived home from work, I hauled wagons of cob corn home from the field and unloaded them. We stopped the harvesting to do cattle chores and milk the cows. "We'll carve the pumpkin as soon as mommy's done helping with the milking," I had promised the girls.

Bonnie was out to the barn several times during milking. "Are you going to be finished pretty soon?" she would ask as she walked into the aisle between the rows of cows. She was so anxious and excited because she was big enough by then—nearly six, to really help with the carving that year. At last, as she left the barn, Bob yelled at me, "What do you mean you're going to carve the pumpkin after milking? Don't you know that I need you to help me unload wagons so we can fill up the corncrib? Where is your brain anyhow? It's harvest. Do you think you can waste time carving a pumpkin with the kids?!" Since the corncrib was almost full, it would take two people to finish filling it, one to run the elevator, which carried the cobs of corn from the wagon up to the holes in the top of the corncrib, and one person to actually be up in the crib to move the corn into all the final, empty corners.

"But I promised the girls. They've waited all week while I've been out helping you. I really think I need to do this with them. This is the last night! As soon as the pumpkin's carved, I'll come back out, and we'll finish off the crib."

"Don't you know we can't waste time? The wagons need to be emptied right away so we can move the elevator and I can go out and finish the corn-picking before the white frost gets too thick!" he responded angrily. "After all, what is more important? Our income or carving a stupid pumpkin with the kids?" He had hollered at me in a threatening way. I knew what I had to do to avoid him striking out at me.

I explained to Bonnie that I had to help Daddy unload the three wagons full of corn, but then I would be in to carve the pumpkin with her and Krista. Well, of course we had some difficulties with the elevator. It took longer than I expected to get the crib full.

At first, while we were unloading, Bonnie came out quite often, "How far are you getting? Are you going to be done pretty soon?" she questioned.

"Pretty soon, pretty soon. I'll be done in just a few more minutes," I tried to appease her. It wasn't pretty soon. One thing after the other went wrong. And Bob became more annoyed each time Bonnie came out to check what was taking mommy so long. "Will you tell that damned kid to stay in the house and keep quiet!" he demanded.

Of course the problems continued. All the corn did not fit into the crib, so we had to move the elevator to put the last wagon of corn on a pile on the ground. As Bob was pulling the elevator away from the crib and out behind the house where we wanted to put the pile, the elevator came very near jumping off of its frame, needing even more repair. While all this was happening, Bob thrust out at me in anger even as I was trying to help him.

Time went by, and at last Bonnie didn't come out to ask anymore. When we finally got the elevator fixed, in the position behind the house where we wanted to put the pile, and the last of the corn unloaded, it was midnight. Bob was ecstatic to be finished with the corn harvest. I was worried about the girls.

I went into the house to find one little body asleep on the sofa with her blanket, and the other little body laid out on the carpet in the dining room, thumb in her mouth. "No wonder Bonnie quit coming to check," I thought. The girls had at last gone to sleep waiting for their mother to come in and keep her promise. I cannot explain the depth of the hurt in my heart at how I had failed them that night as their mother. After all, a promise is a promise. Yet if I hadn't helped Bob, I would have surely set myself up for another beating. I knew that. What could I do?

I carefully picked up each little, limp body and carried it up the stairs, putting my girls gently into bed. I covered each with her own "blankie." Neither one woke as I gently brushed her head in a silent good night and said a prayer to God, thanking God for taking care of my two, little girls for me. I went back downstairs, washed up, and got ready for bed. Bob came in all excited and feeling wonderful. I showed him the kitchen table where Bonnie had taken the initiative to spread out an old newspaper, put the pumpkin in the middle of it, and get out the pumpkin carver along with a large spoon for removing the seeds. He just complained about those dammed kids always wanting something!

After Bob went to bed, I reached up onto the top shelf in the bedroom closet and brought down the two, stuffed ponies I had picked up at a sale intending to give them to the girls for Christmas. I quietly placed the pink pony under Bonnie's arm and tucked it partially under her blanket. I laid the light green pony under Krista's arm and tucked it under her blanket in a similar fashion. The tears welled up in my eyes as I did so. The pain I held inside made all of my muscles ache. I then went downstairs and carved the pumpkin so that it would be ready for Halloween night. If I hadn't been there to carve the pumpkin with them, I at least wanted to surprise them with it in the morning. It was past two o'clock by the time I crawled into bed. And the next morning, chores time would come early. I lay awake in bed, wishing I would have had someone to talk to about this, feeling terribly guilty, and feeling a deep, deep sadness. As I crawled into bed, the mattress shifted a bit. Bob woke a little as the mattress moved. "What the hell are you doing up?" was all he muttered before turning over and going back to sleep.

I lay awake in the dark for what seemed hours. I was thinking about how wrong everything had seemed to go that day. I lay thinking about how wrong everything always seemed to be with Bob. Was I really a witch? Did I really jinx things, as Bob said I did? I had heard these lines enough by this time to fully believe them. In addition I now knew I was also the world's worst mother! My tears were my prayer that night as I cried "in groans too deep for words." Yet I never considered leaving Bob. Was it shame or fear that kept me there? Maybe both. Maybe both.

I was operating on borrowed time by the time February of 1983 came around, worn tired by work, winter weather, and bills that were overdue. Bob was constantly verbally deriding me and complaining about one thing or another. Nothing I did ever seemed to be right as hard as I tried. The farm economy had plummeted, and my checks never went far enough. The cattle had suffered from the cold of winter. It just kept on snowing and blowing, and it seemed that winter was never going to end.

One evening the hell I was expecting did finally break loose. I had gotten home late from work. The girls had been crabby and bickered over supper. Another cow had a serious milk infection, which required a veterinarian's expertise. And the barn cleaner broke. We were trying to get it fixed late after the milking chores were done. It was being uncooperative, and I wasn't strong enough to pull several feet of heavy chain the way Bob wanted me to pull it. Then it came. A shove to the cement floor, some kicks to the chest, a push into the gutter, and more stomps and kicks. The barn fork, used to remove manure by hand, came flying my way, the handle striking me in the hip. With some more swearing and bellowing, the incident came to an end. Bob went stomping out of the feed room door and to the house muttering about how I had looked at him and what a weakling I was. I had no chance to worry that he would wake up the girls, whom I had put to bed before we had started the barn cleaner project. My mind couldn't even think that far.

It took me awhile to get my breath back because one of the kicks had come very near my diaphragm. Once I was able to breath again, I pulled myself up out of the gutter, dirty and covered with manure. I moved slowly, both because I hurt all over and also because I did not want to disturb the cow, whose legs were even with my head, and scare her into kicking me in the face. I went into the milk room and washed my face and arms. I took some paper towels and cleaned the worst of the mess from my jacket and jeans. I checked a few places that hurt to see if there were any broken bones. Finding myself intact, I made my way to the house. When I got there, I found Bob lying on the bed watching television. "What the hell took you so long to get to the house?" he asked calmly. I couldn't believe that he could be so unfeeling and unloving towards me. He acted as if he had no recollection of what had just happened between us out in the barn. He even joked about my being covered with manure.

I left the bedroom, closing the door behind me. I went to the phone and called my parents. What was I hoping for? I guess in some way I was hoping that, with my dad's scolding, Bob would cease to be abusive. I was hoping the increased exposure of Bob's behavior to my parents would somehow help them help me deal with it, or at least they would believe and understand should I make such a call again. I had hoped my dad would be stronger with Bob, somehow instill a little fear like he had with us girls when we had misbehaved as children. I certainly didn't want my parents to call the sheriff. I certainly didn't want to leave my husband, or, if I did, I didn't want my feelings made known.

While they were on their way, I finished washing up and put on some clean clothes I grabbed from the hooks along the basement stairs. I threw the dirty clothes into the washer. I checked on the girls. They were sleeping soundly. I put some ice on a couple of bruises, especially on my lower ribs and hip, which hurt immensely. I took a couple of aspirin and wrapped myself in a blanket on the sofa and waited.

At the sound of my dad's voice, Bob came out of the bedroom. I explained to my dad what Bob had just done to me. I was crying as I did so, much to my embarrassment since I never liked to cry around my dad. My mother asked if I thought I needed to go to the doctor, while my dad talked to Bob. Looking their direction I noticed that Bob spoke calmly with my dad. He acted calmly. My mother asked about the girls and seemed satisfied when I told her that they were asleep upstairs. Then they went home.

Perhaps I just wanted a warm, caring presence when I was hurting so badly. My dad's presence was not strong enough to comfort me or threaten Bob. But at least my calling them had not angered Bob further into beating me some more. Their intrusion into our space that night had instead thrown Bob off his abusive track long enough for him to get through his siege without further violence. And although I was disappointed that they weren't a more powerful force in ending the abuse, I was simply relieved that the episode was over and wanted to get it out of my mind as quickly as possible—which I did.

By the time the sun was shining brightly on the following Saturday, the hurt Bob had caused me was pushed far out of my reality. So when out of the clear blue sky Bob suggested that we go to a nearby town and get some badly-needed, new kitchen chairs, I was very pleased and was no longer thinking about the beating at all. On the way back from town, with two kids and four chairs in tow, we stopped in at my parents' farm. They were very surprised that both Bob and I acted like nothing had happened earlier in the week. They were surprised that it had been Bob's suggestion that we get new chairs. I think they were baffled by the entire situation. I could tell by their facial expressions that they were inquisitive about the situation, but I knew that my bringing up the beating would only turn Bob against me again as soon as we arrived home. So I kept my mouth shut. Besides, it was no longer important enough to matter. I loved the new chairs. They were so much more comfortable than the old ones and didn't fall apart every time I moved them. I was so pleased with Bob that day that the beating dimmed until it was out of sight altogether.

Later I learned that my parents had talked to a pastor about the fact that there was ongoing abuse in our marriage. My mother informed me that the pastor had advised them that the problem was between Bob and me as a couple, and that they needed to let us deal with it. That's about as bad as the advice to a beaten wife to go home and pray about it and try to keep things calm. One needs to remember, however, that this abuse was happening in the early 1980's, and society as a whole, much less the clergy of the church, had no real training in what to do in such situations. Laws protecting abused women and children were just coming into the legal system. There appeared to be nothing I could really do when Bob blasted the dining room chair to pieces in a fit of anger but get it repaired. There was nothing I could do when he put his fist through one of the windows of the china cupboard but replace the glass. There appeared to be nothing I could do when he beat me up, but nurse my wounds.

A highpoint in my life, which I think was a major factor in keeping me going, was my job. I had moved to the position of a Program Coordinator at the program for adults with disabilities in the county in which we lived. My job was to devise learning programs for disabled adults. I performed my job well. My clients liked me. The staff, who worked under me, liked me. My boss liked my work and my ability to relate to the clients. And the Board of Directors was pleased. If I lacked love at home, I certainly received it at work from the men and women whose lives I was responsible to help organize. And my income was steadily increasing along with finally receiving some health insurance coverage. Both Bob and I were pleased about that.

Also as a family, Bob, I, and the girls would sometimes go shopping on a Saturday to a fairly large town. The girls would get a few new clothes or shoes for their growing bodies. I might get a new sweater or pair of slacks for work. We would stop at McDonald's for a Happy Meal, which always thrilled the girls, before returning home. A few times I would even get a babysitter so that Bob and I could attend a neighbor's or friend's wedding dance. And we continued to have our drives, piling the four of us in our old, big, green Chrysler, going to the Dairy Queen for ice cream, and then seeing the wonders of nature so near our farm. And while Bob continued to admire or criticize the fields of crops he was seeing along the way, I sucked in the smell of freshly mown hay or blooming wildflowers or pointed out to the girls a swan on the lake or a gull hovering above the water.

But while there were still some good times in our marriage, there were many more, jagged peaks downward. Although I didn't realize it at the time, my love for Bob had faded greatly, while the episodes of hitting, verbal put-downs, hollering, and name-calling increased.

Since I didn't think that there was any way out of the situation, I gradually gave up hoping, gave up feeling, and, I think, in a way gave up living. I no longer felt like stamping Bob dead. I no longer felt like arguing or fighting back. I no longer felt anything at all regarding the abuse. In fact, I didn't even remember the abusive episodes until much later. I simply put them in a place of my mind far out of memory, and I went on living. I felt a great heaviness in my heart like a growing cancer, but I put that out of my mind as well. After all, what good did it do to dwell on all these things? Later, much later, after all the memories of the abuse came flooding in on me, I learned that I had disassociated them, the term psychologists use for the ability to separate abusive episodes into a compartment of the brain out of immediate memory. That is how I survived all of the years of abuse. I also learned that no amount of stress in life is cause for abuse. Abusive behavior is never to be excused. The abuser chooses to be abusive. It is that plain and simple.

By this time it had been many years since I had received any flowers—not since before I was married. "Thank you" never came out of Bob's mouth. In fact he often told me, when I reminded him that I thought a thank you was in order, that he didn't have to say thank you nor did he have to say I'm sorry. "After all, I never do anything wrong," he'd retort. It had been forever since I had heard a compliment from him, other than his bragging about me in other people's company, which I later came to learn was a way of boosting his own self-esteem. I thought to myself one day, "Have you told me lately that you love me?" I certainly didn't remember hearing an "I love you" for a very, very long time. No, the word "Love" had gone out of Bob's vocabulary. I didn't expect to hear an "I love you" for many more years to come, maybe never again.

Psalm 25
Prayer for Guidance and Deliverance

To you, O LORD, I lift up my soul.
O my God, in you I trust;
 do not let me be put to shame,
 do not let my enemies exult over me.
Do not let those who wait for you to be put to shame,
 Let them be ashamed who are wantonly treacherous.

Make me to know your ways, O LORD;
 teach me your paths.
Lead me in your truth, and teach me,
 for you are the God of my salvation;
 for you I wait all day long.

Turn to me and be gracious to me,
 for I am lonely and afflicted.
Relieve the troubles of my heart,
 and bring me out of my distress.
Consider my affliction and my trouble,
 and forgive all my sins.

Consider how many are my foes,
 and with what violent hatred they hate me.
O guard my life, and deliver me;
 do not let me be put to shame, for I take refuge in you.
May integrity and uprightness preserve me,
 for I wait for you.

Pondering

You hit me once,
then twice, and
more.

Although no sound
touched the sky,
I screamed so deep inside
my muscles ached
until my body numbed.
Reverberating waves
passed from cell to cell,
between the membranes
of my mind and heart
until they touched
my soul.

There they rested
in silence,
quieted
at first by fear,
and then,
through time,
by loss of memory
of even the event
which hurt them so.

From our infested bed,
at last
I cried for understanding,
warmth, and love,
Finding none,
from portals of infamy
pain broke wide open
spilling like gushing rivers
flowing to the open sea,

If only I had known.
If only you had cared.

October 1997

Six: Living A Lie

Four days before Christmas in 1983 the barn cleaner came to a jarring halt as we were running the day's manure out of the dairy barn. Cleaning sloppy, stinky manure out of the chain and iron flights, which pulled the manure from the barn gutters up into the manure spreader, with our mittens, we began to investigate the situation as the icy-cold wind bit through our jeans. Bob climbed up to the top of the chute where the motor that drove the apparatus was located.

"A bearing is out," was his observation as both he and I shivered in the freezing weather.

Two days later, he ordered the bearing and picked it up. In a wind chill of minus sixty, Bob and I sat perched atop the barn cleaner chute, I holding tools and him taking the ice cold iron apart and trying to get it back together. The manure had not been cleaned for two days, and the gutters were overflowing. My job was cold from lack of movement, sitting in a crouched position on top of the chute in the path of the northwest wind, and holding icy, metal tools in my hands which bit even through my heavy clothing and mittens. My eyelashes froze above the scarf that covered my nose, cheeks, and mouth. Yet I had the part of the job in which I could keep my mittens on. Bob at times had to remove his to have enough agility to remove a stubborn bolt or nut. I would sneak into the barn every once in a while for a brief warm up. But Bob sat atop the chute the entire time. His body groaned as he tried to both breathe in the cold and put his strength behind a wrench to remove barn cleaner parts that were cemented together by frozen manure. His fingers bit with pain when he momentarily would hold them to the warm breath of his mouth.

After we successfully replaced the bearing, we retreated into the house to warm up by the large, old, iron radiators in the farmhouse, and rest from the difficult task. Our bodies shook as the coldness came out of them, and I warmed up some soup to help warm us from within.

Deciding that we had had enough of the frigid cold that day, we waited until the next to actually run the manure out of the barn. With the gutters filled from four days of cattle urine, the solid manure was not always enough to keep the liquid going up the chute. Bob worked outside pushing the watery manure up the chute with a pitchfork while I stomped fresh straw into the manure mess on the inside to give it a little more solidity.

Bob came into the barn to warm up before hauling the load of manure away. There was no arguing or abusing that day. We had gotten the job done together, he and I, and exhaustion was the only feeling we experienced as I hurried into the house to check on the girls and he went to dump the manure behind the grove. We had worked as a team to get the job completed like we did on so many other occasions. The girls had spent those hours in front of the television playing, which was the case so much of the time that neither they nor I thought anything of the neglectful parenting they were experiencing. The farm came first. I knew it. And by the time the girls were three and five, they knew it as well.

That day was indicative of that entire December. It had been twelve degrees below zero already on December twelfth when Bob and I took the girls to see Santa Claus. We would not have even attempted the trip into town had we also not needed to check in with Bob's parents, who were elderly and having health problems. I was making daily stops to set up medications and to check in on them. It had snowed and blown hard the evening before, so the four of us cramped ourselves in our four-wheel-drive pickup to get through the banks of snow that had drifted onto the gravel road that led to the highway and into town. The force of the pickup thunked against the hard snow banks as the pickup's force hit one after another along the gravel road leading to the tarred, county road which had been plowed.

We had experienced three weeks of temperatures below zero by Christmas Eve. You can imagine how the machinery needed to feed the cattle and clean the manure out of the barn worked after such an extended period of frigid weather. You can also imagine the strain it put on our emotions, especially on Bob's moods and his abusiveness.

Christmas Eve was a blizzard, and church services were cancelled. When I stepped out of the house on Christmas Eve night to do cattle chores, the world was one blur of white. An airplane passing high above out of sight sounded like a monstrous, freight train blasting my ears from all directions. It was a frighteningly lonely sound. And I prayed as I pushed my weight into the wind as I proceeded to the barn that if God wanted to destroy us, he should just do it. The day-after-day toil in the extreme cold had worn me to desperation.

On Christmas Day the terrible streak of weather broke. Temperatures climbed all the way up to three degrees below zero with bright, shining sunshine. Compared to what we had just been through, it seemed like heaven. We spent an enjoyable Christmas Day with Bob's folks and family, all of whom I loved dearly. Yes, I had been through some very tough times, both workwise and with the abuse in our relationship, but whatever was too hard to bear I simply disassociated out of memory. And life went on as normally as it could considering the drastic weather we had been facing. We moved into the new year having already been through the worst weather of the winter season.

Although it may seem unbelievable considering the circumstances in which I was living, by the time 1984 rolled around, I was beginning to say to Bob that I thought we should have another baby. I would try for a boy one last time! Bob was reluctant and said he had already been through "enough hell" with our first two children. But I was persistent. Perhaps this baby would be a boy. Besides, I had always wanted a family of three children. All the hitting, kicking, name-calling, hollering, swearing, I had disassociated from, pushed below the level of retrievable memory. I simply had put each episode out of my mind even as it was happening to me.

Although Bob will say now that I raped him (Hah! He was a most ardent participant in the process), by May I was pregnant. I took care of myself as well as I could through a tough summer of hard work unloading hay bales, walking bean fields for weeds, and carrying corn silage in to the cows with a bushel basket. I finally went to the clinic to hear the baby's heartbeat in late August.

Mild labor pains woke me early on a beautiful day in January of 1985. And after feeling their regularity for more that an hour, I woke Bob, saying that I felt we should get started with the morning chores as I thought this was the real thing. He didn't question me as the baby was already five days overdue. Her actual due date had turned out to be a whiteout, and we were relieved that I had no labor during the blizzard.

As I fed calves that morning, I had to stop what I was doing every so often to lean against a building or another solid object as a wave of labor passed over me. But the morning was warm and simply beautiful. Since it was still dark outside so early, the yard light was shining on the powdery snow, making it appear blue and pink against the early morning sky. Bob, fearing the worst after my short labor with Krista, drove me to the hospital before he milked the cows, thinking he might have to make the delivery himself if he didn't.

Once I arrived at the hospital and was placed in the labor room next to a woman who was having her first baby and was screaming loudly with each contraction, I felt so sorry for her that my own labor stopped completely. In the meantime Bob had gone home to milk the cows, put Bonnie on the school bus, and take Krista to my parents. He had then returned to the hospital hours later only to find me in bed with nothing happening. By early afternoon there were still no labor pains (or so I thought).

By two o'clock Bob was getting nervous. "Don't you know that I need to grind feed for the cattle today!" he stated loudly. He had not planned ahead so the feed supply for the cattle was empty.

Go home and grind feed," I told him. "You know where to find me when you are finished." I sent him home. His worry and complaining were not helping me anyway.

By 2:40 p.m. I thought, "Am I ever going to have this baby?" "Can you give me something to get this labor process started again?" I asked the nurse as she brought in a fresh pitcher of ice water.

"Well, let's check how things are coming." She replied.

"I'm not feeling any labor pains," I responded. "But I'm here, and I'm ready to get this over with."

Checking me, she said, "I don't think giving you anything will be necessary. You are already dilated to six, and labor seems to be progressing smoothly. We should have a baby in a couple of hours."

She was right except that it was not hours but minutes. Amy was born forty minutes later without the help of any medication. It was a very methodical birth as I felt little or no pain throughout. If I had been in labor all along, I had not been feeling any pain. I think by then I was so used to living with pain from all the instances of physical beating that I was able to separate the labor pains from my consciousness. I was able to leave the pain of my body by disassociating from it.

I'll never forget when the nurses laid the chubby, little body on my chest so that I could get a look at my third daughter. Her beady, big, blue eyes looked directly into mine. Her round Dahlke head was covered with downy, medium-brown hair. I fell in love with her instantly. One of the nurses had asked as I was being wheeled into the delivery room, "Should we call Bob?".

"No, he's home grinding feed so he won't hear the phone anyway," I responded, not feeling that I was being cheated as a wife in labor by not having the baby's father at my side.

Bob had not been any help or comfort to me through the births of the first two babies, so I didn't see any need to call him for this one. And, after all, he would just be angry at being disturbed while he was doing necessary work. No, I did the laboring alone. And, to tell you the truth, I was relieved to not have him there.

Bob arrived with Bonnie, who had just gotten off the school bus, less than an hour and a half after he had gone home to grind feed. But by the time he returned, I was already in my hospital room. The baby was being cleaned up. "What sex is the baby?" was his first question to me as he entered the room—not whether the baby was healthy or even completely formed.

"It's a girl," I answered knowing that very fact would be such a great disappointment to him that knowing his baby was healthy and had been born without complications would shadow in significance. Upon hearing that it was another girl, he leaned back against the wall and said nothing. Bob's body manner stated clearly how displeased he was.

An excited Bonnie chatted with me. "What does the baby look like? Can I see her? Look, here's a picture I made today at school," as she shoved a manila sheet of construction paper with a crayon drawing of a baby carriage in front of my face. It didn't take long before a nurse wheeled the glass-encased, nursery bassinet into my room and laid the baby, clean and pink, into my awaiting arms. Bonnie was thrilled with her new sister.

In a short time Bob said, "I've got to get going. It will take me longer to do the chores tonight—alone." Then he left with Bonnie. He did not return that night after evening milking.

I'm not sure now that he ever really did bond with Amy in a fatherly way. She was a source of embarrassment for him. Three girls—how embarrassing for a farmer yearning for a son! She was another mouth to feed when we already were struggling to survive monetarily. She was an addition to the commotion in the household, and I wasn't always available to help him when he needed me. Of course, there were those extra years of daycare that we would have to pay for on her account since there was no question that I would be returning to my job.

Two days later, following some argument with the nurses and doctor about whether or not I needed Bob's approval, I had a tubal ligation. I fed Amy early that morning, and the surgery was performed while Bob was home doing cattle chores. Bob did not come to see me before the surgery. There was no one but the nurses around me in the recovery room. Certainly I was not sad that there would be no more babies in the Dahlke household. It was clear to me by that time that Bob wouldn't be either.

And while I was glad to be on my own during labor, there aren't words to describe the feeling I had the evening of Amy's birth as I faced the juxtaposition between the joy of just having been given the gift of a beautiful, healthy infant and the emptiness of being abandoned by the baby's father at a time we should have been sharing happiness together. I felt very alone as I lay in my hospital bed holding my new little sweetheart. The nurses would come in and make their comments about my swee, beautiful baby and visit briefly, but it was not like having one's mate there to share those precious moments. I was bonding with our new child. As she lay and made squiggly faces sleeping in my arms, I was there alone to take in those special, beginning moments of her life—alone and lonely.

February came in with roaring, frigid temperatures and strong winds. The first three weeks that I was home from the hospital with my new baby were very cold and snowy. My surgery was on Thursday. I was out in the barn on Saturday evening, staples in the incision on my stomach. I had a whole four days off from my duties on the farm.

We had a major blizzard around Valentine's Day. The strong winds had blown one of the calf pens three feet deep with snow. The calves could hardly get out of their barn much less get to their watering tank. Although I had been sent home with instructions not to lift over ten pounds for three weeks, I moved a large, heavy, wooden gate out of the way in order to dig a three-foot-deep path from the calf barn to the water tank, lifting and throwing the solid, snow pack up and over the drifts to my sides. I didn't dwell on the fact that I might be injuring myself. If the calves couldn't get water, I knew Bob would yell or injure me in some more hurtful way. I simply did what needed to be done and didn't think about it. God kept me well and gave me strength for the task. Bob never even said thank you.

So the winter went by, I out doing chores as usual, Bonnie going to first grade, and Krista home with me and the baby. By then Krista was old enough to wind up the baby swing, so, if Amy was awake, and Bob needed me outside, she would keep a watchful eye on our baby for me.

I took three months off from my job after Amy's birth. The finances were looking a little better, and I did not want to repeat what I had gone through after Krista was born by returning to work too soon. Amy slept well and was soon on a regular feeding schedule. Krista liked her cartoons, played with her dolls, and set up farmyards, houses, and carnivals with her people stuff. She would keep a watchful eye on our baby for me. As long as I was available at Bob's beck and call, the household remained fairly stable. When there were incidences of abuse, I would block them out of my mind even as they occurred.

As the girls grew, I continued to work in my Program Coordinator position, I continued to work outside on the farm with Bob, and I carried the major responsibility of raising the children. In 1985, through a special program for those who financially qualified, money was available to make energy efficient improvements on the house. Bob initially balked at the idea of building on an entry and laundry area, putting in some new exterior doors, and putting some combination windows on the house to cover the many windows for which there were no longer any storm windows. He complained, "First you think you want a new baby, and then you want to work on the house on top of it?" But I went ahead and borrowed the money even with him saying, "You're going to be responsible for all of it!" And I was.

I lined up the builder and the masonry people. I spoke with the lumberyard and picked out the windows and doors. I even did all the measuring and drew out the floor plan. It was not until summer, when my dad came over to tear off the old, deteriorating porches that Bob took some initiative to lend a hand. He still complained about it, but he did help. And even years later, when he required me to do some labor on the farm for him, he always said, "You owe me! I tore those porches off the house in the heat while you sat on your duff (hah!) in the house."

The late 1980's were a time of both joy and turbulence in our marriage and on the farm. We were raising three young daughters and caring for Bob's aging parents. I was completely immersed in and enjoyed my job. Financially, we were more stable than we had been for a long time. I didn't think about the daily grind with the farm, the chores, the cattle, the girls, the household tasks, or my own job. I think by this time, I was operating on automatic pilot. Bob did have his episodes though. His temper hadn't resided nor had his mood swings. I had just perhaps learned to accommodate them better. But there were times . . . a wrong look, a non-agreeing comment, working too slow, working too fast, a broken piece of machinery, not being available at the moment he needed me, not noticing that he needed me, cattle getting through the fences or out of the gates—these are just a number of the things that could and would set him off.

To get kicked, pushed, and stomped into a gutter full of manure was common. He often tore the scarf, which I usually wore to cover my hair while doing chores, off my head and used it to choke me or threw a rock, or a corncob, or a fork forcibly at my head. If it hit its target, Bob would be satisfied. I would wash up the injury, bandage the injury and go on with life.

One time Bob really became angry because I disagreed with his ideas about the best way to feed corn into the feed grinder. The shell corn and the cob corn, which were used to make the feed, had been outdoors in their respective wagons through a warmer day that had produced some snow. In the warmth of the sun, the snow had melted into the corn. When the weather turned cold, this wetness from the melted snow turned to ice. When the corn went into the feed grinder, the heat of the machine would melt it into a sticky, sloppy substance that continually clogged up the auger in the shoot. We constantly needed to stop the grinding process to clean out the corn—an exasperating and tiring chore. We decided to take a break and went inside the barn to scrape the aisle and prepare the barn for cleaning.

"I think the feed grinding would go better if you didn't try to stuff so much of that wet and frozen corn into the auger at one time. Feed it in slower. It will take longer, but in the long run we'll get done faster because it won't block up so often." I explained as I pushed the manure with the scraper out of the aisle and into the gutters.

"That'll take too long! I want to get done before it gets dark. Besides the grinder should be able to take that corn whether it's wet or frozen. I say we stuff the corn in faster so it doesn't get a chance to stick to the sides of the chute. Besides, it wouldn't be sticking at all if you had remembered to put the wagons in the shed before it snowed on them. It's your fault. You're always forgetting important tasks."

"I'd say, if you wanted the wagons in the shed, you should have thought of putting them there. You are, after all, the one who needs to have feed ground today. Sometimes you need to think . . ." I didn't get the last word out of my mouth before I looked up as he raised the barn fork, which he was using to put bedding down for the cows. His face took on that wild, fierce look as he set his jaw tight under his beard. His eyes sent daggers. His nostrils flared. I can remember thinking at the time that he looked oddly like a mad bull. We were in the barn, just the two of us. The girls were in the house. He stopped what he was doing, threw the fork to the side and came rushing towards me. Running through the milk room, I let the outside door shut in his face and headed as fast as I could go in my rubber boots over the wintry ground towards the house. He tackled me with a flying leap sending me down to the ground hard face down on the frozen earth. He then took my head between his two, large hands and pounded it forcibly into the sharp, cold ice. "To you, O Lord, I lift up my soul. O my God, in you I trust . . . (Psalm 25)" These words were passing through my consciousness before the world went black.

The next thing I remember was seeing the expanse of the barn and farmyard before me at ground level. Bob was, thankfully, nowhere to be seen. I checked to see if I was breathing. I was. I brought my hands up from my sides. Yes, I verified to myself that I could still move them. I pushed up on my hands to lift my limp and aching body. As I did so, I noticed the blood-soaked ice below my face. Bringing my body to a semi-sitting position, I lifted one hand to feel the left side of my head. The scarf was frozen hard against the side of my hair. It felt numb.

Gradually I got myself up and walked gingerly to the house. Coming in, I was glad to find the girls playing with their toys and watching television. They hadn't looked up as I had peeked in on them. I went back into the entryway and looked into the mirror above the hand-washing sink we had put in when we had built onto the house. My scarf was frozen with blood against my bloodied, matted hair. Since I now was in a warm room, the blood was starting to melt. It dripped down from my scarf and hair onto the sink. I remember the sight of the brilliant, red drops against the white porcelain. Without thinking about the extent of the injury, I carefully removed the bloodied scarf, noticing the stark contrast between the redness of the fresh blood and the turquoise blue of the scarf's printed background.

I lowered my head to the faucet and let the clear, cool water rinse over my head and hair. For a while the water ran red into the drain hole of the small sink. But gradually, it changed to pink and then cleared. I gently patted the area with a clean towel. I was alive, I decided. "Everything is all right," I assured myself as I removed my boots and set them on the rug in front of the warm radiator. I changed into fresh, clean clothing, and washed my face, arms, and hands. I rinsed out my bloodied scarf and hung it over the tub next to the washing machine to dry. I put the dirty clothing I had just taken off, along with some others out of the laundry basket, into the washing machine. I then went into the kitchen, took a couple of aspirin with a glass of cool water and sat down on a kitchen chair. The warmth of the furnace felt good against my chilled cheeks. And my fingers were tingling as they warmed up. "It feels good just to sit here in my stocking feet," I thought as I watched the girls play.

Bob came home with our red, Chevy pickup some time later. I had put the clothes in the dryer by then, and its steady hum was comforting in the background of my mind. He took off his boots and jacket and walked though the kitchen in a manner no more out of the ordinary than had nothing ever occurred outside that Saturday afternoon. He went into the dining room and lay down on the couch, while I cleaned up the snacks the girls had left on the kitchen table. Nothing was said of the episode. Gradually, the scab on the side of my head under my hair healed and disappeared.

If I had any feelings of hate towards him by then, I was not cognizant of them. If anything, I felt numbness of my entire body, a feeling of nonfeeling. I even commented to my secretary, who displayed her emotions easily and often, at that time, "I don't feel anything. Nothing seems to affect me." And it didn't. I was like a walking robot going through the motions of living but not feeling any reaction to the life going on around me. I didn't feel sad or angry, nor could I respond with jubilance when Bonnie would bring home a report card with all A's or Krista, who was always very shy and withdrawn, would perform her part bravely in a pre-school Christmas program. I never hugged the girls and praised them for their abilities and honors as I saw other parents do. I simply didn't feel those emotions. I had completely shut the emotional side out of my life. I hope the girls will someday understand and forgive me for this neglect. I hope they will be able to work beyond it so that, when they have their own families, they will be able to hug and praise their own children. I'm still working hard at that even as my girls are adults. I'm sure they will be affected to some degree for years to come.

Winter turned into spring, and then summer, and autumn, and soon back to winter again. So the years passed. The girls grew as Krista joined Bonnie in elementary school, and Amy started preschool on some of the days while I was at work. My job remained constant and fulfilling. The farm with its steady and unwavering routine was just another regularity of life. Nothing changed, not the routine, not the drudgery, and definitely not Bob's up-and-down moods. To me all of it was so normal. Because I disassociated myself from the abusive incidents, I was able to go on with my work and my duties outside and to function as a wife and mother as well. Later, I would ponder on all of these incidents—much later when the infesting incidents spilled into my awareness and began crippling my life.

It was not until 1988 that I hit a major snag in what I thought was normal life. That was a particularly devastating year in two major regards.

Bob's elderly parents, along with my grandmother, died that year. Bob's mother died at the end of May, my grandmother at the beginning of June, and his father in October. This was hard for both of us. I had done much of the day-to-day care of his mother before she moved into the nursing home. Even after that, I continued to stop to visit and attend to her needs often after I finished my workday. Although in failing health, she was overjoyed when the girls also came to visit, and, with frail arms and great joy, held Amy as a young infant. Bob's mother sank into a deep depression the final years of her life and no longer spoke to anyone. Yet she would smile and experience joy in response to seeing the girls.

I loved her deeply. Yet, I had done much of the grieving for who she had been as she was in the stages of dying. So, when the actual passing occurred, I was mentally prepared and even glad that her time of suffering was over. I also had a very strong faith. I knew the words of the promise of resurrection would be for her too. She was in God's care now.

Bob, on the other hand, had been busy with the spring planting when her health was quickly failing. So when the day of her death came, his grieving work just began. He never let me forget that I went back to work the day after her funeral, leaving him alone with his grief. I thought perhaps I should have stayed with him. I guess I just didn't realize how affected he was by her death. He never really showed that kind of emotion, and he hadn't asked me to remain home with him. But, for the rest of our marriage, he never let me hear the end of it—how I had abandoned him in his time of need.

Bob's dad died in mid-October. Most of the crops had been harvested by then, but there was still some plowing that needed to be done. Bob was in the middle of arranging for someone to tile out part of the land so that it would have better drainage in case of large amounts of rain. I went with him to make arrangements with the head of the tiling crew the day of his father's visitation. He didn't seem to be grieving at all, which surprised me. It was not until after his father was buried that the reality of his dad's death hit him. Once again I had returned to work, having done my grieving as his father's health had been failing. I felt good that I had visited with his dad one last time in the hospital just shortly before his death. Bob had not been with me.

1988 was also a year of extreme drought. The autumn farm work was easy because there was not much to harvest. Instead of ending the summer with enough hay in the hay barn and shed for the cows to eat all winter, there were only small stacks, which we knew would never last until the next year's crop came in. In fact, we had brought in the entire second crop of alfalfa bales from one of our large fields on one rack instead of several loads, which would have been a normal harvest. It was obvious that the coming winter was going to be a scant one both feed-wise for the cattle and money-wise for us.

It was no wonder then that, as the colored leaves floated down, covering the ground with a rustling blanket that year, Bob's temper was ready to flair more quickly than ever. It took very little to set him off, and I went out of my way to make sure that I didn't. Then again, as I so often did during my married life, I turned to the Psalms for assurance: *To you, O Lord, I lift up my soul. Do not let me be put to shame, do not let my enemies exult over me. Make me to know your ways, teach me your paths. May integrity and uprightness preserve me, for I wait for you"* (Psalm 25). By repeating a fitting passage from the psalms to myself, whatever my struggle, I could let go of the hurt and shame, find the value in life, and go on coping.

I think this is why, for me the autumn brought more peace than I had ever experienced. I was often drawn out to the gravesite where I experienced a sense of presence which filled my longing and lonely soul so that I could go on. With Bob's parents' deaths, something had touched me deep inside, something very great, far beyond me and this world of tension and drudgery. I had a definite sense of God. God was with me as I walked the green-brown carpet of grass and felt the warm, autumn breeze gently brush the hairs on my cheeks. That year also, the words of two Psalms I had learned as a child were often in my thoughts. "The Lord is my refuge and strength, a very present help in time of trouble . . ." (Psalm 46) would go through my mind as I helped Bob with yet another task that angered him. "I lift my eyes to the hills, from where will my help come? My help comes from the Lord. He visits me day and night . . ." would be on my tongue as his fist would fly, hand strike, or mouth spit at my face. These words filled me with a power and strength that was almost beyond my human comprehension. Along with their power came a sense of total peace, that my entire being, my entire life was in God's hands, and that I would be kept safe whether I lived through the attack or died during it. This feeling gave me an utter calmness as my mind left my body, as if I were an angel, looking on from afar.

I lost a client to death that spring. He had been hydrocephalic, and the shunt, which allowed for drainage of fluid from his skull, had, unknowingly and unexpectedly, closed up. He died very quickly. The only warning signal that I had seen was his vomiting in my car as I drove him to a progress review.

"I think there's something wrong with Dan," I reported to the nurse at the group home in which he lived telling her of his sudden illness in my car. Despite a doctor's visit, he was dead in a few days. I found myself bewildered, surprised, and deeply saddened by his death, not only because of my work with him, but also because of the close relationship I had developed with his family. In a day, all that work was for naught. He was gone. Yet again I felt a certainty in the promise of resurrection for him. I wrote a long letter of my thoughts and faith to his mother, who was deeply moved by my words.

Although I had thought about ministry in some far off, unreal way at times in my adult life, that autumn I felt both a sense of God's presence with me and a calming peace that was beyond my explanation. From what seemed out of the blue, I said to a co-worker late in October at the end of an exhausting day of meetings and work with clients, "I think I need to go into ministry." I can remember her responding, "I think you should. You would be good at it."

I went home, and life went on as we moved into winter. I had a job, a life, a husband, and three, young children. Certainly a change in careers that would require several more years of study on my part was out of the question. I let it go, thinking that the feeling was just a response to the losses of the year.

In 1989 we built a large machine shed to house our equipment. In 1990 we put up a larger silo. Although Bob was overjoyed by the improvements on the farm and the difference they would make in the overall farming operation, the ups and downs of his moods continued. I often felt like I was walking the top edge of a fence, not knowing which way the fall would be next. We had fun times as a family, going shopping, eating out, going to a nearby lake to swim on a balmy, summer afternoon. We also had times when it seemed that nothing I or the girls did was right in Bob's eyes. The erratic nature of his emotional behavior was both hard for the girls and for me. I think that it also greatly confused them. One moment he was this playful dad who would take them somewhere or fool around with them. The next moment such a stream of deriding criticisms would spew forth from his mouth that it froze them in terror.

One of those hot summers, with the oats harvest in progress, he got angry with me while we were preparing the barn to run the barn cleaner in order to remove the days' manure. He was angered by having to quit what he had been working at to perform this daily and mundane task. "I don't see why you can't do this without me. All you gotta do is back the spreader under the chute and press a button!" Yet I was afraid that, without a person to watch at both the lower inside curve of the gutter and at the top of the chute as the chain turned unloading the manure onto the spreader, something would go awry. I would be blamed when it broke. It was very hot and humid that day, had rained in the morning and the sun had come out steamily in the afternoon. The sweat was rolling down my forehead as I worked, and I could feel it trickle down my back under my plaid, cotton blouse.

As we worked we were discussing the most recent illness causing death among some of our young calves. "I don't see why you can't keep a calf alive!" he hollered.

"I've given them the medicine. It doesn't seem to be working." I answered. "I wish you would let me call the veterinarian. I think we have a problem that needs professional help."

"We can't afford to keep paying all our profits to the vet. You should be able to take care of a calf without having it die!"

"I've tried everything I know how to do. I think we need to call the . . ." I never got the word out a second time.

In a fraction of a second, he rammed the large, metal blade of the barn manure scraper into my bare leg. The blood came streaming out as Bob stomped out of the feed room door. Quickly I grabbed a piece of brown, paper towel, which I had scrunched up in my pocket. I pressed it on the wound, clumsily making my way to the milk room walking in a bent over position, holding the towel on the wound below my knee.

Once in the milk room, I took some clean paper towel, ran it under the cold water faucet, and pressed it to the wound. It quickly filled with blood. I did the same thing with another, and another, until finally the blood's flowing slowed. As I saw the towel remain fairly clear of blood, I lifted it gently away from the wound. I was petrified by the depth of the cut. If I pulled the skin apart, I could see the bone between the skin's smoothly severed edges. Holding a folded square of clean, white paper towel from the roll by the hand sink in the milk room over the wound, I slowly and carefully made my way to the house. My coming in and needing to dress some wound was so routine to the girls by then, they may have looked up at me briefly, but were quickly again absorbed in play and afternoon cartoons.

That particular wound took several changes of dressings and several days to even begin to improve. Not only was the skin severed, but the bone was also bruised. This made walking both painful and difficult. And, I did momentarily think of when I had had my last tetanus vaccination since manure had been injected into the wound along with the blow. But never did I think of going to the doctor with it. No, the wounds Bob inflicted on me I cleaned, dressed, and allowed to heal. Only Bob and I knew what had occurred to cause the wound in the first place. And most times, I don't even think he remembered doing the wounding deed.

There was a time in the early 1990's, which also stands out in my mind. I had come home late from work, and Bob was extremely upset because of it. It was his birthday, and besides stopping at the hardware store to buy him a gift, I had taken the girls to the dentist that day. Although most people understand that for such appointments patients are at the mercy of the medical providers, Bob blamed me for scheduling the appointment on his birthday. For children in the town near where we lived, dental appointments were set up automatically. I suppose I could have called and rescheduled, but the girls did need to see the dentist. It just happened that the appointments were on the say day as his birthday. Besides, we had nothing special planned for the evening. I figured I would bake a cake while I made supper, which we would enjoy after evening milking.

"What the hell did you make an appointment for on my birthday? Besides, they don't need to see the dentist. They have perfectly good teeth. That just costs us money and wastes time! Anyway, it's my birthday, and now you've ruined it!" was his angry greeting as I drove onto the yard after a busy day. I rushed to change clothes and get out to the barn to help.

I was trying to hurry with evening feeding in order to get back into the house and get supper started. I crawled up the ladder into the hay barn to throw down some bales of meadow hay for the young stock. Bob was still griping about the late hour and the dentist visit as I did so. After I climbed up and was busy with the bales, he pulled the ladder out of the hole from below saying, "This will teach you to come home late on my birthday!" his angry voice followed me up the ladder. I called for him to put it back. I needed to get down, not only to finish the feeding chores, but also to get back into the house to get supper made and check on the girls. "See what you're going to do about this!" was his reply as he walked out of the barn, got into the pickup, and drove away.

Stranded in the hay barn, I wondered what to do. I thought maybe one of the girls would wonder what was taking so long and come out to check on where her mother was. None did. They were busy watching their late afternoon television shows and doing homework. Even if they had noticed, the girls were not big enough or strong enough to raise the ladder back into its position so that I could climb down. And who knew when Bob would return. Surely when he arrived back, I would need to have supper on the table. I had to think fast.

Throwing bale after bale of straw down through the hole to form a pile in front of the cows' heads below, I was able to form a mound that I could climb down on. I made my way out of the hole carefully, not to disturb the haphazard positioning of the pile of bales, which would send me falling to the cement floor below.

Having made my way to the floor, I then stacked the bales in the corner calf pen so that the cows would not pull them apart and make a huge mess. Finally I was free to get done what needed to be finished before milking.

Supper was just ready, and I was setting the table when Bob arrived home. I had baked a cake and the gifts the girls and I had picked up for him following the dental appointment were on the table. He gladly accepted everything presented to him. He never said a word about what he had done. Did I expect him to by that time in our marriage? No, an apology for any misdeed or pain he inflicted on me was no longer an expectation on my part. I was already very skilled at putting the incidents out of my mind and going on with life.

One particular behavior of Bob's on more than one occasion terrified both the girls and me. Throughout the time I had known Bob, he had always had a problem if another vehicle passed him. He would become very upset by this simple occurrence. Since we lived in an area where there were not any freeways and very few four-lane highways, usually we were in a situation in which the lane beside ours was for oncoming traffic. Often as the vehicle, which was passing us, moved up beside us, Bob would step on the accelerator, speeding up so the passing vehicle could not pass. "Oh, so you think you're going to pass me. See if you can get by this!" he would chant almost excitedly. Early on in our relationship I learned that it was best not to say anything. His backhand could come rushing from the steering wheel to my face.

Certainly the behavior was childish. It was also quite dangerous. This especially proved to be true on one particular occasion. As a family, we were returning home from a shopping trip to one of the larger towns some twenty-five miles away from the farm. The car was full of kids and packages. The girls were busy looking in the bags and admiring some of the new items I had purchased for them. Bob was annoyed by the noise and the commotion they were making in the car.

Although I was sure we were going the speed limit, another vehicle pulled up behind us and moved out to pass. Before I knew it, Bob stepped the accelerator to the floor, making it impossible for the vehicle to get by. We continued side by side for, what seemed to me, an eternity. The girls, noticing the car's increase in speed, looked up from what they were doing to watch.

We were now moving into a curve in the road. The other vehicle was not yet dropping back nor was Bob slowing down to allow it to get past us. A large truck was approaching in the oncoming lane as we rounded the curve. The conditions were set for a head on collision. Yet Bob persisted. The girls were panicking in the back seat as they were witnessing the two vehicles, ours and the one parallel to us, moving head on into what seemed to be imminent contact with the approaching truck.

"Dad, stop it!" Bonnie scolded from the back seat.

I reached out for Bob's arm with a gasp that he should let off the accelerator. He didn't heed my cue. The approaching truck sounded its long, low horn as it began to slow up before the vehicle beside decided to slip back into the lane behind us. I breathed a sigh of relief as the truck whisked safely past in the opposing lane.

One of the girls said, "Dad, you could have caused an accident!"

"Yah," another chimed in, "you could've gotten us killed!" But he paid no heed nor did he change his behavior.

A similarly dangerous situation occurred on Christmas Eve of 1992. Bob was especially grouchy in the late afternoon and evening as we were trying to get the cattle chores done early in order to make it to the Christmas Eve worship service. In order to get to church by 7:00 p.m. we had to milk the cows early. Often when we needed to change the milking time, Bob would not be pleased, and we would all know about it.

This Christmas Eve he held off until the last minute to start with the milking, so there was no extra time for something to go wrong or to take longer than usual. Well, something did take extra time. We returned to the house to clean up for church later than I had wanted to so our getting to church in a timely manner was delayed. And Bob certainly did not hurry himself in any way to make the process easier. The girls were anxious. After all, it was Christmas Eve. "Come on, Dad. Hurry up!" they were saying, which made him move more slowly than ever.

By the time we climbed into our club cab pickup to travel the four-and-a-half miles to church, Bob was both angry and mean. He was yelling at the girls, criticizing and calling us names. When we arrived at church, the girls and I were terribly anxious and stressed. I remember there being a big, heavy lump of fear at the top of my chest, a feeling I was experiencing more and more. Bonnie was crying in the back seat.

We rushed into church after the first hymn and found seats. Bonnie was not with us. She was so upset that she sat out the entire service in the pickup. Krista, with tears in her eyes, spent the service lying on the sofa in the Fellowship Hall. Amy hung close to me, knowing that we were on thin ice.

By the time we left church, it was snowing heavily. As we turned out of town and onto the highway, it was hard to see. Large snowflakes were hitting directly into the windshield. Bob, who had behaved normally with other people at church, moved into his angry mode as soon as we climbed back into the truck. He was boiling mad. Once out on the road, he pulled into the opposing lane and sped up heading into any oncoming traffic. The younger girls hollered for Dad to stop it. Bonnie sat terrified against the back seat. By God's grace, nothing came along to hit us head on before we turned onto the gravel road that led to the farm.

Although we were barely able to see our mailbox, which indicated where we should turn into our driveway, Bob purposely passed by it. He drove up to a neighbor's box—a neighbor, whom he both envied and despised. He hit the brakes, jerked the shift lever into park, jumped out of the truck, and with the vicious look on his face that had become so familiar in the eighteen years I had been married to him, kicked that neighbor's mailbox as hard as he could. The wooden post holding the box cracked off at the level of the frozen ground. "Let's see how happy they are about that!" he said triumphantly as he jumped back into the pickup, jerked the truck back into gear, made a U-turn in the middle of an intersection in the snowy, blind night, and with his family as witnesses, sped back to our driveway and up to the farmyard.

Bonnie was so upset by all of this and was crying so hard by the time we returned home, instead of opening her gifts, she went up to her room. The other two girls opened their gifts in a somber mood. Bob continued to rant and rave angrily as he changed his clothes and headed out to the barn to feed the cows their evening meal.

In the meantime my parents came over. By the time they arrived and made their way to the house, Bob had returned from outside, he had become his normal self again and was conversing with them as if nothing had occurred out of the ordinary that night. And, aside from my mother noticing Bonnie's tearful eyes when, at my call, she came downstairs, my parents never knew the danger and fear that we experienced that Christmas Eve.

The quick changes in Bob's emotions and behavior, the difference between what was happening privately in our family and the image he portrayed of himself to the public were terribly confusing to the girls, especially to Bonnie, who was maturing herself by that time. One minute we had this angry, vicious, and often violent beast on our hands. The next minute Bob was a gentleman, smiling and greeting people as if nothing had been happening to upset him. Later, I learned in therapy and domestic abuse groups that this kind of Dr. Jekyl and Mr. Hyde behavior is typical of abusers. It is a kind of crazy-making that keeps the abused person in such a state of disarray that she cannot focus on the steps necessary to remove herself from the situation. She is walking on eggshells at all times trying to prevent, ward off, or lessen the next abusive episode that is surely to come. In a mental state of chaos, she literally cannot act to get away even if she should want to.

As I reflect back now, the years from 1985 to 1992 were marked by turbulent behavior on Bob's part, and the incidences of abuse increased sharply. I just didn't think about it at the time. I simply went on with life.

Sometimes the tenseness would grow so strong that I would do or say something that most certainly would make Bob angry, like ask him what he had done all day while I was gone at work. That would usually set him off because he didn't want to be accused of blowing the day away, something he often did. This left all of the cattle work to be done when I returned home from work. I knew his temper would flare, but I was prepared to flee to an area of safety until I felt the certainty of danger had passed. I would find refuge in a field grown tall with corn, or behind a building, always shifting my position so that I would not be visible from any angle. Sometimes, especially after dark, I would hide in or behind one of the hay bunks, which stood out behind the barn on the cow's cement platform, either covering myself with hay or slowly creeping around its perimeter by the glow of the yard light in order to remain out of sight. My behavior would maneuver the abusive episode in a way that would make it more controlled and actually safer to endure, taking the tension of an oncoming onslaught out of the air.

What the girls really knew of or thought about the abuse, I don't know. I know that I tried to save them from as much of it as possible. But when Bob threw a glass at me while we were eating a meal at the kitchen table, or a pitcher of milk or Kool-aid, there was no way to avoid their seeing what was happening. If one were to have made a line graph of the time between 1985 and 1992 to illustrate Bob's behavior, it would have looked like a piece of tightly-kinked rickrack.

I dealt with the stress as each incident required and as time passed. Sometimes, after a severely abusive episode, I would return to the house and find myself angry and scolding towards the girls. I know I caught myself doing that, and for that, I hope they will forgive me. More and more as the years went by I found myself nervously knotted up inside, a heavy lump at the top of my chest. For a period of time, I experienced troubling stomach upset and continued tension in my jaw. I continued to suffer severe bouts with bronchitis and episodes of unstoppable coughing to the point that I thought I would die from an inability to catch my breath. Never did I associate these physical problems with the anguish of my life.

Since I was a Christian woman, I never even considered the possibility of divorce. I had been taught that divorce was wrong. It never even entered into my thinking that God would not want me and the girls in a situation that was not life-giving and certainly, at times, was life-threatening. Yes, I did begin to pack a few times. I did get the girls into the car to go to my parents' house a few times, but I did not follow through. I never called my parents back to our farm after the incident in which they told me that there was nothing they could do, that Bob and I needed to get help for this ourselves. But how could or would we? I knew even the suggestion would either lead to denial or more abuse on his part. So I said nothing.

I did pack some clothes for each of the girls in a black, garbage bag and kept it under the folded blanket in the trunk just in case, hoping inside myself that such a time would never come. I did, on occasion, actually get into the car and leave the farmyard, with the girls unsuspectingly at play in the house, to escape a certain episode in which I knew a beating was coming. Bob would then often rush into the pickup and speedily catch up with me, trying to run me off the road or ram the back of the car with the bumper of the pickup. If the neighbors ever noticed any of this, they never said anything. They never came to help me.

Although laws had been passed in the 1980's to protect women from abuse, and I knew vaguely of them, I also never considered calling law enforcement. Both shame and fear bound me from doing so. I didn't know of any groups in my area that worked with abused women, so I also didn't know how to get help. I knew the nearest women's shelter was more than forty-five miles away. I also knew that if I ever did call for any kind of outside help, Bob would kill me.

No, I was left alone to deal with a violent and erratic husband. I never told my co-workers—until later. I truly did not realize that what I was living wasn't a marriage. What I was living was a lie.

Psalm 46
God's Defense of His City and People

A Song

God is our refuge and strength,
  a very present help in trouble.
Therefore we will not fear, though the earth
should change,
  Though the mountains shake in the heart
of the sea;
though its waters roar and foam,
  though the mountains tremble with its tumult.

There is a river whose streams make glad
the city of God,
  the holy habitation of the Most High.
God is in the midst of the city; it shall not
be moved;
  God will help it when the morning dawns.
The nations are in an uproar, the kingdoms
totter;
  he utters his voice, the earth melts.
The LORD of hosts is with us;
  The God of Jacob is our refuge.

Come, behold the works of the LORD;
  See what desolation he has brought on
the earth.
He makes wars cease to the end of the
  earth;
  he breaks the bow, and shatters the spear,
  he burns the shields with fire.
"Be still and know that I am God!
  I am exalted among the nations,
  I am exalted in the earth."
The LORD of hosts is with us;
  the God of Jacob is our refuge.

Seven: Road To Damascus

In the Bible there is a story about a man named Saul, a devout Jew, who persecuted the early Christians. When Saul was walking along the road to Damascus, he was struck by a storm, a force from God, in which God not only changed his name to Paul but after which his entire life took a new path. Paul, Christian evangelist and author of many letters in the New Testament of the Bible, ended up converting many nonbelievers to Christianity. In fact, he was the primary apostle to bring the good news of Jesus Christ to the gentiles. It is through Paul's proclamation that we, who claim to be Christians today, have our roots. Although I didn't know it as my life moved into the summer of 1993, I was by then traveling down my own road to Damascus. My life would take a turn in what still seems to me today a most unbelievable way.

The turn began with the vengeance of cool and rainy weather that rolled in with the spring of 1993. It was weather never before seen by Bob or me in our now almost twenty years of farming. Four times we purchased soybean seed that spring, each time choosing a variety with a shorter maturity season. The first time the weather delayed the planting. The second time, the seed rotted in the ground before it could break through the rain-beaten soil. The third time, so much of the field where the soybeans had been planted was drowned out by flooding rains, the field needed to be replanted or we would get a half of crop for sure. After the third disaster, the weather never did cooperate to plant a fourth time. I rushed out on Bob's demand to purchase the seed as Bob said "before it's all bought up and we can't get any," but it didn't matter in the end. With uncooperative weather all through the month of June, by the time the fourth of July rolled around, we knew it was too late to replant the crop, much less harvest it. That last purchase of soybean seed, too late in the season to be returned, was like giving money—money we didn't have—away. The rotting, tattered bags probably are still laying in the shed on the farm with age-old, musty seed flowing out of them.

The cattle were also greatly affected by the persistent cool and rainy weather. Even though by 1993 we had a cement platform on which the cows could exercise and eat hay, the rain along with manure on the platform formed a soup on the cement, which, even if removed almost daily, seemed to infect them just by looking from beneath. The local veterinarians were making daily calls to the farm. On top of that, for a reason which remained unknown to us, the cattle were failing to breed. This would in the long run cause a loss in production as cattle that don't breed must either be sold or must milk longer between calving, decreasing the amount of milk they produce. Less milk meant less income.

The rains also spoiled much of the alfalfa crop, which is a mainstay in the diet of milking cattle. Much of the alfalfa rotted on the field until the nutritional value had been washed out of it. Bob would swear as he'd put on his cap and sweatshirt to go out and chop the once valuable but now useless, rotted crop back onto the field. Since we couldn't make the alfalfa when we wanted to, we were short on fodder for the animals. Sometimes we resorted to hauling in mounds of wet, green alfalfa that had not been baled, which we then forked by hand into the barn to feed the cattle.

Sickness ran rampant in the baby calves that summer as well. It seemed that the young newborns would be healthy at birth and would thrive while on their mother's milk only to weaken and die once I placed them on a formula-based, milk replacement. I struggled with them in what seemed an endless endeavor to figure out the problem. I tried every remedy and vaccination I could think of to fight whatever battle was besieging them.

Of course, with the young calves dying right and left, Bob was not pleased. Yet, when I begged him to allow me to call the veterinarian, he denied the request saying, "The vet bills are already too high!" And they were. The veterinarian bills were eating up whatever profit the cattle could produce. Bob called me "calf-killer, calf-killer!" over and over again. Didn't he realize that I too cared about the health of our young stock, that I too knew how devastating their deaths were to our overall profit on the farm? Didn't he know that I too cared whether they lived or died, that I did not like dragging a little one that I had nursed from birth out to a pile to burn or bury? No matter how hard I tried to explain what I was trying to do to keep them alive, or no matter how I begged for him to help me with them, he didn't listen nor did he help. "Calf-killer, calf-killer!" was all I heard over and over again. I wondered how I had managed to take care of my own babies without killing them.

I finally did call the veterinarian at the risk of an onslaught from Bob. The veterinarian found salmonella bacteria, a bacteria that is deadly to young or weak animals, in the calves' nursing formula. He said that this was not uncommon as there were no guidelines for quality in the importation of milk product for animal feed. He also stated that the milk product was imported because it was less expensive to use imported milk product than to use product made in the United States. All cattle feed companies did so. It all seemed unfair! Both to the calves and to me!

By the time the fourth of July rolled around, Bob was behind both in making the alfalfa crop and in cultivating the weeds from the corn and soybean fields. As a family, we had always celebrated July Fourth with friends of my family with whom I had grown up. We planned to do so this year as well—at least I thought we had. On the day of the Fourth, Bob went out cultivating while I prepared food and clothing, packed up the card table and chairs onto the pickup, and mixed lemonade.

"It's time to start getting ready!" I signaled the girls to start getting cleaned up and dressed for the picnic. I then went out to cue Bob that the time was approaching noon, which was when the picnic was to begin.

"It's time to stop," I yelled to Bob as he circled with the tractor and cultivator close to the road where I was standing. No response. I stood there as he made another trip up the rows of soy beans and back towards me.

"It's time to go to the picnic!" I hollered above the sound of the tractor as he approached again. But still no response.

The third time I signaled with my arms to get his attention. Again he turned the tractor to make another pass though the field. But knowing he had both seen and heard me, I decided if I went back to the house, he would soon come.

When he did finally come home, his face black from dirt and sunburned from the rays of the sun beating on him, he was angry. "I don't see why I need to stop for this dumb picnic. You know I have to get the work done!" he yelled as he took his dear, sweet time in cleaning up and getting dressed.

The girls were getting impatient. "How long is it going to take Dad to get ready?" they asked again and again. I could sense the feeling of anxiety welling up in my upper chest and a tightness developing in my throat as I tried to indicate to them to be quiet and wait patiently while he cleaned up.

When Bob was finally ready, we drove off in the pickup. It was already past noon. I was feeling anxious about not getting to the picnic on time with the food I had prepared for the potluck. I was also feeling anxious about Bob's mood, which seemed like it was about to burst at any moment. When one of the girls again expressed impatience, Bob's mood did burst. He pushed the accelerator of the pickup down to the floor, passing other traffic on the roadway, even when there was oncoming traffic, narrowly getting the vehicle back into our lane in time. There were more than a few close calls. Along with the intense speed, so much verbal abuse flowed from his mouth that the girls sat in stunned silence. I tried to reason him back to a tolerable mood, but it wasn't to be. Although he never lashed out at me as I thought he might, the verbal accusations, the put-downs, the names, the swearing—all broke the mood of festivity for the day.

By the time we reached the picnic, my eyes were red with tears, and the girls didn't feel like picnicking. They sat quietly on the chairs I took out of the pickup box. Bob sat himself down at a table by himself and didn't speak to anyone. With him in this kind of mood, I knew I had better bring him a plate of food. I also knew I had better sit by him. Otherwise, I would for sure get it when we got home.

His mood lightened somewhat as the afternoon progressed, but he still accused me of talking about him behind his back when I was in the house helping to wash dishes with some of the other women. He became angry and shot daggers at me with his eyes when I later exited the house because he thought I had been inside too long. The short time I had been in the house doing dishes with these other women, my friends from childhood, had been like a breather from the tenseness of being in the presence of his foul mood.

Even though I made an excuse to leave the picnic early, Bob complained all the way home as he drove at a speed well above the limit. "What a waste of time when I could have been home getting some work done!" he expressed as we sped along. "Don't worry. I'll do all the feeding chores so you can go out on the field until the cows have eaten and are ready to be milked," I tried to calm him. I expected a beating when we arrived home. I am sure I didn't get one because, although completely tired out from both the day and its accompanying stress, I volunteered to do all preparation chores. Allowing Bob the time on the field seemed to simmer him down so that milking time was tolerable.

The girls had had enough of him that day and spent the evening out of his sight. When I came back in the house after milking, I washed up, cleaned up the dishes from the picnic, and went to bed, feeling again this uncomfortable, nervous, tightness in my upper chest and throat. Bob soon followed wanting to have sex. I let him. It wasn't worth fighting against it. I had had enough of his bad moods for that day already!

Then came a truly destructive storm in mid-July. During the storm, Bob, I, and the girls had retreated to the water-flooded basement to sit on some pieces of dry cardboard to wait out what seemed to be an unceasingly strong wind. When it quieted, I crawled up the basement stairs giving the girls instructions to stay put. I passed through the kitchen, completely dark as the electricity was out, to look out of the bay window of the dining room. Although on most nights I could see the row of lights of the nearby town more than four miles in the distance, on that night I could see nothing. The rain was coming down so heavily that looking outside was like looking at a solid, black sheet of nothing.

I knew the fields were flooded when I looked out of the bedroom window as the sun rose.

All I could see everywhere was lake upon lake on what had been the crops we had managed to get planted and keep alive to that point. My heart sank down through my knees and the pit in my stomach hurt. The tightness in my chest that I had become so accustomed to by now became even tighter still as I looked out, and I felt what I would call a nervous fluttering in my throat. Remembering back to a day before we were married when we had agreed that we would farm for awhile and, maybe, later on do something else, I said to Bob that morning, "It's time to move on, do something else."

He retorted, "We're never moving on. We're never going to do anything else! This is all we're ever going to do!" At that moment, my heavy heart with all of the nervous, fluttery feeling sank down and right out from under my feet.

The farm wasn't the only disaster that year. There were also rough times at my job. With government cuts in spending and the moving of clients out of the state hospitals in an attempt to downsize and cut costs, my place of work had continually been receiving clients with much more difficult problems. The clients were not only more disabled, but many also had severe behavioral issues. At the same time, all raises in salary were denied due to financial difficulties. As well, management seemed unsympathetic and unresponsive to cries of staff for outside assistance in developing behavioral programs.

As a program coordinator, I had asked for the assistance of some behavioral therapists to work with my staff on a few very tough cases. In these cases the behavioral problems were not only preventing clients from progressing in their education but also threatening the safety and well-being of staff. I also asked for some outside, professional people to help staff deal with the situation and to help them debrief after particularly disturbing episodes had occurred. All of this seemed to fall on deaf ears. Is it any wonder that several staff members, who had worked for the program for more than a decade, were quitting? Yet, management did not intervene, choosing instead to hire new staff, who would come in at a lower salary. This put me in a position of constantly needing to train and retrain staff in addition to all of my regular duties.

I had two client cases that summer which were of particular concern and which had me particularly puzzled. I was finally allowed to call in some behavioral professionals to help me with these cases. I had attended a number of care conferences on their behalf. Yet, the difficulties persisted.

When I finally learned the causes of the problems, I was devastated. In each case, the cause was a diagnosis of depression even though the indicating behaviors were very different. "I know what depression is like," I thought to myself. I had lived with my mother's recurrent depression during my childhood and later in my adult years. I knew what kind of pain it brought both to her and to those who were around her. Perhaps I too acutely felt my clients' pain because I had become too emotionally connected to their care. Perhaps the abuse my staff had endured from these clients brought up unpleasant memories for me. Perhaps management's unsupportive attitude reminded me of my own unsupported struggles. Perhaps I was trying alone to give my staff the support they needed to keep going without getting help for myself. I was touched by both my staff's tears and their anger in regard to the clients *and* the management. I just wanted to make it better! After all, nothing ever affected me! I never felt anything! I was immune to the stress that all of this was putting on me—or was I?

It seemed the smallest occurrence would anger Bob enormously that summer. For example, one evening the electric fence wasn't working. During milking chores, I looked for the trouble spot in hopes of getting it fixed quickly, which would still allow for a somewhat restful evening. I walked around the perimeter of the fence more than once. "I just can't find anything that would cause it not to work," I continued to tell Bob as I returned occasionally to the barn to see how far he was getting with milking. Bob was becoming more and more angry since he knew that if I didn't find it while he was milking, we would still have the fence problem to deal with afterwards. Besides, he wanted me back in the barn to set up the milking units for washing. "You dumb idiot! Why can't you figure anything out? I might as well send a rat's ass out to do the job!" When he and I were both at the end of our rope, I finally noticed the spot. The electric wiring was barely touching the metal supporting post in one, simple but inconspicuous place causing it to short out right along the feeding platform.

As I was fixing the problem, I was nervous. "You'd better hurry! I'm on my way to plug the fence back in!" Bob yelled. Bob would often go and plug in the electricity as a joke—a cruel, mean joke—when I had hold of the wire. He was threatening to do it again, so I was hurrying, trying to move the wire before he got back to the calf barn where the electric cord was located. I had this churning feeling inside—a churning, restless feeling. The feeling didn't go away after I finished with the fence repair escaping the electric shock Bob had in mind to inflict. It didn't go away after I finished the milk room clean up. No, that feeling stayed with me for the rest of the evening, even long after Bob had gone to sleep on the couch. I finally took a few aspirin, in hopes that they would make the feeling less noticeable.

That restless feeling was my companion that summer—a terrible, anxious companion. At times at night it would be so intense I wouldn't be able to sleep. Oftentimes in the daytime, I ended up taking aspirin, which would seem to help temporarily. I was beginning to think that something was wrong with my heart. That would be all we would need to make Bob's temper boil! No, I would not go to the doctor with the problem. All I needed was to breathe more deeply, get more rest, and try to stay calm, I told myself. And I tried to do these things. But, as the summer wore on and Bob's temper continued to flair like a roller coaster run wild, the feeling was ever more intense. My efforts to calm the restless feeling were futile.

Although I kept up my regular schedule of daily chores, taking care of my growing family, and performing my job at work, as a balmy, wet July turned into a summer-soaked August, I found myself more exhausted than I had ever been. The weather was unrelenting, Bob's moods and abusive behaviors steadily increased, half of my staff quit to find other jobs, and the problems with the few difficult clients with whom I was working continued unabated.

The last week in August of 1993, I was completely exhausted. The feeling of restlessness was a constant companion. Try as I might, I could not sleep at night. Bob was angry at me in the morning, saying, "For God sakes, if you worked harder, you'd sleep at night! Your carousing around is keeping me up." It was, which wasn't helping either. The less I slept, the less sleep Bob would get. And the less sleep Bob got, the more his moods turned for the worst.

The last Sunday of August, a Sunday when Bonnie had gone along with the other 4-H members and their parents on the bus to the performance at the state fair, I found myself at home on the farm struggling with the cattle and the mud as usual. We had spent much of the week, after my work day at my job, baling, unloading, and stacking the alfalfa, which should have been long done by then. The tension I had been feeling in my chest from the stress had begun to make my heart race.

I learned earlier that week that Bonnie would be performing in a musical at the state fair. "Can I go along on the bus to watch Bonnie? I asked Bob. "I'll have to be gone for evening milking but . . ." I didn't get to finish the request before he vehemently denied it. "You have no business there! You don't need to be at the state fair, especially after dark!" he retorted.

When I went into my bedroom crying, Bonnie, then fifteen, followed me and asked me, "Mom, how can you let him boss you around like that?"

I answered her that it was okay. "You know how your father gets when I do something he doesn't want me to do. I saw your performance at the county fair," I assured her.

"It's okay," I repeated as if to convince myself that missing something so important to my daughter would be okay after all. I tried to tell myself that it was. I would stay home as he wished. Bonnie walked out of the room and up the stairs. By that evening I was exhausted. I felt trapped, and there didn't seem to be anything that I could do about it all.

That Sunday, after morning chores, I found myself crying for no reason. I lay down on the bed, exhausted from the usual morning routine, and the tears streamed down my face. Bob, who was ready to have sex following morning chores, yelled at me, "What the hell are you crying for now?" I had no answer. I did not know why I was crying, and I didn't know where the tears were coming from except that I could tell they were coming from a very deep place indeed. My entire body ached as the tears flowed. Yet the tears came warm and wet, following their river down my cheeks and onto the cool, soft pillow. I was already far along the "Road to Damascus," and the storm was about to strike. I later journaled of that summer's experience on the farm: *"If something is destroyed overnight, it is a great loss, one grieves the loss, then gets on with life—whatever direction that life might take. It is final and decisive! The frustration and exhaustion created by the incessant rains was more like a slow death. To try and try and try—to be dangling on a string of hope and to see that hope dashed again, and again, and again. To watch a person so close to you who lives his occupation, his farm, experience that frustration, to bear his anger, to see his tears, and to experience his suffering alongside him and not to be able to console—that is what I was living. A victim alongside a victim! So powerless . . . so powerless!" (November, 1993)*

As I moved into the first week of September, at my job I was busied with client progress meetings. This meant long, late days at work on top of a busy autumn schedule on the farm. With the girls just beginning a new school year, there was that added stress as well. On Tuesday, the ninth of September, following a long and deeply moving meeting regarding one of the clients whose case I had been working on ceaselessly, a co-worker asked, "Are you all right? No offense, but you look awful." I went into the restroom and looked in the mirror. My face was an ashen gray. Bags hung blue under my eyes. My cheeks were drawn tight. I went home, did my evening chores, made supper, tended to the girls' needs for the day, and went to bed.

That afternoon I fell into a very deep and very great abyss, and along with the fall nothing—and yet everything—changed for me. The decades of abuse flashed before me like the video of a horror story. That day as Bob and I lay on the bed following evening chores, I looked over at him and saw him as a vicious enemy who was trying to destroy my life, who was strangling me little by little until my breath was disappearing altogether. That evening I realized how I had neglected my daughters in order to pacify his demands. I also realized that even my youngest child, Amy, then eight years old, had surpassed her father's emotional maturity. The train which I was riding—the train that Bob set in motion by his dreams for the farm and his abuse—even before our marriage nineteen years earlier—the train which was now traveling full speed ahead made an abrupt stop. I veered off the tracks at a ninety degree angle, and my life made a right turn. I met God on the "road to Damascus." That day I fell into a hole deeper than the earth. Yet, at the same time, I experienced a piece of heaven, God's presence with me like never before. God was surrounding me as the tears streamed warm down my cheeks onto the pillow, and the peach color of the walls glowed with a divine presence in a surreal way as the three, light bulbs on the old, brass fixture above the bed shone down on me.

Ministry called me that evening and long after the lights were turned off for the night. It filled my thoughts. "I have seen God and lived," I thought as I buried my face into the coolness of my pillowcase and remembered an Old Testament verse with a similar phrase. Whatever Bob was saying bounced off me like a noisy radio wave hitting an impenetrable surface. Without ever getting off the bed, I knew my farming days and my marriage were over. I boarded my own train. And it was going in a different direction. And, although my life was usually so busy and filled with people that alone had been a blessed, though rarely experienced, retreat, now to be alone was frighteningly devastating. I longed for the place where *"There is a river whose streams make glad the city of God . . . God is in the midst of the city; it shall not be moved." (Psalm 46)*. I felt God was in the midst of my life and of me. I was sure God would come to my aid *"when the morning dawns."* Yet, I longed for someone to hold me, care for me. I longed to be loved.

I continued to spiral both downward into depression and upward into the oblivion of heaven until mid-October. There would be days, when I would function almost normally, interspersed with days in which I might just as well have stayed in bed. I felt dizziness when I tried to force myself to think hard or get a complicated task finished. I had completely disappeared. I felt like I was no longer a person with identifiable characteristics.

I had disappeared into a cement-block wall—Bob's cement wall. Yet, at the same time, I felt a oneness with God and an extreme peace which I will never forget and which I continue to experience on some scale even today.

Yes, I had met God on the road to Damascus on that early September day, and I had been changed.

Time To Be

Time,
Time to BE,
just to BE,
I need time to BE with ME—right now.

Time—
To lay back and watch elephant clouds
drift slowly through the big, blue sky,
To feel the breeze whisper against my cheek,
softly . . . gently . . .quietly. . .

Time—
To watch a beetle running thither and fro,
aimlessly, pointlessly scurrying everywhere
and nowhere,
To feel the sun surround me, hug me tight
warmth . . . glowing . . . peace . . .

Time—
To feel giant snowflakes lightly land
on sleeping eyelashes,
To draw angel wings on smooth, white banks of canvas,
freshness . . . cleanness . . . gracefulness . . .

Time—
To imagine magical fairytale worlds
where princes kiss my hand and bow,
To dance in lace, organza gowns,
flowing . . . swaying . . . dreaming . . .

Time—
To feel the Spirit's presence surround me,
fill me from within,
To listen for the Father's voice within my soul,
stillness . . . silence . . . ECSTASY.

Time,
Time to BE,
just to BE,

I need time to BE with ME,
Time to just be ME—
right now.
July 1994

Eight: **Abyss**

In mid-October I attended a training conference for my job with my co-program coordinator. The conference was held in a city about an hour's drive from the farm. The arrangement was that I would meet my co-worker in a town near her home, and she would drive the distance to the workshop. As I drove the miles from the farm to meet her, I began to steadily feel more and more dizzy. As I passed through the blocks of a town on the way to the one in which I would meet my co-worker, I was having trouble focusing on the road. I felt an intense sweat over my entire body followed by a shivering sensation. My mind was also greatly confused.

Truthfully, I don't know how I made it the twenty miles to meet her. I had no cognitive control of the car at all. I pulled off to the side of the road to get some air, try to get rid of the shakes, to regain control of myself. The fresh, cool morning air against my face helped. I have just faint recollections of what I saw along the way. It was as if I—the cognitive part of me—wasn't really there.

To make matters worse, I passed through a length of streets that were under construction. New sewer pipes were lying haphazardly along the right hand side of the streets along the curb. There were roadblock markers scattered among them. I felt an intense fear as the street would become foggy in my view, and would catch myself at the last moment before hitting the debris head on. I would straighten the car out and get back on track only to find myself having the same experience again. My salvation was the early hour of the morning and the lack of traffic.

By the time I arrived and climbed into my co-workers van, tears were streaming down my cheeks. They were intensely hot against my unusually cool cheeks. I had no idea where they were coming from. The unexplainable tears flowed the entire fifty miles to our destination.

My co-worker, the same person who had noticed my ashen-gray face the day I had come out of that important meeting in early September, had watched me as I had spiraled downward during the succeeding weeks. She had seen that I was not eating which had resulted in a significant and noticeable loss of weight. She had watched as I struggled to concentrate and work through the tough issues at my job. And she had noticed I was quick to cry. I had been the one, after all, who could deal with anything. Nothing affected me!—until now. As she talked with me that day as we drove, she was calm and reassuring. I felt safe with her as she guided the way to our destination. The focus of the conversation was my imminent need for some type of professional intervention.

After one glance around the large hotel room where the conference took place, I remember nothing except my co-worker's calm suggestion that I get help. I know that during the presentation I leaned my head into my hands, elbows resting on my knees and felt the world whirling around in my head. I fell into a numbing sleep that lasted the length of the day.

After ten hours I arrived home exhausted, weak, and with an intense headache. I took a few aspirin and lay down on the bed. It was late—almost six o'clock—time to tend to the cattle. But I couldn't make myself move.

Before I knew it, Bob came in. Angrily he marched into the bedroom, face set in that fierce, stern way that I had become so accustomed to. He yelled, "How can you think you can lay around when there was work to be done. Don't you know how late you came home!" He grabbed me, shoved me out of bed onto the floor, and started kicking and stomping on me. The kicks landed on my thighs, abdomen, and groin. It seemed unreal to me, like I wasn't really there. Yet, when he retreated back through the bedroom door and into the dining room, I dizzily and dutifully got to my feet, put on my chore clothes, and went out to work. I don't know how I did chores that night. I trembled from deep inside as I did them. I came in, cleaned up, and crawled into bed, the girls still watching television in the dining room. If they knew that something was wrong with me, they never said a word. I must have dozed off quickly because I have no memory of the rest of the evening at all. I seemed to be quickly losing my grasp on my own sanity and an abysmal crater lay before me.

In later journaling I wrote of the work I continued to perform throughout the autumn:

"During this time I had taken a few days off from work to haul silage wagons for my husband. For the state of mind I was in, I did expertly well—every complicated step with the machinery. But I can remember the tears running down my cheeks as the tractor lights flashed the rows of frost-nipped corn in the dark of the night. This was all a total waste of my time—the farm, the chores! If I had to do it again tomorrow, the next day, "forever", I would be sick! Again, and again, and again—I simply couldn't do it. Yet I did.

During this time at my job, I kept all prearranged contacts, sent out reports, held and attended meetings, planned activities, directed staff—whatever needed to be done. I don't know how I did it. It was just too hard, too routine, too worthless!" (November, 1993)

Autumn moved into winter, and, although I could function enough to get my daily work done in a minimal manner, I continued to lose weight.

And I shivered so! I was always shaking and shivering as the weeks passed slowly by.

In December, really feeling I needed help to get past whatever it was that besieged me, I called a mental health provider's office and made an appointment. When I told Bob that I had done this, he was extremely angry. He said. "There's nothing wrong with you that a little hard work won't take care of. You need a therapist as bad as you needed a hole in the head. What's wrong with you is all in your head." He was so angry and so persuasive that the next day I called and cancelled the appointment.

"After all, I'm okay," I told myself. "I'm working every day. I'm doing my chores. I'm taking care of my family," I thought trying to convince myself that whatever I was going through I could handle on my own. I had done some reading, and I had concluded that I was depressed. "But I'm still functioning, aren't I?" I told myself. "Sooner or later," I thought, "I'll shake this terrible plague."

All the while I felt that God was very near me. I could feel God's presence breathe on me in a room, a warm heaviness that made me know that I was not alone in this.

"God is right here with me," I thought. I wrote: *"I feel a oneness with the presence of God at a level in the world but also yet beyond it—an indescribable presence, a oneness with the suffering of Christ. I feel like I've stepped beyond reality. The messages of the Bible hold such deep significance. Their meanings are so much deeper. I have an understanding of it all much deeper than ever before."* (November, 1993)

I also wrote about both the experience of falling away from the reality of daily life while also moving closer to God and a Hope. In my illness, God gave me "Time To Be"—time to step away from the drudgery and worries of this life, if only in my mind. In doing so I experienced God's presence with me in a way I can only describe as ecstasy.

Along with the feeling of God's presence came a powerful call to ministry. The urge to enter the formal ministry of the Church was tugging at my soul. It was doing more than just tugging. All I seemed to be able to think about was the call to ministry. It consumed my thoughts in a way that I didn't think anything could. I didn't know yet that that inner voice and that sense of presence would be the factors that would save my life—that my call to ministry would also be the pathway out of my life of abuse.

Not receiving any professional help or medication for my depression, I was trying, in any spare time I could find, to read and learn anything and everything I could about the condition. By December, I found several books which helped me to understand that what I was going through was real. While the cold winds of January had their way with the world outside my house, I wrote my thoughts to validate for myself both the depression and the feeling of God's presence I was experiencing.

I write at the risk of sounding like I have really and totally been losing my mind. Yet, I know that I have not, and all I write is truth—truth of experience and feeling. I write to bear witness to the powerful influence my faith has played throughout this entire experience. God has not given up on me but continues to push and prod me.

Initially I remember feeling very, very tired. It was as if the entire weight of the world was pressing against my mind and body, and I had nothing left to fight against it. I think I was able to recall every difficulty, every unfairness, every infraction, which I had encountered over several years, in extremely clear detail. It was all vivid, as if it had all happened yesterday. I remember the weight of it all—the extreme weight of it all!

During those days, certain hymns kept going through my head. "I Lay My Sins on Jesus" was the first. The main focus, however, was not on my sins, but on someone else's. And, my thoughts kept going to the part of the verse, "I lay my wants on Jesus, my burdens and my cares, he from them all releases, he all my sorrows shares." Burdens, cares, sorrows—that is where the focus rested over and over again. The second hymn, which kept going through my mind was this; "If I have done somebody wrong today, if I have gone in my own sinful way, if I have led one foot to go astray, Dear Lord, forgive." I searched for the wrong I had done. But, in reality, I felt that, instead, someone had terrifically wronged me.

At the same time, I felt that I was being slowly and totally consumed by an ever-present, engulfing serpent from which I was too weak and tired to release myself. I wrote of the experience, and once I had written about it, I was able to be mentally released from this phase.

Once released from the serpent's grasp, I moved into a second phase, which was not so dreadfully heavy as it was phenomenally and profoundly sad. It was during this phase that, instead of coping with difficult situations, I would cry.

I could not sleep throughout all of this time. At night I would cry—not me on the outside—but me way down deep. My soul was crying. My soul was crying and I didn't know why. I couldn't stop it. "Be Still My Soul," a hymn from my grandmother's funeral, went through my mind over and over again. "Be still my soul . . ." But it wasn't still. It was crying.

I remember very little of one week in October. That week I was in deep distress. I was standing beside life as the observer, looking at what was going on. Sometimes I lay in bed awake all night. I was tired, very, very tired. And I cried. Where does life end and hell begin.

116

I felt like the pieces of a puzzle in my mind had been torn apart, and there had to be a missing link which would somehow bring me back. I read books, collected pertinent articles and materials, sorted through magazine articles, and looked up information in medical dictionaries. I was on a mission: a mission to again find myself, a mission to reconnect with the life I was seeing go on around me.

Finally, well into one Sunday night in mid-October, in a book describing a Christian view of the spiraling phases of suffering, the missing link—that factor that pushed me under—became explicitly clear.

That factor was Bob's ongoing physical, mental, and verbal abuse, and the realization that I did indeed now experience what truly was depression. I physically shook at the discovery.

Following the discovery, not being allowed by Bob to get any medical help for my depression, my writing took the form of processing both what I was learning from my reading and what I was learning from the experience of living with it.

For now, I need to begin to learn to dream again. I need some dream to carry me through this day into tomorrow. To kindle a dream has become most difficult for me. I have had lots of practice—years and years of it—of putting dreams on the back burner and gradually letting the flame go out, or snubbing out dreams quickly and fiercely so that the let down feeling can not even occur. After all, what really is a dream that you know will never come true—disappointment! I'm a realistic, practical person, on my own to sink or swim, overloaded, heavy-laden. Where is the dream? What is the dream when one is tired, and a dream-come-true only happens to someone else? To dream—me! My impractical soul dreams in its solitude—beautiful, mystical, poetical pictures, which no one can destroy, make fun of, or take away. But me, the practical, logical one—do I dare to dream? God, help me learn to dream again! . . .

As for the farm, I cannot affirm it. Oh yes, I continue to do the work as I have throughout this whole, sordid affair. But, I keep all thought or emotion out of it. Perhaps last summer was just one, final blow to any warm, emotional attachment I may have clung to. We are now in the deep of winter. Last year's doom is buried under snow—its residual effects being fed to the cattle. My husband occasionally speaks of spring plans. He need not speak to me, however. In some mute sense of responsibility, I suppose I will assist with the work come spring. But as far as the farm goes, I cannot affirm it now. Maybe in the spring, when the iris leaves spring from the flowerbed mulch, when the cabbage moths play on baby broccoli plants, when newborn kittens cry from a slumbering haymow—maybe then I will be able to affirm it . . . maybe. God help me affirm it

What is life for me these days? Truthfully, there is not one morning when I wake up nor one evening when I go to bed that I do not think of this entire ordeal—to define and redefine who I am and where I am, to give it credibility. My mind has traveled a thousand pathways in a short time, and it has been a most difficult journey. My heart is healing but remains very cautious. And my soul—my soul is wide open to a presence, whose knowledge and power is quite beyond me, yet, which I trust completely. (January, 1994)

I found, as winter wore on, that I was still struggling intensely. I felt like the puzzle, which I had put together and called my life, had been violently overturned, and the pieces of *me* were scattered everywhere. I was trying to gather them and put the puzzle back into place. I thought that, if I just tried hard enough and concentrated deeply enough, the pieces of my life could be put back as they had been and that then all would be well. I felt an intense need to make sense of all that was happening.

Even in the depths of the confusion and sadness, I knew one thing to be true. I was desperately in need of love—not some romantic notion, not some sexual feeling. I felt desperately in need of being held in someone's arms and told that everything was going to be all right. I needed help sorting out this maze of sadness in which I was lost. I needed someone, who would be willing to be with me in the depths of my sorrow. I needed love—that unselfish and total caring of one person for another, one person encircling their arms around the other with a hug, an embrace of kindness and reassurance.

Although I knew that love was the cure for the malady, which had overtaken me, love was not forthcoming. Certainly it wasn't coming from Bob, who was constantly on me to snap out of it because there was work to be done. And, although I worked professionally with people on a daily basis, I was in a position of authority over most of them. My co-program coordinator was supportive to a point. I had no close friends. It had been so many years since I was allowed to go out with any girlfriends, I couldn't name anyone in whom I could really confide to save my soul. And my parents had made it clear long before they didn't want to help me.

No matter how much I read, and learned, and wrote, and tried to lift myself out of the depression, I couldn't do it. And, although I had partially discovered the source of my intense pain in my recognition of my own depression and the ongoing abuse, I had not yet figured out what to do about it. I felt an aversion to my marriage and husband. I won't call it hatred. It was more that I was disinclined to be anywhere near Bob, to hear his voice, or be involved with his work on the farm. I had a deep desire to be disconnected from him in any way possible.

Although I loved my children and my clients, I also felt the need to be away from them as well. How they read this at the time I am unsure. I didn't dislike them or make a conscious decision to avoid them. I simply had all I could do to make it through the routine of each day.

As much as I wanted to be loved, I also wanted to be alone. And during the Christmas vacation of 1993, I often locked myself in the bathroom, where I would sit in silence against the wall while my children played and watched television downstairs in the dining room, and Bob made joking comments towards them. I could not be in his presence. I needed to be away from my children's presence and their neediness. I needed to be alone. I needed time for me.

There was just one dimension of my life as I fell into the abyss, which I give total credit for easing the fall during those months. Someone at church had suggested that some murals would look nice on the outside, plain-brick north wall of the church for Christmas. Amazing as it may seem, it was Bob who told the church council about my artistic abilities. I had not painted anything but house walls and farm buildings for almost twenty years. But that autumn, I began painting two four by eight foot, cathedral-shaped, stained-glass-like, Christmas murals. It kept me going through each day to know I would spend the quiet hours at the church after evening chores were finished, and the girls were in bed.

While I painted the great, golden-yellow star shining in the midnight sky, the drape of mother Mary's gown, the haloed, infant Jesus sleeping below the rough, brown beams of the stable's frame, and the angel's wings spanning the sky over the sleepy shepherd with his crook in one hand and a lamb in the other, the Spirit moved around me in the church. I had a definite feeling of presence, which I found not at all frightening, but instead, very comforting. The project ignited in me a passion, which I had thought to be totally dead after all the years of drudgery. It was the beginning of an intensely creative period of time in which my artistry was flowing in both visual and verbal forms. I was still, however, swimming at the bottom of a deep, deep pit. And, the abyss would become deeper before I would begin to find my way out.

Journey With The Serpent

I am just returning from a long journey. It began some weeks ago when I found myself in an almost overwhelming and constant battle with a mysterious, dark serpent. During the initial steps of my journey, the serpent of which I write would encircle my feet, lashing out at them, teasing me. It concerned me and maybe even frightened me a little. But moreover, the pathway that I walked with the serpent at my feet was lonely and void. My steps were empty and hollow. The more I tried to step, the more meaningless the steps became. As I walked the pathway, I imagined myself shouting, "Hey, I'm here! Would somebody notice . . . listen . . . hear!" Not one head would turn my way, not even a glance in my direction.

At last I didn't even try to step anymore. I couldn't bear the serpent's taunting and teasing. The burns on my feet from the lashing of his forked tongue hurt the depths of my being. Tears formed around my eyes, a deep burning from within. Would the serpent not leave me alone if I stood perfectly still, silenced by its taunting?

Like the browning leaf following fall's first frost, fragile and delicate, clinging to life by a single cell's strand, I stood motionless, daring to hope that the absence of movement would lead the serpent to believe that I no longer had hopes of pursuing the fulfillment of my life's travels or that I no longer cared. It was at this time that the serpent no longer lashed at and taunted me from beneath. It instead began its slow and silent slither upon my feet, wrapping itself tightly around my ankles, and stretching its long, elastic scales up my legs, grabbing me at the waist, reaching for my arms, trying to entrap me in its bleak and dismal doom. It felt cold—so very, very cold that I shivered way down deep. And no longer did it tease me in its taunting sort of way, but it ridiculed my very being, and all that I have stood for, and all I have aspired to do . . . or be . . . or think. I began to wonder who I was and where I was, or if I really was at all.

The serpent surrounded me during the light of day with its dismal thoughts, its perverse and ugly ridicule. But it was the dark of the night I really feared, for it was then that the serpent crawled with me to bed and lay with me in stone-cold silence. My eyes froze open. Every shadow of the darkness pressed deep and heavy upon my chest. The hint of morning's rays relieved me of the terror of night's shadows, but couldn't pit its strength against the serpent's might to lighten up its hold.

In the stillness of the morning air, the serpent crept around my head, encircling my mind, confusing me, bewildering me. My thoughts were muddled. My clearest sense of all that was good, and fair, and wonderful was clouded with the trail of tears I no longer could hold back. The tender, growing plants around my feet, the very flowers from my being irritated me simply by their presence. And if they dared to utter just a word or even flitter in the breeze, my skin began to ache. "Be gone with you! Be gone with you all! Can't you see this serpent is devouring me, and I can't deal with both you and it. Please be gone," I begged.

As the sun rose into glory in its bright, blue sea of home, the serpent slowly slithered towards my heart and tried to grasp my soul. So pressed down I was by its weight within my chest, I couldn't eat and only drank the stream of tears encompassing my being. "Serpent! You terrible dark, dank serpent! How dare you?" I screamed with all the strength that I could muster. "How dare you try to take my soul? My soul belongs to . . ." I paused. My breath stopped short. I glanced towards the window.

The sun stood high in triumph having conquered morning insecurities. Its rays, like searching arms, were reaching through the window glass, almost touching me. No, now they were touching me. I could feel their warmth on the outer extremities of my limbs at first. The warmth radiated over and surrounded me, slowly yet sternly, colliding with the serpent's ice-cold grasp. My inner being shivered as the pulse of warmth beat its way through every organ and cell and came out tingly at my fingertips. My head was pounding, but my mind cleared. "My soul . . . belongs to God," I thought. "Get out of here, serpent! I have no space for you!"

In an instant the grasp was gone, the burdensome yoke lifted. I sighed, filling my lungs to a capacity I no longer thought I had the strength to gather. I was surrounded by a pervading peace, a fullness, a satisfaction I can't describe in words of any form. My tears dried. The sun was indeed shining, casting warmth throughout the room. The cheerful cries of those of my own being were calling me, "Come see, Come see." I got up from the sofa, suddenly feeling very thirsty from the journey. The sun beamed at me contentedly through the window at the sink. I have journeyed long and deep in a battle with a dark, disgusting serpent. I am so very weary from the battle. And I am so fragile as I step that the slightest breeze may rift me from my path. But I have emerged, and I am at peace . . . because my soul belongs to God."

October, 1993

Nine: **Death Watch**

I laid my head back against the seat of the skid steer loader that was parked in the garage. For an instant the thought of wanting to be dead passed through my mind. It was early December of 1993, and that first suicide thought came to me very innocently. During chores that evening, Bob had milked a fresh young cow that had had her first calf that day. It was the first time she was milked, and much of her thick, first milk was still hanging in the pipeline when I started the washer. Bob had already gone to the house, and I was on my way there when I thought I should really wait for the first rinse cycle to end and then start it over again to make sure the line cleaned properly. Since the garage was between the barn and the house, and the skid steer loader was sitting in the garage, I decided to sit down on its seat while I waited. I sat there for a few moments, and with the temperature below zero, I soon began to shiver. It was then that just for an instant, the hopeless endlessness of it all overtook me. I thought of how easy it would be to wander out in the dark of the middle of the night, find a very private spot on the farm, and freeze to death. It was a fleeting thought, which passed almost within the instant that it had entered my mind. It was accompanied by a quick surge of adrenaline—a feeling of ex-citement instead of fear.

Again in the wee hours of the early morning of December 28, 1993, the thought of my own death came, only with more fury. Sleepless, I was standing with my face pressed against the knife-cold window of the door to the outside entry, gazing into the black of the night.

The snow was swirling in patterns on the icy, cement sidewalk, which pathed away from the house and out onto the snow-packed gravel of the farmyard. I rested silently, nose and forehead against the pane, decorated with frosty spirals around its outside edge. I watched—and I watched.

The gusts of wintry wind pushed the powdery snow, which had fallen peacefully during the daylight hours before the darkness had come and settled itself over everything like a heavy, iron blanket. Between the gusts, the powdery wisps would seem to retreat back to their places of origin. And, as I stared into the white, blackness of the night, the movement of the snow had a hypnotizing effect. Something much greater than myself seemed to be out in the bleak, coldness of the night. It was alive. It was breathing. With each breath, snow particles were swishing across the side-walk and then retreating, back and forth, again and again.

Lured by the breath of the swirling snow and clothed only in my cotton-knit nightgown, I could feel the breath of the wind as it sent the snowy whispers forward and back, pulling, pulling at me. Surely it would not be so difficult to walk out into the cold, find a private spot on a blanket of frozen white to lie down upon, and gently, peacefully, go to sleep once and for all. Surely it would not be so difficult. Oh, how I yearned for such a sleep, to be rid of this torment once and for all.

I grasped the tarnished, gold doorknob and turned it, stepping gingerly with my bare feet onto the frost-covered, wooden platform just outside the door. Two or three steps forward down onto the sidewalk, with an icy-northern gust slapping me back into reality, I startled myself as I found myself shivering in the wind, toes becoming numbed by the sub-zero cement mat under my feet. Retreating back into the safe warmth of the kitchen, I thought about what I had just done. Oh, how I wanted to go through with it! Oh, how I wanted to be freed at last from the on-going monotony of life! Oh, how I yearned for the peaceful sleep that would last forever!

I didn't do it that night. No, I turned back into the dining room, grabbed the knitted afghan from the sofa, wrapped it over my shivering body, and curled up in the rocker-recliner by the bay window. I started to rock. I rocked, and I rocked, and I rocked until the great heaviness of heart I was feeling began to be rocked out of my body. I rocked and rocked as the night went on forever, crawling back into bed just shortly before the radio started blaring the morning news, signaling time to get up for morning chores. As I bundled myself into my bulky, chore coat and pulled on my insulated boots, I thought of the lure of the darkness of the night. I wished I had gone through with it.

During the bleakness of the Christmas and New Year's festivities that year, I was lured to the window again and again to watch the snow breathe its life in a beckoning way. Again and again, I would picture myself curled up securely, secretly under a tree in the woods, along the ditch bank, behind a building—wherever a hiding place might look alluring. I would imagine myself lying down that one, last, final time and peacefully drifting off into the slumber of eternity, free from my abuser, free from the monotony of life with him with its familiar rhythms of explosion and retreat. Yet, each time I moved forward to go through with my own self-destruction, I would back off before the act was performed, kept from doing it by some force over which I had no control, kept in what seemed like an eternity of misery. The wintry winds of January closed in around me like a prison of blizzards, whiteouts, and seclusion from the safety of the outside world, and I wrote:

"Whistling wind . . .breathing, calling, luring, beckoning . . .
My destiny is in its hands."

Of course, I kept my pain secret from the world around me. I performed my job in a perfunctory manner. I continued to do the necessary, daily chores with the cattle. I even cared for my children in a perfunctory manner. Throughout, I could not stand the sound of my husband's voice. Every word, every action, every advance towards me, whether in love or malice was like a poison, which infested and ate away at my insides like cancer—a slow, slow death. Sometimes the gaze of my children's eyes towards me, when I was particularly miserable, would let me know that they knew there was something drastically wrong with their mother. But they were silent. They were bearing my misery with me—in silence.

By the time New Years passed, I was obsessed with my own obliteration. And everything that caught my eye seemed to become a tool by which I would or could end my misery once and for all. I climbed to the top of the hayloft, gazed out the window to the frozen cement below and contemplated. I climbed to the top of the silo chute, looked downward toward the ground some forty feet below and contemplated. Every time I pulled a knife out of the kitchen drawer to cut up meat, or vegetables, or fruit, the thought occurred to me of what I might do with the knife instead. I studied the veins on my wrists trying to decide exactly which ones would do the quickest damage if severed with the blade. A few quick swipes with a freshly sharpened knife would surely do the job, I thought! I kept the shards of glass from a broken picture frame. I held a particularly pointed shard up to the vein in my neck and contemplated as I looked in the mirror. My face was pale and thin, my mouth drawn tight across my face, my cheeks sunken. The bags under my eyes hung heavily as tears formed among my eyelashes. "Surely God knows my pain and will forgive me for this act of violence—and surrender—against myself," I thought as I contemplated. Again, I was stopped, if not by a child's voice calling for mom, by a force quite beyond me that seemed to hold my hand from moving at just the important moment. Always these thoughts and the accompanying activity were filled with a sense of excitement, a thrilling shot of adrenaline.

I am not where I appear to be, nor am I who I used to be. I am both here and there, and yet I am not either place. Where I walk you cannot choose to join me.

For where is one who is no longer one alone but two apart in different spheres? My soul is basking in the peaceful splendor of God's presence, my body left behind in earthly waste. Somehow, somewhere, I stepped over a line I did not know existed. Now I walk divided, imprisoned in a body, which cannot join the heavenly realm where the soul has felt the warmth.

And why should the soul desire to stoop down again to wasted drudgery, where not even dreams dare to live? I will not let it do that. I cannot. For what purpose? Because I cannot let the soul live in death where the body is entrapped, I stand an empty shell.

In restless anguish, I cry in pain. No one can understand this. The silence deep inside screams in torment seeking to be understood. The messages of me must come rushing from my fingertips onto the canvas now! The time is short! For how long does a vacuum exist without its contents? Not long, I say. Not long. (February, 1994)

I remember the night that I wrote this. Bob had rushed off to church council following evening chores. The girls had gone to bed. It was past eleven, and Bob had not returned as yet, which was not unusual. He and other men on the council often stopped at the bar uptown for a few beers following a meeting. I was left to myself to indulge in my own thoughts. It was quiet, and I was alone on the bed with only the bedside lamp shining its dimness into the room. For some reason, writing seemed to be a release of the anguish for me. A pen and notebook had become my best friends. It seemed that if I could put some of the feelings down on paper, I could release myself from their bondage and breathe again. I was totally miserable. Writing this particular piece was very freeing for me. I experienced an awakening in the fall of 1993 when, all of a sudden one early September day, all of Bob's abusive behavior came flooding into my consciousness. It was as if I had been brainwashed for two decades. After that the entire world as I knew it came tumbling in on me. I struggled with the sudden and overwhelming knowledge of the abuse. I struggled with the on-going toleration of its continued presence in my life. I struggled with the Christian value that marriage is a sacred bond, not to be destroyed by anyone or anything. And as a result, I struggled with trying to figure out what to do about Bob's almost constant put-downs, name calling, belittling, and physical attacks.

I was deeply depressed, which made it nearly impossible for me to even think about the abuse at all. But, I also knew I couldn't ignore it. If I did, I would die, either by Bob's hand during one of his fits of anger or, now most certainly, by my own. My soul and spirit had already essentially died. The shell of a body that was going through the motions of living was miserable. It seemed I was stuck between a rock and a hard place, and the only way out was for me to exit this world. What was at least as frightening as the suicidal thoughts is that, most of the time, this entire process towards death was below the cognitive level of thinking. "DEATH, DEATH, DEATH" was the only chant I heard. My mental and physical energy went there.

By September of 1995, I considered myself to be living in exile. I had not carried out any of the life-threatening activities I harbored so near in my thoughts. Anything and everything I laid eyes on continued to be a weapon whereby I might end it all. I didn't go anywhere without a razor blade handily packed along. I ended one of my poems written during that time with the words:

" . . . *Exile, exile, God, why must I walk in exile when I'm ready to come home?"*

The pain, for the most part hidden from the outside world, was so intense, even I, who had developed such a high tolerance for pain over so many years of malicious abuse, could barely breathe under its weight. Yet, this was an emotional pain. For the first time in decades, my emotions had been awakened—awakened to a reality of living death. My mental, and emotional well-being were constantly being challenged and shattered by the person, who should be holding them in the special recesses of a loving and caring heart. My husband was destroying my ability to reason by making me think that I was crazy, saying I was a *mental case*, that I was incapable of having any rational thoughts of my own. I was also dependent on him, or so I thought, for both my means of a living and my life. After all, hadn't I been told repeatedly that I could not make it on my own, especially with three children. Bob had not only beaten my body repeatedly by this time in our marriage, he had beaten down my self-esteem, my ability to think and reason for myself. He had destroyed my ability to decide between right and wrong, good and bad. I was like a helpless infant in the hands of a destructive tyrant.

Not only were my mental capabilities eaten away, I was besieged by shame as well. No one should ever know about the abuse or about my mental state by this time. We lived in a small, rural community in which almost everyone was somehow related or at least, knew everyone else. Bob was a respected member of the community, both in town and at our church. For heaven's sake, he was serving on the church council! And I was going to somehow accuse him of abuse? Even if I did, no one would believe me. And certainly, I wouldn't do such a thing. After all, I, too, was a respected, professional person in the community. I worked with law enforcement and social services all the time through my job. And I was going to admit something terrible was—had been—going on in my marriage? We, Bob and I, would be the gossip of the entire town. What would happen at church? At my job? With Bob's family?

Certainly, even if I could get past the shame, I would open myself up to even more abuse if I ever said anything.

Late one February evening, after I had arrived home from taking the girls to a 4-H meeting, I was especially miserable and struggling. The tears streamed down my cheeks as I tried to make preparations for the next morning. It was a tremendous labor on my part just to move and breathe. Bonnie, by then sixteen, had been washing up by the sink in the entryway. She came into the kitchen in order to pass through on her way to go upstairs to bed. Only the entry light was on. I had been working in the dark without thinking. I saw the outline of her body come into the room against the light in the background. Trying to pretend I was all right, I turned my back to her, hoping she would pass through quietly. She didn't. I'll never forget the way she looked at me that night and what she said. In the darkness from across the kitchen table, she said to me, "Mom, you've got to get some help. You need help!" There was such a look of concern in her eyes. Here was my teenage daughter telling me I needed help. My own spouse had told me I didn't need any help, that I could snap out of this myself. Yet, here was my child telling me to get help. How desperately I needed to hear the words that came out of her mouth! How desperately I needed some support in getting through all of this and going on with life!

That night, as I lay in bed, I thought of her words and what I might do to get help. The next day I made a call, a much-needed call, for help. I made an appointment with an intake person through a mental health agency, which was offering assistance and counseling to farmers and/or their spouses who might be struggling with emotional and mental difficulties resulting from the stress of the floods of 1993. I made an appointment. I had finally taken the first important step to getting through my misery.

The day of the intake appointment dawned bright and sunny, if still snowy with a blanket of white covering the ground. I was going through the rudiments of morning chores. The plan was that I would take off early from work to travel the forty-five miles to the place of the appointment. I had told Bob I was going as I never did keep secrets from him. That was a mistake!

Somehow, Bob and I got into a discussion over my going during morning milking. He was complaining both that I had made the appointment, and that now that the day had arrived, I was intending to keep it. "There's nothing wrong with you that a little more hard work won't cure," were his words, as well as, "and do you know all the miles you're going to put on the car, and how much gas it's going to take. Gas costs money you know!" he continued. I quietly walked out of the barn through the milk room and went to the house. From the phone in the dining room, I called to ask my dad if he would take me to the appointment. Then it would not put miles on the car or cost us money for gas!

My father had known I was struggling with the depression since fall. He also, back in the corner of his mind, knew I had been living with abuse my entire marriage. I guess I could feel angry that he had this knowledge and did nothing, but I think he was as confused about what to do as I was. On this morning he readily agreed to drive me to the appointment. He agreed to meet at work, and we would go from there.

I went back to the barn only to find Bob still carrying on about the appointment, the car, and the gas. I somehow found the courage to tell him that, indeed, I would keep the appointment, and that I had arranged for my dad to take me—so it wouldn't wear out the car or cost us the gas money! He didn't say anything at the moment I told him, but when I went up in the hay barn to throw down the morning feeding of alfalfa for the cows, he pulled the ladder away from the hay hole, went out of the barn, and drove away with the pickup.

I was both baffled and confused about what I should do. Maybe I should have backed down, I thought. That would have avoided the conflict, which left me stranded in the hay barn once again. But no, something inside me was telling me I needed to carry through with getting help. Otherwise, I was surely going to die. One would think that I might have felt anger at Bob at this time, but, strangely, I didn't.

As quickly as possible, I threw down enough bales to crawl down to the ground floor, spread out the alfalfa for the cows, and quickly cleaned up in the milk room. With the girls already on the school bus, I hurriedly washed up for work with the intention of getting away from the farm yard before Bob came back. If I didn't, I would surely be beaten, and I knew it. I did manage to get away quickly enough. I arrived safely at work with no sign of Bob or the pickup along the way. Later he called me at work.

"You're still certainly not thinking of keeping that appointment! Do you have all that sick time to take away from your job? If you do, then you should call in sick and stay home to help get something done around here," he hollered at the other end of the receiver.

"I'm going, and you can't stop me," I said as I hung up the phone. With other people in the background of the conversation, there wasn't much he could do. After lunch, my dad picked me up as planned, and I was on my way to getting help. I would deal with the consequences later.

The intake did indeed prove that I was clinically depressed and in need of medical care. I began taking some medication for the depression and also started seeing a therapist, Susan, who over the course of time, became very special to me. She understood both how depressed and suicidal I was. She also came to realize my strong faith in God, which I could talk about freely with her. I told her I was feeling a strong call to ministry.

I can remember complaining to Susan that talking to Bob was like talking to a cement-block wall. I can remember telling her about his extreme verbal and emotional abuse. But it took a number of sessions over a period of months before I even hinted that there was any physical abuse. Yes, Bob was controlling. Yes, Bob hollered and called me names more than I thought he should. Yes, Bob derided the girls for being "lazy." Yes, he even on occasion threw objects in anger. But I would not admit that he was physically abusive as well, and that he had beaten me on numerous occasions over a period spanning two decades. I think Bob trusted the fact that to admit the physical abuse would be too shameful for me, so he began not to fight my going to see her. I know he also trusted the fact that I believed that marriage is sacred and divorce unthinkable. He did not worry that I would leave. I'm not sure if he was incapable of such a thought, or if, indeed, it had crossed his mind, but he certainly didn't acknowledge it.

Because of the crop disaster of 1993, we had very few, financial resources. We had cattle to feed, machinery to fix, seed to buy for the new crop, and a family to provide for. The stress continued. And Bob, trusting that I would not tell the therapist any major secrets, had no reason to change his behavior even if he could have. He was perhaps more careful where he laid a black-and-blue bruise, but he still managed to get his punches in.

Even more devastating than the physical abuse were the name-calling, the swearing, and the verbal put-downs. They bruised me in the heart. And it hurt worse in the heart than on the arm, shoulder, back, or ribs. I felt all the hurt now—every bit of it. It all piled itself on top of all the past episodes, which were now all too clear in my memory. The immense feeling of tension between my commitment to my marriage and the reality of the abuse was only slightly lessened by the medication. And death continued to appear to be the only way out.

I can remember, during those months, contemplating suicide from a religious perspective. Religiously, I had always been taught to believe that suicide was totally immoral. Now I struggled with this belief. God—the God who loved me—could not be so cruel as to make me suffer as I was. Certainly God knew my pain. Certainly God could understand that I just couldn't live with this pain any longer.

I look back on the last seventeen months and reflect on the continuum of thoughts I have experienced as part of the depression. . . I need to write to relieve myself of the burdensome-ness of the thinking and also to prepare those who know me that they might understand even in a slight way, that, should I take such a course of action in a moment of panic or utter despair, it will not be that I have not struggled with the right and wrong of it. It will not be because I have lost my faith in God, or that God has abandoned me in any way. What I am saying is that in my humanness, such an act could be possible. I don't write this to frighten anyone, but to make real how very real the self-destructive element is.

My depression is, for me, a walking and living 'emotional' death, and at times, a physical death would seem more merciful. In the thoughts of suicide and wishes for self-extinction, I have found no fear of death itself. The fear, rather, lies only in the possibility of not finishing the job when it is attempted.

I want to make it known that I have been fighting a valiant battle with this illness. My life is neither ungodly nor do I lack faith. God has ministered to me throughout the affliction. God has shared my sorrow and cried with me in my pain. God has daily walked closely by my side. My faith has become stronger, my spiritual growth has been immense. I thank God for God's comforting love, and in no way blame God for the illness—the human body is very weak. But God gives strength to the soul.

I have courageously pursued earthly forms of healing with no one to support me by my side. I have treated the illness medically but have concluded there does not seem to be a magic bottle of pills that will take this away from me. I have worked closely and conscientiously with a very special therapist, who has helped to relieve the intensity of the pain, helped me to understand and see through the affliction, and cared about me when I have not been able to care about myself. My despair is not ungodly.

Yet, I cannot say with certainty that in a moment of utmost despair and panic, suicide would not be a mode of action. I cannot say that I will not desperately cry when I go to bed that I would not have to wake up in the morning. I will say that the depression has shown me death in the face of life, and within it, I have been given a glimpse of an eternity that is infinitely more wonderful than any experience here on earth. I will continue to pray that God hold onto me tightly that I might experience the wonder and balm of eternity in God's time some day, and that God might bring some peace while I wait for that timing. But I know God will understand regardless of what the future holds. It is my hope that important 'others' in my life will in some way understand also.(March, 1994)

On a sunny, summer morning in 1995, I stood out on the little, country cemetery that once had been the sight of our family's church. I felt a kinship with those lying in that cemetery, especially with one lying buried in the far corner, outside the row of evergreens that demarcated the cemetery's boundaries. The man's stone had no name and faced the opposite way of the other stones. I had been told that he had been buried that way because he had committed suicide. I stood over his marker and felt a oneness with this unknown person who had died long before I had been born. Perhaps he too had felt my pain. Perhaps he too had despaired to the point of death. It seemed to me that to ostracize a person who was perhaps ill and in terrible pain in this way was not a Christian act at all. Where was forgiveness? Where was Christian understanding? Where was grace? I felt ashamed for those who in ignorance had performed such a shameful act!

I returned to this man's grave often, feeling some sense of peace as I did so. It was there that the sunrays reached down to touch the overgrown grasses in the way they had when I was a child, escaping the criticism being tossed at me in my childhood home. The sunrays had reached down then to touch the water in the ditch as I had sat on the bank. And in those rays, I knew that God was with me, even as a young child. And so it was when the sunrays again reached down that I knew God was present for me—again. There was a bright-golden, shining light, and with the light came a glimpse of eternity. It was peaceful and pleasing, and I longed to follow that light just as this man had once done. After all, I understood his hurt, and I felt he understood mine.

I longed to come to "eternity" to meet this like-minded one. I wanted to hear his painful story. But even beyond my own suicide thoughts in connection with these comforting, be they morbid visits to this one buried beyond the bounds of my own church's cemetery, my religious beliefs were, by my own experience, being tested.

Even today my thoughts on the subject are shaped by my own experience. When I hear a story on the news or see an article about a person who has gone through with a suicide, I certainly am not judgmental. I know what the feeling that leads to suicide is like. I've been there and still am often close to those thoughts today. Suicide results from an illness of-

132

ten, but not always, brought on by the stress of life. If a person lives with abuse of any kind, without emotional support, and often without love, depression is often prevalent along with accompanying thoughts of suicide. Signs around the city say, "Treat Depression, Prevent Suicide!" I wish it were as simple as it sounds. Unfortunately depression is a pervasive illness. Support to overcome it must be consistent and ongoing. Also unfortunately, medical insurance often does not admit that depression is in fact a medical illness. As a result, often the expensive treatment is either poorly covered or not covered at all. I have learned this in a very real way as even the insurance I have through the church body for which I am a pastor pays for very little of my ongoing care. I no longer believe that suicide is a sinful act. Rather, it is an act of desperation of an illness that often results from lack of love, encouragement, and support. It is the literal acting out of the death the inner being is already experiencing. I believe God forgives those who commit suicide. I believe there is a place for them in God's kingdom at the heavenly banquet. God probably loves people all the more when they come to God in desperation. I continue to feel empathy for cases of suicide.

Finally, it would be this transformation in my thinking, not only on suicide, but on abuse and divorce, that would both dissolve my marriage and save my life. I had come into contact with the God of *grace*, not a God who sat in judgment. Since the resurrection of Christ, grace has both fulfilled and superseded law. Living in a state of grace, I was able to move forward in God's love. I set up an appointment to visit the synod office and the seminary to find out what the requirements for becoming a pastor were. I began to peruse the seminary catalog. I wrote letters to pastoral candidates to gain their perspective on seminary study. I was taking baby steps forward even while I was holding the delight of suicide as the only way out. I was sure that this "grace-filled" God would hold on to me tight and never let me go.

To my husband:

You Wonder Why I'm Angry

I spoke my heart, and you made fun of me.
I painted pictures, and you chided me.
I wrote fairy tales, and you told me how I wasted time.
I filled my life with poetry, and you laughed at my idiocy.

I designed dreams, and you called me "dreamer."
I molded lives, and you mushed my sculptures.
I wiped tears, and you made them flow again.
I built up people, while you tore down souls.

I cradled hearts, while you toppled rockers,
I soothed the hurts, while you bruised the head.
My life is measured by inches of caring, your life by dollars and cents.
And, you wonder why I'm angry.

Nothing I've ever done is "good enough."
Nothing I've ever earned is "money enough."
Nothing I've ever said is "worth hearing."
Nothing I am is anything you want.
It seems apparent that I am nothing to you.
Yet, I am good enough to help you reach YOUR goals!
And, you wonder why I'm angry?

You have done all these things, and yet, you say you love me.
Pardon me, but I don't understand.
I have not made life as it is,
Yet, I have learned to find life within its context.
And I will not let it go!

Just don't ask me again why I'm angry.

July 1994

Ten: Turning Point

Sometimes as children, on those rare occasions when my family went to a city with stores that had escalators, my sisters and I would experiment with climbing up a down escalator. Unless we moved quickly, the escalator would take us down before we ever reached the top by climbing each step along the way.

That was life for me in the months, which turned into years, following that flooding moment of recognition of the abuse in my marriage and at the beginning of the treatment for the depression, which had besieged me so. There was progress forward, only to be followed by retreat. I didn't know it at the time, but even though I did move backwards a distance for each few steps I took forward, I was gradually inching my way to both health and freedom.

Never have I undertaken such an ordeal of healing and trying to decide to continue *living* again than I was facing by the summer of 1994. I was miserable—to the point where every moment, every performance of necessary duties as a mother, program coordinator, wife, and farmhand was a burden. The abusive behavior of my husband continued, and I had no way to stop it. My job was no longer rewarding, but I knew that we needed the income now more than ever because of the crop failure the summer before. In addition to carrying these burdens, I was feeling called more strongly than ever to attend seminary and enter into formal ministry in the church. The monotony of my life in comparison to the strength and urgency of the call to ministry was stifling.

When I would discuss all of this with my therapist, she would say, "It can change. But you have to be the one to make it change." I would leave her office. I would return to the monotony and misery of my life. Each day would continue in its usual, predictable way. I thought one night as I was dumping buckets of silage into the bunk in preparation for the morning cattle feeding, "How is this going to change? Aren't I performing daily the same things I have always done—each day framed by morning and evening chores, mothering the girls, doing my job at work, cleaning manure, dumping feed for the cattle, tending the young calves, and taking care of household duties sandwiched in between? Isn't everything as it always has been?" I thought. I could not see a way out. Yet, I was stepping out onto a new path surely and carefully, inch by inch without realizing it.

The suicidal ideation did continue as did the visits to the cemetery to visit the grave of the one who had died by his own hand. Although I managed to hold onto my job and perform perfunctory duties on the farm, I would often escape to watch the water flow in the open ditch which passed through our land. I would even go to a nearby lake, crawl through the overgrown grasses, and contemplate entering, never to return again. I felt a strange pulling sensation as I stood on the lake's edge and watched the silent rippling of the water's breathing in its timeless motions. I learned a young woman in her teens, who had lived on a farm near ours, had drowned in that lake before I was born. It had been an accident. But if someone could be pulled under by a current or whirlpool within the water of the lake once, it could certainly happen on purpose to someone who was too miserable to go on living.

I felt that, while the train of life was roaring straight ahead on the tracks that had been laid for it, I had turned off those tracks and was now traveling at a right angle. And try as I might, I could not change the direction that I was now set to go. Since I could neither change nor could I remain the same without rotting from the inside out, death appeared to be the only answer. Besides, I had seen in both the sunshine and the dewshine something far greater, far more wonderful than the monotony of this life. In the bright, golden light on the water, I had glimpsed "eternity." In the motion of the waves, I felt the breath of a loving God, who embraced me like no one in my earthly life ever had. And one August day as I sat among the daisies and black-eyed Susans growing wildly along the lake's edge and smelled the freshly cut hay from the field across the road, I knew God was with me. I was not afraid. How I wished this person named Delores who had drowned could reach out from her heavenly home and pull me into the rush of water to eternity as well.

But I did not walk into the water that day. Some power quite beyond me held me back. I went home to my daughters, my job, and the drudgery of the farm.

Yet there was a change in me even if it was most imperceptible. My life was no longer ruled by the demands of the farm. I felt called on at my church to serve in numerous ways—working with the youth, serving on committees. I got involved in Bible study at a depth like never before and made banners for the worship space. I even became connected to Augsburg Fortress Publishers. I submitted materials to become a curriculum writer, and I did some stained-glass gift designs for them. God was calling me to spread the message of God's love like never before. In order to do that, I needed to understand it and be able to translate a message of grace in a world where religion seemed a sort of perfunctory responsibility, a generational tradition, and a Sunday morning, social gathering. I needed to help people turn their religion into a living faith that would feed every moment of every day of peoples' lives with grace.

That was also the year I submitted a poem to the American Library of Poetry and had it published. I, whose voice had been quiet for two decades, was beginning to speak through my actions and writing, through my artistic abilities, as I designed two more large murals for my church for the Lenten and Easter seasons and supervised their painting. I, who had only read newspapers and magazine articles for two decades, was also beginning to read again—not just anything, but books and anthologies, which I felt would, in some way, give me answers to what I was experiencing—books that would give me insight into the God who had come into my darkness with a marvelous, glowing light.

It was in my search for meaning that I ran into two writings by Walt Wangerin, Jr., which spoke loudly to me. In one writing Wangarin stated that the question was not whether one would suffer on this earth but rather *how* one would suffer. He said that in unearned suffering (which I definitely felt was true for me) I would find an opportunity to connect the loving God of grace to a world badly in need of redemption. I asked myself, "Is God calling me to be a healer in a world that knows hate and anger, slander and hurt all too well?" In another excerpt Wangarin wrote that if a person cannot align her goals and values with those of the world, the world will seek to destroy that person. I found a depth in these writings that touched my heart and soul. The world and my husband—particularly the world of my husband—were putting me to death, slowly but surely.

The struggle with life in the world as I knew it stopped for me when I fell into the depression. Nothing mattered anymore! Nothing! But God had touched me in the depths of my despair. God had nudged me into realizing that the true value of life is not in possessions, or power, or prestige, not in the farm, or a paycheck, or looking good to the community. In the grand scheme of things, it became clear that none of these things really mattered. What really mattered was that people would hear the message of God's love and mercy, that people would experience through the love of each other the love of God. What mattered was that we, God's created humanity, would make use of each moment we are given to share, by our words and through our actions, the message of God's abiding presence with us and with this world. Only in that sharing, only through our hands and our hearts, could the kind of world that God had envisioned at creation and the kingdom of God be experienced.

That is not to say by my recognition of that need or my call into ministry my world was instantly changed. It was not. I could go about my daily tasks with a renewed sense and spirit knowing that even the mundane chores of life are precious in God's sight. But the depression was very real and ongoing. It made those tasks most difficult to carry out. It felt that daily life was a continual climb uphill. And Bob's abuse did not fit into the picture at all. I tried to explain to him that he was abusing me and, in turn, the girls. I tried to tell him to stay calm, that God's love would see us through the difficulties, and that he did not need to get so upset, that he did not need to worry. But, it seemed that the more I tried to express the message of God's grace and love to Bob, the more he resisted it. "What are you, some kind of religious freak as well as being a mental case?" he ridiculed.

I still could not see a way out. I would not consider divorce. In my perception of the Biblical teaching, divorce was clearly wrong. Neither could I change Bob. If anything, the abuse increased, especially as my feelings and actions were no longer aligned with his priorities. I talked with my pastor during those months, and although I did not reveal the extreme abuse that I was living with to him, I did tell of my displeasure with my marital relationship. "I feel that I can't talk to Bob about anything that is important to me. He simply doesn't listen. As hard as I try to express myself, he doesn't hear me. Everything he talks about seems so superficial while my thinking and feelings are so deep," I complained. My pastor ask me, "Have you ever thought about divorce?" bringing up to me that possibility. But I didn't even want to consider it at the time. His suggestion did, however, in the grand scheme of changes that I needed to make in my life, open the door to the possibility, even if I did not see it as such at the time.

In therapy I was encouraged, "You need to find and take hold of your anger towards Bob." But when asked to express my anger, I could not do it.

"I don't feel any anger," I said again and again.

My therapist encouraged me to write. She gave me an assignment—an assignment to write about my anger. And so I wrote the letter to my husband, "You Wonder Why I'm Angry" which he never bothered to read even though I put it in plain sight.

Yet, although I used the word "anger," I didn't really feel it. Because the span of time of the abuse had been so great, I felt nothing anymore—no anger towards Bob, no anger over the physical attacks, no anger at being called those terrible names, and no anger about the verbal put-downs. Except for a feeling of aversion to Bob and the pain of the depression, I had become numb. I had seen that numbness in the eyes of people on television or on a poster who had lived in abject poverty. I had seen that numbness in the eyes of innocent citizens who had fallen victims in war-torn countries. I had seen that numbness in the eyes of persons who had lived through the torture of concentration or refugee camps. I had seen that numbness in the eyes of soldiers who had been stunned by the face of battle and killing. I identified with that numbness. A person bears the beating and goes on with life. The sensations of fear, of violation, and of hurt have been taken away. All that is left is the numbness—a numbness like a living death.

By July of 1995 I was beginning to make changes in my life. The persistent call to ministry translated into my beginning the process of being accepted at the seminary. In the fall of 1994 I had a meeting with the synod office to find out requirements. In March of 1995 I had my approval interview. In April I filled out the application and wrote the essays for seminary admittance. In May I was evaluated to be suffering from mild depression, and it was recommended that I continue my therapy. By early summer I had begun to study the synod and seminary requirements for my Master of Divinity degree and had begun the process of being rostered by the church. Since I felt an obligation to Bob to help with the summer farmwork, and also needed to continue to earn income from my job as long as possible, I took Greek through independent study. The plan was that I would complete the first course in Greek during the summer, still working full time. Then, in the fall I would begin commuting to the seminary to begin the four-year regimen leading to ordained ministry.

Bob criticized me every step of the way. He continued to ridicule me when I would study the seminary catalog to become more familiar with the requirements. The day I went to the synod Bob chided me, "I don't see why you're wasting your time and putting miles on the pickup to go there. You'll never be able to be a pastor anyway!" One time he even grabbed the seminary catalog out of my hands and threw it across the room where it crashed against the bedroom wall.

One particularly hot and humid Saturday in July of 1995, Bob's anger about my seminary plans came to a head. I was at my computer by the table in the dining room working on a Greek assignment. The girls and Bob were also in the dining room. The television was on. The ceiling light was still on because it had stormed briefly that morning, and the cloudy skies were still darkening the room. I needed the light to see what I was doing. The fan, sitting on the divider between the kitchen and the dining room was oscillating a badly needed breeze back and forth into the non-air-conditioned room. It had been humid and hot for several days, and the house was sticky and stifling.

What started out as a conversation between Bob, as he lay shirtless on the couch in the dining room, and my two younger girls, who were having cereal in their pajamas as they watched Saturday morning cartoons, soon turned into Bob complaining about how lazy and worthless they were. The second crop of alfalfa had not been baled. The cows needed feed ground before their evening meal—a hot and tiring job even in good weather! Some piece of machinery needed fixing (There was always some piece of machinery that needed fixing!). The cows had not yet been given their morning feeding of hay. The list went on and on. "Why can't you kids help out more?!" was Bob's complaining query. "Why can't you be more like (the neighbor's kids)? You kids are so lazy and worthless!"

The next thing I knew, he was up from the sofa. He had slipped his belt out of the loops in his jeans and was right in front of Krista's fourteen-year-old face, threatening to hit her with it. Krista, attacked by both Bob's words and his belt, fought back. She grabbed the other end of the belt and whipped it back at him, hitting his shoulder.

I stood up just as Bob whisked past me through the kitchen and into the entry way. I followed him, "What do you think you're doing? Don't you know how hurtful your criticisms are to the girls? And why take out your belt? You're the adult here. Krista is the child. You're the one who should be setting the example for them! Do you know how hurtful it is to be compared to someone else like that? Your criticism is destroying them?" my questions trailed after him. As I did so, he had slid on his boots and had taken a few steps towards the door. I thought he was (finally) going to go out to get some of his work done.

Instead, as I followed him towards the door, he quickly whirled around and attacked me. He slammed me into the clothes washer and landed a few punches into my stomach. As I turned my back to him, he shoved me further into the clothes dryer still fisting me over the shoulders, back, and arms. As I fell to the floor, he gave me one final kick in the right thigh. Before I realized how severely he had beaten me, he was out the door, driving away in the pickup.

I got to my feet gasping for air, trying to regain my wits, and rested against the laundry appliances. The girls, who had not seen the beating but had heard it from the other room, were in tears. Krista was afraid for her life in anticipation of Bob's return. Quickly pulling myself together and with Bonnie safely at work, I told the two younger girls to finish their cereal and get dressed. Although my parents had not been involved in my abusive marriage for more than a decade, this time they would be. Not even thinking of myself, I knew I needed to get Krista to a place of safety. I called my parents, "Bob just beat me up and threatened Krista. I'm afraid for all of our safety. Are you going to be home? We need to come over now!" With that I hung up the phone, and we were on our way. The girls, sensing the danger in my strained tone of voice, didn't need to be told to hurry. They were ready in just minutes.

"What's going to happen to us? What's Dad going to do when he gets home and we aren't there?" they questioned me.

"It'll be alright," I answered, although the big knot in my stomach was growing larger with each passing mile. "We'll only be at Grandma and Grandpa's house until Dad calms down." But inside, I really didn't know what was going to happen. Would Bob be enraged when he came home and found us gone? Would he be waiting behind some cornfield at some intersection on the way to ram us with his pickup? Would he come up be-hind the car and push us into the ditch?

Bob was nowhere to be seen as I drove the miles to my parents' farm, and I was relieved to make it there without further attack. With my dad's help, the girls settled in watching television and eating some treats. With a tear-streaked face, I briefly told my parents what had happened. "Bob has just been in such a foul mood lately because of the weather and my plans that there's just no talking any sense into him," I said.

"Where did he punch you?" my dad asked.

"In the back and shoulders, and then as I fell, he punched me in the stomach before he drove away," I answered.

Looking worried, my dad made no reply. At my mother's request he just got some potatoes up from the basement and started peeling them for lunch. I went and sat down on the couch in the living room next to the girls. My parents went about the tasks they were busy at in the kitchen, clearing the breakfast dishes from the table and making some plans about increasing the volume of lunch to accommodate the kids and me. Although I may have seemed calm on the outside, my insides were churning as I thought about what I should do. "Should I return home? Should I take the girls with me? Or . . . should I call for help? Should I do something about this situation—should I call the sheriff's department?" I thought. I could call law enforcement in such a situation. I had learned that in therapy. Such behavior on Bob's part was assault, even if he was my husband. And there were legal consequences for assault! But what will doing so do to my marriage?" I wondered. "How much abuse will I be in for afterwards?" It never occurred to me that I would not return and not con-tinue being married to Bob. That was unthinkable! Yet, he had violated me physically—again! And this time he had openly and blatantly violated Krista, and by association, Amy, then ten years old, also. I felt that the girls were in more danger now than ever before. I decided that I would call my therapist for support. "Dad, can I use the phone for a long distance call?" I asked.

Since it was Saturday, my therapist was not in. Instead I talked to the on-call therapist, not really knowing if I should trust her. "Does she really know my situation?" I wondered.

"What Bob did to you is wrong, very wrong, you know that. But you are the only one who can do anything about it. You have to be the one to act! You know what to do," she added.

"Can't I get in touch with Susan? I need to talk with Susan. She knows more about this," I begged the on-call person.

"This is her Saturday off. We have to follow our procedures. I heard what you told me, and I know that you know what to do," was her reply. To one on the outside of the situation, it may seem like a simple act to call law enforcement when one has been brutally, physically violated. But an abused woman, especially one who has lived with the very present and real danger of ongoing abuse for as long as I had, is nearly paralyzed to act. The very thing that woman needs to do, she cannot do because she has lost her own sense of power to do so.

As I sat back on the couch with the girls, I noticed nothing of what was on television. I also didn't notice the fact that the girls were sitting like frightened urchins on immobile perches. I sat there for what seemed to me to be hours before finally getting up. "Dad, can the girls stay for a few hours while I take care of a few things?" At his nodding yes, I proceeded out to the car, leaving the girls in my parents' care. I had decided that I would drive the ten miles to town, I would use my key to get into my office at work, and from there I would call the sheriff. Then I would wait to give the sheriff some time to start out to the farm before I would return without the kids.

This I did. I drove the miles from my parents' farm to the small town where I worked. Nervously I worked my key in the lock to enter the building. Reaching my office with an almost unbearable fright in my stomach, I picked up the receiver. My hands were shaking so much I was barely able to push the numbers to dial. I didn't notice how shallowly I was breathing until the dispatcher picked up the phone on the other end. I barely had enough breath to get the words out. "My husband beat me up," I blurted out to the dispatcher. "I need an officer out to the farm right away." (I didn't need to say more. In the small, rural county in which I lived everyone knew where everybody lived.) Then with a great heave of relief, I put down the receiver. I leaned back in my office chair feeling almost dizzy from my call, and I waited. As I waited I thought about what I had done and the ramifications of my actions. I could get beaten to death for this act of treason! And the shame of having my community learn the truth, as they most certainly would, crawled over me. But I did not call back, deny my statement, or tell the sheriff's officer not to come. I did not do that! I had made the decision, and I was sticking with it. My arms trembled so badly that I had to place them on my thighs as I sat in the chair to keep control of them. In fact, my entire body was trembling. Was it out of fear? Was it out of anticipation? Was it because I did not know and could not predict what would happen after the sheriff department's visit? Or, was it because taking this step was like stepping into a huge vacuum of future of which the ending was unknown? I could feel the adrenaline coursing through my entire body as anxiety gripped me. Yet, I was determined. Bob had violated me. And now he was directly violating my children! Now I both knew it and could no longer live with it. This time I would not back down! I had reached a turning point!

Eleven: **Glimmer**

"Your husband wouldn't do such a thing. I've known him since he was in high school." These were the words the sheriff's deputy said as my husband and I and two law enforcement officers sat by my kitchen table that hot, humid July afternoon. This was the response I received in answer to my call for help from the physical beatings of my husband. This was the authorities answer to my plea in the rural county of southwestern Minnesota where our farm was located!

I sat at the table, cut off blue jeans rolled above my knees and my oldest daughter's, deep aqua, Mickey Mouse t-shirt on top. My husband, having been asked into the kitchen of the house by the officer, was still bare on top, sweaty and dirty from the task of grinding cattle feed, the task he was busy with when the sheriff's deputies and I had arrived within minutes of each other. In his usual style, my husband had left the scene of the beating and gone on with the day's duties as if nothing had occurred.

What may actually seem most unbelievable at this point is that I sat back in my chair and wondered, "Did I dream all of this up?" Thoughts of whether or not the beating really happened fluttered in and out of my mind as I was trying to hold onto reality while at the same time deciding if I was telling the truth. In the seconds which passed, I watched the episode again and again in my mind, rerunning it repeatedly, as if to prove even to myself that, yes, my husband had punched me repeatedly in the stomach, abdomen, and over the shoulders and back. Yes, the force of his punches sent me banging not only into the clothes washer but also into the dryer and down onto the laundry basket, filled with laundry waiting for its weekly bath. I could remember feeling the squishy softness and smelling the damp, somewhat musty smell of the laundry-filled basket compared to the hard punches of my husband's fist and the cool, smooth surface of the laundry appliances. And then there was that red mark on Bob's shoulder from the belt buckle Krista had hit him with as she defended herself against his threat to her safety. No, I decided, Bob had hit me not just once but repeatedly and hard.

"I'm telling the truth," I told the deputy.

"Do you have any bruises?" was the deputy's next question.

I had not examined myself beneath my clothes. I had not even thought to do so in the time which had elapsed between the actual beating and the deputies' visit. I looked at the length of arm extending from the short-sleeved t-shirt, first right and then left, and at the portion of my legs extending from my cut-offs. "I don't see any YET," I admitted to the deputy, as he eyed me in a scrutinizing manner. "I will have bruises!" I offered in my own defense. "Just wait until tomorrow or Monday. There will be bruises," I stammered.

I knew that I would have bruises galore—maybe some were already making their appearance if I were to have looked more carefully. But, the deputy was not interested in giving me time to do that. And I was not thinking clearly enough to insist on having that time.

Meanwhile, Bonnie had arrived home from work to find the sheriff's deputies sitting at our kitchen table, heard the conversation while washing up and passed by to go to her room to change clothes. And although she had paused briefly with a look of disgust as she walked into the pantry on her return from work, she had simply gone on with her business before leaving to stay the night at a friend's house.

Then the deputy stood up from his chair at the table with his buddy in law enforcement and said to both Bob and me, "It's a hot day. Tempers flare. Try to calm down now, and just do your work." Then both he and his friend-in-crime put their spiffy hats back on their heads, taking time to make sure they were officially placed, and marched as a pair out of the kitchen door and back to their car. They drove away down the farm's driveway as I stared in disbelief.

Bob chided as I turned around and headed back into the kitchen. "I told you they wouldn't do anything! Now get to work! You've already made us late in getting the chores started!"

I looked back at him as he sat bare-chested with a reddened, belt-buckle shape etched into his skin near his broad, left shoulder. He rested on that chair at the kitchen table like he was the indestructible king of the world, and I—I was his meager, submissive serf. I looked at him for what seemed to me to be an eternity. I was not confused at this point. No, I had been in therapy for sixteen months by this time. I had seen the abuse wheel [Appendix I], which described to me all the ways in which one person can abuse another—which count even if the two people are married! Although the sheriff had briefly confused me by his confident assertion that my husband had not—could not have beaten me, my mind had cleared. Yes indeed, Bob had beaten me! He had emotionally and verbally abused both Krista and Amy, even threatening Krista with physical abuse. I had acted to protect my children, and he had beaten me for it!

Instead of putting on my chore shoes and going out to feed the cattle, I marched past Bob and up the stairs. I quickly opened the chests of drawers holding Krista and Amy's clothes and grabbed a few shirts and shorts along with their pajamas, which were crumpled in piles on the floor of their bedroom. I walked briskly down the stairs and lifted my pillow and pajamas from our bed. I grabbed a pair of jeans out of the drawer, a shirt from the closet, and stuffed my gathered possessions into a bag. I walked right past Bob, who still unbelievingly sat by the kitchen table, stunned. I stepped quickly down the steps and the sidewalk, got into the car, both slamming and locking the door, and wasted no time in leaving the farmyard. Would Bob follow me as he had done on those occasions before when he had beaten me and I had driven away? I didn't even take time to think about it. I was out on the open road before I knew it, heading back to my parents' farm and to my children, whom I knew would be frightened to death over my absence and for my safety by this time.

The girls were not happy about spending the night at my parents' house, especially under such uncomfortable circumstances. "Mom, can't we go home?" Krista begged.

"We don't want to stay here overnight," Amy chimed in. But we had no choice. We made the best of it, me consoling them before they went to sleep that "everything will be all right."

In my mind, I really wondered if everything would be all right this time. For one thing, I had called the sheriff's department and accused Bob. And now for another, when he had told me to get to work, instead I had packed up clothing for myself and the girls and had driven away. What would the future hold? What kind of trouble had I gotten myself into now? What's going to happen to me? The girls? What about my marriage? What are people going to think? Going to say? Those were the huge questions weighing down on my crazy, mixed-up mind. The only call I made that evening was to my pastor, who had come to know some extent of the abuse. "Bob beat me up. We're spending the night at my parents' farm," was all I told him.

That evening was an uncomfortable one. First of all, my parents had made it clear that once my sisters and I had graduated from college, we were to be on our own. The idea of returning to live at home once we were adults was not an option. Also, since I was rarely able to visit them during the years of my marriage because of Bob's incessant demands that I be at home to work, I was no longer familiar with the surroundings. I felt like an intruder. As well the girls were not comfortable there. My parents had taken care of them on rare occasions, but staying with my parents was certainly not part of their regular routine. They wanted to be home in their own rooms and in their own beds. Also, I could sense my parents nervousness that Bob might cause an uncomfortable or even dangerous scene at their farm, which was more than ten miles from the nearest town and even farther from the sheriff's department. My dad would not be able to stand up to Bob's strength.

That night, as I crawled into one of the extra beds in the pink-floral, wallpapered bedroom that had been mine as a child, tears streamed down onto the pillowcase as I prayed for deliverance from this horrible, incredibly awful life. Surely, God knew I did not want to be alive any longer. Why couldn't he just take me up and out of this mess of life that was more burden than blessing? I would be happy to just not wake up in the morning! As I prayed in my exhaustion from the difficulties of that steamy-hot, mid-July day, an indescribable sense of peace came over me as I sensed the presence of more than my children sleeping in the room. That peace covered me like one of my grandmother's cool, cotton quilts, and I drifted off to sleep amid the smell of my former existence and the smell of the undisturbed ages of time that had permeated this rarely used space in my parents' house.

The hazy appearance of the world the next morning, a Sunday in mid July, dawned humid and cloudy, which seemed most appropriate to me as my mind was filled with a foggy mist as well. And certainly no one but God knew what this day would hold.

I went to church allowing the girls to sleep in, tucked safely in bed in Grandpa's and Grandma's upstairs. They had not gotten to bed early so were sound asleep when I left. And, if they had slept anything like I had, they would not be in the sort of mood that I either needed or wanted to deal with that morning. Besides I did not know what they would say to others about the entire ordeal, and I was not ready yet to let anyone, especially the people who I needed to meet and work with on a regular basis at church, in on the entire, horrible affair.

I scanned the rows of vehicles for Bob's pickup as I entered the church's parking lot. No silver and gray, extended cab pickup was anywhere to be seen. Would he come later? Follow me out of church, and work his destruction on me when we were out of range of anyone else's sight or hearing? Only God knew.

I walked into church and sat down. This did not appear unusual as Bob would occasionally not attend church if there was hay to be cut or other important field work that needed his attention—or even if one of the cattle were sick which would require him to remain home to wait for the veterinarian's call. I knew everyone at church, having attended there for the entire twenty years of my marriage, so I simply sat down and waited, with a careful eye out for Bob, for the service to begin. I found the organ prelude to be especially welcoming and calming on that terrible Sunday. I allowed myself to take a few deep, calming breaths as the service began with no sign of Bob.

After the service the pastor caught me on my way out of church. "Where are you going? What are you going to do?" he asked concerned. My plan for the rest of the day was complicated by my husband's family's reunion in which I was to play an important role.

"I need to go back to the farm. Bob's family has this reunion this afternoon. The stuff I need to bring is there. I need to bring it as I promised," I answered. With a concerned look on his face, he asked about the girls. "They're safe," was my reply. "They're going to spend the day at my folks." Then I set out for the farm—my own home—with fear and trepidation but also knowing that I had a responsibility towards Bob's family.

Bob's relatives gathered every other year for a reunion. Each time that they met, one of his aunt's or uncle's families organized the gathering. Bob's family just happened to be in charge that year. Bob's sisters and I had met earlier to lay the plans and send out the invitations. My duties were to provide plates, silverware, napkins, and relishes, which I had purchased and which now rested, bagged and ready to go, on the counter in my own kitchen. I had made a commitment, and so, I had an obligation to fulfill it. And I would do so. What kinds of questions would come at the reunion or if Bob would show up for it and what he would do, I did not know. I prayed as I drove that everything would be all right and the afternoon would be a smooth one.

Of course on my arrival there were questions from my husband's family. Where was Bob? Was he coming later? Where were the girls? I told his family the truth of what had occurred the day before—the entire, messy truth of the beating, the sheriff's call, and going with the girls to my parents. "Krista and Amy will not be coming, and I'm not sure about Bonnie." I silently hoped Bonnie would come because she was to bring the orange drink in a large thermos from her workplace. "And Bob," I added, "I have no idea what he'll be doing. I didn't spend the night at home, and he was sleeping on the couch when I picked up the supplies. We haven't talked since the incident."

Most of his family seemed not to be very surprised by the words of truth that came out of my mouth that Sunday noon. But one of his sisters sat quietly on the picnic bench facing the long table, which had been tableclothed for the many foods that family members would bring. She said nothing—nothing at all. I had always felt closest to this sister so her silence disturbed me. And the look in her eyes was one of disbelief. Was it disbelief that he hit me or that I would call the sheriff on her baby brother? Or, was it disbelief that I had been living with this for more than two decades and had never let the secret out? I will never know. She has not talked to me about it in the eight years that have passed since then.

Other relatives—cousins, aunts, and uncles—asked where Bob was that afternoon, as he never did come to the reunion. As unbelievable as it still seems to me, I was quite frank about all of it. "He beat me up yesterday, and I spent the night at my parents. I don't know if he's coming. No, I don't know what's going to happen between us." These were all statements of truth. The real fact was that I did not even know what I was going to do after the reunion was finished. Would I go back to my parent's place? The younger girls were there. They would be waiting for me. Would I go back to the farm and face Bob? What would I say to him? What would he do to me? The questions haunted me, but if someone would have suggested that divorce loomed on the horizon, I would have emphatically denied it.

In spite of all of these internal questions circling through my mind, I cannot say that I did not have a good afternoon. I had always enjoyed Bob's family immensely in the many years of my marriage. I was close to his brother and sisters. Sometimes I felt much closer to them than to my own family, who were scattered farther away, and whom I seldom saw. Since plans were already made for my start of seminary in the fall, and I was already doing my Greek studies, there were questions and conversations about that. I was excited about the possibilities for growth and learning that loomed out on the horizon, even if I could not figure out how my call to ministry and my response to that call would fit into my life.

Bonnie did come bringing the beverage as planned. Knowing she had witnessed the ordeal with the sheriff's deputies, I was relieved to see that she was holding up as well as she was. She stayed for a brief time and chatted with relatives, all of whom were kind enough not to bring up the matter between her father and me in their conversations. Then she left early needing to go to work. At least, I thought, she will be in a safe place—her work site—when, after the afternoon's festivities, I return to the farm and my house to face Bob, which is what I had, in the end, decided to do.

When I arrived back at the farm, Bob was just getting up from the couch in the dining room where he had evidently spent the entire day. He said very little to me as he saw me come through the entry into the kitchen. In fact, what he did say had nothing to do with the events of the day before. His questions were about the family reunion—who was there and how it went. He did ask me what I said about his absence. But when I told him that I had told them the truth about what had happened between us on Saturday, and that I had told at least his brother and sisters and their spouses that I had called the sheriff, he didn't say much of anything. It was like it didn't even affect him that word was now publicly out, at least among his family, that he was physically abusive. He proceeded into the entryway to put on his chore clothes and boots. He then went calmly out the door to begin the evening chores routine with the cattle. Almost as I had been programmed by the decades of routine, I changed my clothes, put on my chore shoes, and followed him out.

During evening chores, we talked casually about the day, but there was no anger between us, neither on his part or mine. It was as if the entire event happened between someone else, not us, the happily married couple, who had celebrated their twentieth anniversary just the year before. After the milking of the cattle and the evening feeding chores were finished, I washed up, changed clothing, and went to pick up the girls at my parents' farm. I can't even remember them asking me about how or when we had settled our differences. Life was all so normal, so routine, it was as if nothing had ever occurred.

I, however, did have bruises and sore spots on various parts of my body. And when I drove to work on Monday morning and tried to lean my head against the headrest, I found I had a swollen lump on the back of my head. My upper arms were black and blue, and there was definitely stiffness in the area of my ribs.

"I have bruises today from Saturday's beating," I said calling the sheriff's office from work. "Could you send an officer out to my worksite immediately after I'm done with work. I'll be here from 3:00 to 4:00 waiting. He needs to bring a camera. He wanted pictures," I told the dispatcher. I told her—she, who was actually my next door neighbor—that I would show the sheriff's deputies the bruises they had inquired about on Saturday. They could take pictures to prove that Bob had, indeed, beaten me.

After three o'clock, when my clients left for the day, I waited for an hour for a law enforcement officer to arrive. None ever came. Neither did anyone call to tell me that they weren't coming. They simply did not show up.

A week later, when the bruises had almost greened themselves into normalcy, a deputy called to apologize that no one had come, making some excuse about people being on vacation and the request being lost in the shuffle. I did not become irate with him like I should have. I did not stick up for myself and continue to push regarding the incident. I didn't have enough emotional energy left in me to fight the county's law enforcement system. But I did file the incident deep in my mind. I was now quite certain that even the legal authorities, who were supposedly there to protect the citizens of the county, would not do anything for an abused wife. And somewhere deep inside without my being even cognitively aware of my own thinking on the matter, I decided I would never be safe on the farm and in my county of residence. My mind was beginning to turn the corner from thinking that I would stay on the farm and with my husband forever to realizing that I must act on my own behalf for my own safety's sake. It had, however, not cognitively registered on the conscious level yet.

For the rest of the summer, I was outwardly performing the functional duties of my life, including completing my first Greek class. Not even being sure if I would be attending seminary in the fall, I worked with a pressure from within that this class would be the preparation and foundation for future studies. Yet, I struggled daily with how seminary attendance would fit into the major scheme of my life. With no outside encouragement to pursue this aching dream, I felt lost in the confusion of the thinking of it all. My husband was not anxious for me to go, and, I think, really only relaxed his pressure on me when I worked out a plan to continue my job while commuting to the seminary, a seventy-five mile drive each way. And certainly, how could I attend class in St. Paul and still be there for my three daughters, attending school in local towns?

In the meantime, the occasions of abuse seemed to lessen. Oh, there were a few verbal altercations here and there as I sometimes felt pressured from within to argue with Bob when I knew that what he was saying was blatantly incorrect. There were a few names slung my or the girls' way when, in the heat of August and the grain harvest, his anger soared if a piece of machinery didn't work as it should, or if one of the people we contracted with to swathe or combine the grain didn't show up at the time he felt was best for getting the work done. But basically things were as calm on the home front as they had been for a long time. I had not suffered any devastating consequences from the call to the sheriff in July other than an occasional deriding remark over my stupidity. But I suffered from a great sense that my life was worthless, and I was slowly and surely being enmeshed in the nothingness of it all.

By the last half of the summer of 1995, following the incident of abuse that prompted me to call for assistance from the local law enforcement authorities, my entire life blurred together in a confusing mire that was both pulling me down with its sinking momentum and yet, out of which I was being transcended by an enormous creativity and a sense of the presence of God beyond all comprehension. Between my full time job, taking care of the girls, and the outside chores and farm work, it would seem that I would have been completely occupied. Yet, because I slept very little, I found the hours to both think and write. And amazingly, even in the deepest depression, there was a glimmer of hope that I could not yet consciously describe but which permeated the writings that flowed from my mind and fingers.

One morning in late July, I was pulled from my bed, where I lay wide-eyed waiting for dawn to issue its first rays of light across the sleeping fields, and, I was drawn out into the early morning by this power that so fully filled and transcended me during these hazy, heat-filled days.

Early Morning Journey

This morning very early, when darkness still held its firm grip on heaven's expanse, I rose up from my bed. In the cool and quiet peacefulness of the morning air, the calling of a restless sparrow beckoned me from my front step onto trails of morning blessing.

As I stepped forth on the chill, damp sidewalk, my bare and empty footprints left a telling trail of this dawn's delicate dance. My feet swished further into overgrown grasses, sprinkled with angel-white and kingly-purple clover blooms. The sweetness of the smell that lingered in my nostrils sank its scented floral fragrance deep within my spirit's depths. And as my feet pressed forward, tiny sprinkles of rainbow drops spattered ahead and to each side, for I upset dew's sleepiness on silent blades of green.

As I rose up onto the gravel-blanketed byway, the sandy pebbles stuck to the moistness of my feet bottoms like glitter splattered in waiting glue designs painted delicately by unknown artist's fingers. When I reached the creek bed, the endless, dauntless rush of water's flow broke the silent stillness. And the blueness of the scurrying stream glowed faintly whitish-yellow as sunbeams quietly broke the eastern horizon.

I briefly rested on a cool but sturdy tree stump, whose telling circles spoke stories of days and ages freely given and so presently taken away again. The increasing power of impending sunrise turned the deep, brown bark a hue of golden richness. And I knew the tannish circles would burn like golden rings of grace in the open expanse of day's bright sun. It was then that I noticed a mother deer, stealthily sneaking an early snack from the carpet of green alfalfa leaves so bountifully and boldly bathing the landscape with luscious luminescence.

Telltale sunrays reminded of time's quick passing, and as I slowly trodded back along the black and muddied field path, the dusty cloud that rose along the gravel lane behind a passing pickup, the cows slow yet sturdy movement towards the barnyard gate and the morning welcome song sung boldly from deep within the robin's breast sent clear and conscious messages. The day's hurriedness and hustle were enjoining me to commence their senseless scurry. And knowing the necessity, despite my heavy hesitancy, I stepped forward, assuming their toxic stride.

Leaving the tangled, untrodden, yet peaceful path, I knew I must rejoin the vicious pace. I am so thankful to have been given these brief and private mo-

ments—such pleasurable moments given to me, just to me, to travel trails in blissful solitude. And yet, I know quite certainly that I have not walked one step alone.(July, 1995)

Later I realized this was God's way to keep me moving forward with the formal ministry process and to keep me taking steps forward out of my present life of abuse. The call to ministry gave me a strong sense of purpose and a goal to work towards. I don't know if I could have taken the actions necessary to leave the abuse and my threatening marriage without God's power for me to effect that change.

I arrived home from my walk to be greeted by the words, "Where the hell have you been wasting time now! There's work to get done!" Bob's words bit in their usual way, but instead of my believing that I had somehow wasted time on my early morning adventure, I felt blessed by it—and sorry for him that he could not see the pleasure that lay before him like a three-dimensional, artist's canvas, that he could only focus on what I saw as the drudgery of life. I spent many more moments either wandering along the ditch bank that ran through our farm or at the nearby lake, experiencing wonder with each journey. Finally, finding that I would not be listened to regardless of how hard I tried to speak, I put the thoughts, that had no place else to go, on paper.

Somehow in my search for meaning during that time, I ran into a bookmark I had saved from my childhood, which was resting among the fine, thin, red edges of my confirmation Bible. It had words on it by the sixteenth century mystic, Theresa of Avila. It said, "From the interior of the soul God makes the spark." Those words intrigued me to such an extent that I sought out a copy of her book, which I had not known of prior to this time but suddenly could identify by name, *The Interior Castle*.

She compared her encounters with God's presence to a poor, little butterfly not knowing what to do with such experiences of divine grace. She wrote, "O poor little butterfly, bound with so may chains that do not let you fly where you would like!" (*The Interior Castle*, Paulist Press, New York: New York, 1979, p.139) I had experienced *ecstasy* in being in communion with the Spirit. Theresa also used the word *ecstasy* to describe the experience of the presence of God. She said that there was an interior knowing of God's presence—one that was difficult to put into the form of words.

Theresa wrote of stages of knowing God's presence and purpose for the one God calls to service: There is first distraction from the things of the world and a wounding as if by an arrow, which is known by the recipient

154

as something precious. The pain is great while also being delightful and sweet. The feeling of God's presence at first comes and goes until there is a continual feeling of companionship. The favor of God is felt by the interior of the soul. Signs come through the senses that awaken the soul and keep it directed. The soul knows with great certitude the favor of God that it is receiving. The experience of rapture turns to service in the world. (*The Interior Castle*, pp.29, 115-117, 152-153)

Her writing confirmed that I had indeed been urgently and forcefully called into ministry the summer before. She verified my feeling of being in the presence of God. There was for me a great pain in the realization of the reality of my relationship with my husband, and how it was holding me back from life. I had been touched by and filled with grace. When I would try to show Bob parts in the book that I had highlighted, which held particular significance to my experience—the messages of pure, unbounded holy love and grace—he told me I was crazy.

Bob's comments, however, left me less and less confused as I read Theresa's writing over and over again. And somewhere or somehow between the constant messages of crazy and worthless, a word from deep within my soul spoke even more loudly; "I have called you by name" [Isaiah 43:1]. I opened my Bible to Isaiah and found this verse—this verse, which I'm sure I had read a dozen or more times before, but which now stood out boldly from the other printing on the page. I was unable to respond at first. I was unable to find my voice, which had been silenced and buried by the years of abuse. But ever more surely, day by day, my response was lifted from within me. My response was becoming the "Here I am" of Samuel, when he had heard God calling in the night [Samuel 6:8]. I knew I was not nearly worthy of either God's presence with me or God's call for me into ministry, but my journey to seminary became ever more clearly mapped as the days went by.

Of course, I had to keep the miracle to myself. My speaking of it brought negative responses from my husband. The threat of the entire prospect to Bob could send him over the edge with his anger at any time. I did not want to endure his wrath any more than necessary. And I don't think the girls really understood any of it—my depression, Bob's behavior, my feeling of "presence" and call into ministry.

I'm not even sure I fully comprehended what was happening to me and the journey that I was called to take. On Labor Day of 1995, I fled the farm, my house, Bob, and even the girls to the solitude of my office. My insides were tied in knots just thinking about the future and wondering what would happen to me, my marriage, and my life. Yet, I had a very real sense that I was taking a step into the future. I could not go back to living as I had before I had had the awakening, before I had had the very holy experience of God's presence speaking from within my soul. In my anxiety I drove to the lake seeking solace, to watch the sunrays touch the water with that brilliant, white light I had grown so accustomed to receiving.

There is a "restless uncertainty" on this day—'the day before'. I'm not sure that words can even do justice to the feeling of "gaping chasm" deep within my chest. For today is a day of dying—dying to the past, the usual, the customary, the routine. And in the dying of today, there is a silent screaming that refuses to allow me to work. The constant motion of my body doing nothing tires me. And my fingers pulse with incessant, useless energy. The screaming within cries in tones of fear, awe, and wonder. I am overwhelmed by nervousness—and I can hardly contain myself. I watch the silent ripple of peaceful waves contentedly held on water's buoyant surface, glowing with white-golden tranquility, safely held in the eternity of their holy creation. God, why do I not feel so safely cradled? Or, in my anxiety, am I pushing you away? A tear is spent in terrorizing uncertainty. One calming tear. Bless me with your peace, Lord, today in this day of dying. For tomorrow I begin to be reborn.(Labor Day, 1995)

From my dark hole of life, I began to see a glimmer of hope—just a glimmer, but a glimmer nonetheless. I, who had learned not to hope or dream, was beginning to look into the crevice of the door God was opening before me even as I was fighting doing so with all my might. And I would follow that glimmer out of my life of abuse and into the world God had waiting for me. It would not be quick, and it would not be easy, but that glimmer would not give up on me. The next day, I stepped forth to follow the light.

God wrapped his loving arms around,
And cradled me without a sound.

Twelve: **Baby Steps**

In the sleepless darkness of the wee morning hours of September 5, 1995, my first day as a fulltime seminary student, I stared into the blackness of the bedroom, running my restless hand along the smooth coolness of cotton sheet beneath me. I watched the red led display of the clock click the time from four a.m. to five a.m. to six a.m. "What am I doing?" I thought to myself, rising carefully so not to wake Bob. I grabbed the outfit I had hung on the closet door before going to bed the night before and went to the bathroom to wash up and dress. My fingers nervously moved over my clothing, shook as they held my toothbrush, quickly clutched the hairbrush, running it through the tangled strands of hair left in the wake of such a restless night. My mind flitted in and out of prayer as I did so—prayer for this new journey I was about to take, prayer that I would find my way safely, prayer that Bob would not be so upset when he awoke that he might start the day with an unkind comment, or worse yet, try to stop me from going at all. I tried to pray for my daughters, who, on the first day of a new school year, would be getting up and going on their way without mom around. But try as I might, I couldn't keep my mind on the words I wanted to pray. My mind was scattered in so many directions, I couldn't seem to think at all

As I descended the stairway, Bob was up and in the process of putting on his chore clothes to begin the morning milking. He looked up very briefly as I passed the doorway to the pantry, which led to the entryway where he was lacing up his shoes. He said nothing to me, nothing at all, just looked up and then down again. There was really nothing for either of us to say at this point. There had been all too few inquisitive words, all too few words of encouragement and support, and all too many harsh words about my foolishness for embarking on such an endeavor. All these discussions were reeked with my own indecision about taking the journey at hand. Two weeks before fall semester was to start my pastor had asked me if I was indeed planning to go. I had responded simply, truthfully, "I don't know." After a pause I repeated, "I really don't know at all."

Now that the morning had arrived, all the words that could be said had been said. I was going. I had heard a still, small voice, God's voice, almost nagging me to follow this path. How would Bob get the morning chores done without me? I didn't know, and it wouldn't be truthful to say that it didn't worry me. It all worried me—leaving Bob alone with the chores, the girls getting off to school without any last minute emergencies, the long drive to the seminary on uncertain roadways crowded with morning commuters, and the entire uncertain future.

Then there was always the question of what Bob would do when I returned home in the evening. Would he be angry? Would there be unkind words or something worse waiting for me on my return? I asked the angels to keep my family in their arms in my absence as I had so many times before when I had left my small daughters in the house alone so that I could help Bob with some necessary task on the farm. This was a journey that I had come to believe, over the course of twenty-four months of contemplation and prayer, I absolutely needed to take.

The sun was just beginning to show its rays above the dark outline of the eastern horizon as I turned from the gravel road that led away from the farm onto the county highway that would connect me with the twists and turns of highway and freeway leading me to the seminary—a way that would become so familiar to me over the coming months that I think the car could have maneuvered the commute without my guidance. As was always the case on a cool September morning in the country, there was a foggy mist above the lowlands that I passed as if bits of cloud had descended and entered the earthly terrain. Against the glow of sky ahead of me, I could see the occasional flight of a mallard or wood duck rising smoothly and magnificently above a slough and over the road only to find habitat among the overgrown reeds and cattails on the other side. A deer, nibbling its breakfast in a nearby meadow, turned curiously to see what was intruding on its peacefulness. Otherwise, there was nothing but the green of grass and the slightly golden tint of autumn on the cropland which I could see more clearly as the sun lifted its light above the dark line of horizon ahead of me—no vehicles of any kind on these small country roads at break of day. Only God's presence with me in the car and in my surroundings as I drove into the unknown.

By the time I reached the city, the sun had risen high before me and there was traffic on every side—long semi-trailers bearing loads of metal and iron pipes, garbage trucks turning out of their night homes to collect the day's debris, and car upon car of workday commuters. I was indeed entering a world that I knew little or nothing about. And my frightened fingers clung anxiously, nervously to the smooth, gray, steering wheel of the '89 red Dodge I had begged my husband to let me purchase the winter before. "What am getting myself into?" I thought as I entered lanes of traffic, cars and trucks rushing by on either side. If ever I had second thoughts, it was when I entered the rush hour traffic of the big city. To make matters worse, the morning sun, shining directly in my face above the eastern horizon, was blinding my reading the large, green signs above the freeways.

And I let out a big heave of breath that God would help guide me through all this. But as I rounded a turn in the highway's maze and traffic cleared a bit, ahead of me was the most marvelous spectacle of high rises and skyscrapers holding their heads in the yellowish, foggy clouds above them. It was my first sight of the downtown area of the city in the early morning light, and the eastern side of every pane of glass reflected a glorious, golden glow. My fingers relaxed their grip on the wheel for surely God was in this place, with me in my car at this very moment.

I made my way surely and safely through every twist and turn of freeway eventually to the seminary grounds, neatly mown, and with mums and daisies. By now the sun was high enough to light the cross above the chapel, and the bricks and mortar of the seminary buildings stood gallantly, elegantly among the green carpet of grass, mighty oaks, and slightly golden maple trees. It was peaceful. I had made it safely. Teardrops formed around the edges of my eyes—out of fright, out of thankfulness, out of wonder. As surely as I walked into the chapel for worship that morning, I did not walk alone. I could feel that presence—that presence, which had become so familiar to me by now. It not only walked beside me. I was engulfed in it. I was overwhelmed by my being favored in such a way, and for the first time I could identify with Mary, Jesus' mother. Carrying the black, vinyl backpack I had purchased so recently, precisely for this journey, I tentatively stepped forward into my new life.

I soon found my time at the seminary to be thrilling and rewarding. I found my studies interesting and insightful. I was being fed a wealth of knowledge and challenged to think in new ways—things that I had not experienced for longer that I can remember. I found that I was not the only second-career student. There were others on this journey with me. I began to form solid friendships that would follow me not only through seminary but beyond it. The lectures, the discussions, chapel, and time spent with books and new friends were life-giving.

Days and weeks passed quickly as the leaves on the trees ripened gold and red and fell from their branches until the whole ground crunched beneath my feet. I thrived on the lectures and the class work, which came easily to me. I relished the quiet hours in the library between classes, where row on row of books waited for my inquisitive mind to find them and open them. I was overtaken by the swell of the pipe organ during chapel and the chorus of singing of my many classmates during worship. Surely God was in this place. I could feel God's presence all around me—in the chapel, in the library, in my classes, among people, who were friendly and likeable. There were no harsh words for me here on campus as there had been at home on the farm with Bob. There was no striking out, no hitting, no punching, no kicking. There was instead a quiet friendliness that spread with the cool autumn breeze, which swayed the drying blooms of the hydrangea bushes and the stems of the black-eyed Susans lining the sidewalk from the campus center to the library.

Although during the first days I felt some relief as I passed out of the busy city with its traffic, and sirens, and rows of houses and back into the peacefulness of the country, that feeling changed as I experienced more and more warmth in my relationships with other seminary students and staff and had positive and friendly encounters with people in the many shops and stores I visited. The people of the city were not unfriendly as I had been led to believe during my years in the country. People, from the gas station attendants to the shop owners to people casually walking their dogs, were helpful and friendly. As evenings on the farm with Bob remained difficult and I saw more and more the difference between his behavior toward me and that of others I encountered on my daily journeys away from the farm and the rural area, I felt a tingle of excitement when I would see the traffic radio sign signaling my entering the urban sprawl. Yes, my children were still in the rural area, and out of love for them, I knew I needed to return home to the farm, but my heart was shifting, adapting, and, yes, even aching for my daily experience of wonder and learning.

What struck me most as I experienced this new life at the seminary and in the city were the interactions between husbands and wives and between couples and their children. I saw fathers in the grocery store, children in their carts, grocery list in hand. I saw couples in the early evening hours walking hand in hand or strolling the baby carriage ahead of them. They were smiling and chatting or laughing with each other. One evening a father was out teaching his young daughter to ride a bicycle. It is little wonder that I found such scenes unusual and would catch myself staring curiously.

At home on our farm, there were few positive interactions. Although I tried as best to give the girls quality time, between my job by which we made a living and the farm work, which stared us in the face just beyond the kitchen door, I had precious little time to laugh and play with the kids. When I did, I was so exhausted I couldn't muscle up the energy to really enjoy and appreciate the time. And Bob had never really had any genuine kind of father care for the girls. His interactions with them usually occurred through me. And certainly, between Bob and me, there was a relationship based solely on work—both the work Bob wanted done and the work I knew needed to be done in order to make some kind of a profit out of the entire ordeal of farming. I could count on my hands the number of dates we had had since our marriage twenty-one years before. Yet, the number of abusive attacks were too numerous to count by any method. It was as if my eyes were being opened for me in a way they had not been for a time longer than I could remember. I think God was showing me that there was a different way of living, a better way, a way of love.

Often, during the hours of commute time, I would argue with myself and with God the pros and cons of staying with Bob or leaving him, staying on the farm and enduring the years of commute or moving to the seminary. I would tell myself that I could not leave my husband, the husband I had promised my life to when I was so young. But a voice in my heart kept telling me otherwise. And although my religious background told me I shouldn't listen to that voice, my new experience of God's grace told me I had to. If I didn't I would surely die, if not by my husband's hands, by my own yearning.

I often went to one of the lakes within the city to savor the peacefulness when I was in a state of despair. The water would always calm me, sometimes so that I could go on and sometimes in a way that would draw me out of this world with all its anger, and heartache, and problems. I was amazed that city lakes had tarred paths around them. When I became aware of the volume of walkers, joggers, and bicycle riders that used them, I understood the necessity. Yet I chose to go to an area of the lake where a long-abandoned stairway led to the grasses of the lake's edge. There I felt torn between my own suicidal ideation and the feeling of God's presence being ever by my side. By late fall, sitting in the brush of one of my favorite, off-the-beaten paths on Lake Harriet, with God's presence so very near at my side, I contemplated suicide.

In private carnival of solitude, I kneel before a pool of glowing wonder, which crosses the expanse of time, hiding sun in shadows of indifference. I dip my cup-shaped palm, breaking mirrored surface into spreading ripples, distorting crystal images, shattering the pane dividing an eternity and mortality of which I belong to both, and yet, not either. I contemplate the entering, of pushing beckoning door wide open, escaping death-like tomb of life,
The sound of a jet flying just overhead broke into my concentration. *Amid the roar of soaring jet, I hear your voice again, O God. I listen yet to song so sweet, and breath of freshness, sweet relief. Surely this is most holy water, Your temple, not my tomb."* (October, 1995)

I finished completely torn by the wonder of it all, its overwhelming intensity, my desperation with my life, and the certain feeling of God's presence with me. And so the year went on, my favorite body of water freezing over into wintry solidity as those who circled the lake's path became fewer and fewer in number.

I continued my therapy for the depression, needing the extra support and encouragement as I began this new venture, now with a new therapist in the city, Jan. Together we identified the many characteristics of post-traumatic stress disorder I carried with me from the many years of living with the trauma of abuse. I startled easily, I had recurrent nightmares, I experienced on-going depression, and I still struggled with thoughts of suicide. It took several pastoral counselors along with Jan's prodding to convince me that the marriage was not safe—my life was in danger as well as the lives of my girls—and that the marriage I had with Bob was not the life-giving relationship God intended marriage to be.

With the coming of the springtime meltdown of the wintry snows and ice, I began a ceremonial burning of household items, a stuffed kitchen goose, unused teaching materials from the storeroom closets, old books, college papers that had been saved, sewing supplies I would never use. All these things and more went up in smoke as Bob worked the fields for spring planting. Other more useful items I bagged until the trunk of my car was full of black, garbage bags, which I gave to charity. Snack sets, dishes, warming and serving trays that were wedding presents I cleaned out of china cupboard drawers. Old clothes I either cut up for rags or washed and folded for quilts, placed carefully in a box, and prepared. Prepared for what—I could not have really told you at the time. I was un-nesting, taking a home apart from the inside out. Without disturbing too much of what showed as our house, I effectively dismantled my farm home from the hidden corners towards the surface. I didn't know what I was really doing or why. I just felt compelled to do it, as if in preparation for something ahead of me.

Although I could not have said with certainty that I was moving, when a classmate in Hebrew class said she was looking for someone to sublease her apartment over the summer, the dull aching I had been pushing below the surface peeked its head above the mire. If the instructor taught any Hebrew of importance during that class hour, my brain did not receive it. It was too busy struggling with the question of whether or not I should express my interest in the apartment proposal.

At the end of the Hebrew class on the fifteenth of May of that first year in seminary, with the sun shining into the classroom windows, I said: "Diane, would you consider renting the apartment to me during the summer?"

"Sure, meet me after my afternoon classes and we'll talk," was her response.

By afternoon the sunny day had turned overcast. Diane and I sat in her '70's model sedan and discussed what seemed simply a dreadful unreality and totally wrong—sneaking behind my husband's back in such a way. I knew that saying yes would commit me to three months rent payments, the money of which I did not know if I had and which I knew I dared not withdraw from our joint checking account. If I said yes, I would have to pay that money whether or not I actually lived there. My entire being trembled inside. "How much is the rent?" I asked Diane again. Despite my fear and misgivings, I agreed to the arrangement, and we made plans to meet at the housing office the next day to finalize a contract.

How could I do such a thing, contemplate living away from my husband and our farm? I trembled at the thought. Yet, although my entire being on the inside was saying "No, you can't, you mustn't," and I both wondered and worried about what would happen with my daughters during the three summer months, some voice spoke the affirmative "yes" from out of my mouth. As my classmate drove away, I was weighed with such a terrible guilt that I could barely walk the short distance across the parking lot to my own car. I drove the many miles back to the farm that afternoon going over and over in my mind what I had actually just agreed to. I was frightened, filled with guilt, and at peace all at the same time.

The next day some part of me that I had not known before walked into the housing office to make the agreement for the sublease valid. That part of me moved my hand to sign the form. "Evelyn Dahlke" it signed in cursive black ink on the correct line of the housing sublease contract.

That evening, when I returned to the farmhouse, I felt both a great sense of heaviness about the future and a great sense of excitement and joy. The two parts of me were at war with each other, and I was nearly immobilized by the inner tension. But again, that part which had signed the agreement, sneaked in the house during evening cattle chores, reached into the dresser drawer under the pairs of folded blue jeans and pulled out the wad of paper bills I had placed there from my paychecks over the final months I had held my job. That foreign part of me then placed the folded bills in a brown envelope from the kitchen cupboard and took the envelope with its contents out to the car. There, it hid the package under the front seat, locking the car door behind it. Having done so, that part of me rejoined the responsible farmwife, returning to the barn to finish with the milking of the cattle. Once there, I and this new part of myself conversed with my husband as we finished the work and washed up for the evening.

The next day after my classes, the part of me that arranged for the apartment took the pile of folded bills and opened a checking account at the bank near the seminary. "What kind of an account did you want?" the bank official asked.

"Just a regular student checking account," I answered nervously, holding the wad of bills in my hand.

Soon the bills were counted. They totaled enough for a month's rent with some spending money left over. It would take care of the immediate future until I could apply for more student loan money. I felt both relieved and nervous as I ordered checks with only my name on them. I felt again like I was not myself as I spelled out the address I would have for the summer on the order form.

"Your checks should come in about a week," the bank official told me. "In the meantime, you can use these," and he handed me a small pad of temporary checks.

I left the bank both nervous and elated. I went directly over to the housing office and paid the first month's rent. With that, the deal was finalized. I had my own space for the summer.

Since I realized the danger that such a living arrangement would put me in with Bob, I knew I had to have a reason—a good, logical reason—for my actions. I could not tell him that I was leaving him. I would certainly bear the brunt of that reason. In reality I did not know for sure if, indeed, I was leaving him. The part of me that had rented the space was not in total connection with the part of me that said I must stay because of a marital commitment I had made some twenty-two years earlier. To leave seemed inconceivable, it could not register on any level of reality for me. Yet, I stopped at the Goodwill store when I left the seminary that day and purchased a bedside lamp, some drinking glasses, a cook pot, and a frying pan, which I hid under the blanket in the trunk before setting out for the farm so that Bob would never know.

The part of me that was moving on with plans to leave went forward. I registered for sixteen credits of summer study. Some part of me had reasoned that with a full load of daily classes through the summer, it would be simply unfeasible for me to try to commute and keep up with the work. I told Bob that this would help me finish seminary sooner in order that I might get back to work sooner.

I had not worked for a paycheck since the October before when I was given the ultimatum at my job to either work fulltime, regular hours or go to seminary—not both. Although I had known Bob would blow through the roof, I had chosen going to seminary saying that I could not take a step backward after I had already taken a step forward. Bob did blow when I got home. I bore the brunt of it, but I neither could nor would change my decision about seminary attendance. I had already struggled with that issue. What was one more beating and name-calling session? I had already decided I was stepping into a new career come what may.

Bob did not beat me up when I told him about the heavy load of class work or about the apartment for the summer. He was busy with spring planting by then, working day and night. Besides saying that he already knew I had gone terribly crazy, he walked out the door and went on with his work. I think it really didn't register as a reality for him, at least not at that time.

The spring and early summer of 1996 was full of so many things other than my seminary class load, it's a wonder that I was able to take the step to move as I did. First, Krista made her confirmation at church that April, and there was the extra work that surrounded that event. Carol, Bob's cousin and a woman with whom I had worked on banners at church and with whom I had become friends, had volunteered to help with house-cleaning and food preparation for the confirmation dinner that would follow. But Carol was unexpectedly diagnosed with liver cancer the day before the confirmation. This pushed all of the work back onto my shoulders. It was not only the house and the food that needed preparation, following winter the farmyard also needed my attention if we were going to have company.

Things didn't ease up once the confirmation was over. Carol was given only six weeks to live. During that time she was back and forth between a hospital in the city, her home, and the local hospital. I stopped to see her as often as I could.

Carol had one brief stay at home during those weeks during which I came to visit after commuting back home. She got out of bed on my arrival, and we sat by her dining room table together. I looked deeply into her yellowed eyes and told her of my summer plans. "I'm going to live with Amy at the seminary for the summer. I have a heavy load of classes," I told her. She said nothing, but her silence spoke as did the worried look that came over her jaundiced face. Unable to bear her stare, I glanced out the window only to notice how very vividly green the grass was outside her house. "Look at the grass, Carol. Have you ever seen such bright green grass?" She continued looking at me, not at the grass, as if to say, "Don't you know, the new grass this spring no longer belongs to me." She had already moved to a new dimension, that dimension that transcends the earthy realities of this life. I said goodbye as she wearily moved back to her bedroom.

The next time I saw her she was almost comatose and in great pain. As I traveled to the seminary after that visit, I discussed with God what I could do to make her final days more comfortable. It was during the moments of that discussion with God that the tape I had playing in the tape deck all of a sudden seemed louder. It was Easter music. "Jesus Christ Is Risen Today" rang loudly, boldly through the interior of my car. I looked down at it. Yes, I thought, the music. Carol, an organist all of her adult life, would appreciate music. And since I had heard that sense of hearing is the last sense to leave when one is dying, she would at least hear the music even if she couldn't respond.

When I returned from the seminary that day, I rushed into the church offices. "Is there an extra tape player around here?" I asked the church secretary, who was busy working on church bulletins for Sunday's service. She looked at me inquisitively. "Carol needs music!" I responded with an urgency that sent the secretary rushing into the copy room to find a tape player. I hurried it with the Easter tape to Carol's hospital room. With her son looking on, I set the player near Carol's ear and pressed play. When the music started, her eyes moved slightly up and over in the direction of the music, and, at the same moment, her labored breathing relaxed. God had told me what I could do for Carol, and I did it. I didn't realize how long the process had taken, or the time I spent holding Carol's limp hand as the music played, so Bob was not pleased when I arrived home later than usual. His unkind words slashed into me like a sword. But I didn't care. I needed to do what I did for Carol. She died on June 1, 1996, six weeks after she was diagnosed.

By that time, I had decided that Bonnie would stay on the farm for the summer. She worked in a nearby town and could drive away from the farm if she needed to. Krista would spend part of the time on the farm and would stay at times with some people from our church. She had a job in town and could either walk or get a ride as needed. Amy would have to come with me. She was only twelve and could not stay at the farm all day, day after day, alone. I knew Bob would not look after her needs. Yes, Amy would come with me, and together we would share my one bedroom apartment in the city, which was so foreign to her. "You can have the bedroom." I enticed her. "I'll sleep in the study."

I made these decisions with deliberation. After evening chores, and after the girls had gone to bed and Bob had fallen asleep on the couch, I would drive to the church, like I had so many times before, and sit in the darkness with only the eternal light burning in the chancel and the fans humming near the high, vaulted ceiling. I could feel the spirit moving around me, like a fresh breeze against the staleness of death. I allowed the tears to flow, something that I was not allowed to do at home. I couldn't hold them back. The contrast of the holiness of God's presence with me in the church against the ugliness and hurt of my life on the farm with my husband pressed hard against my chest. But after some moments of breathing prayers into the darkness, the heaviness of the suicidal thoughts would lessen. The answers I so desperately needed for my family's welfare would come. I would return home to find Bob still sleeping on the couch as he had been when I left. I would put on my pajamas and crawl onto the edge of my side of the bed so that Bob would not feel enticed to disturb me when he would come crawling in beside me. There I would stare into the blackness of the bedroom until my eyelids would finally close in sleep.

The day after Carol died and one week before I moved, Bonnie graduated from high school. One of the top-ranking students in her class, she spoke at the commencement exercises. I listened to her speech with great anxiety. Although I couldn't have been more proud of my oldest daughter on that day, I felt like a betrayer sitting next to Bob, like the entire scene was a fake one. Soon people would know the truth, I thought. I would be shamed and disgraced for moving away from my husband. As part of the ceremony each of the graduates gave a rose to their parents. For some graduates, both parents went up to receive their rose. For others, only a mother or father did so. I went up to get the rose from Bonnie by myself. It was a beautiful rose, large and white, and she looked me in the eyes when she gave it to me. Overwhelmed, I carried the rose, not back to my place next to Bob's, but out of the auditorium and into the freshness of the hallway. There I rushed towards the school's front doors. The partial sun had been covered by stormy, rain clouds, and a heavy shower had just burst open from the weighted skies. With tears streaming down my cheeks, I smelled the summer rain as it descended on the shiny sidewalk. I wanted to run out of the building, away from this life, scream my misery for all the world to hear, and end it all at that moment. I felt so guilty, so ashamed, so overwhelmed, so helpless. "God, how can all of this be happening to me?" I silently cried.

I pulled myself together to rejoin Bob in the hallway. He muttered something about my disappearance as we headed out into the subsiding rain. With the girls in tow, we made the motions of being the happy parents of a graduate, appearing at the numerous parties we had been invited to that afternoon. It became very stuffy—humidly hot—after the rain shower passed, so I wasn't sure whether it was the weather or my misery that was making it difficult for me to breathe.

The next day I met with Carol's family to help plan her funeral. After that the days moved into a big blur. I sat at a table in the fellowship hall at church writing my message for Carol's funeral and my sermon for the coming Sunday. I had agreed to do the service for our pastor while he took some vacation time. The children were having Vacation Bible School so every so often a line of bubbling children clad in brightly colored shorts and T-shirts paraded through like a train. I was there in body but my mind was far away, disconnected from what was going on around me.

The Wednesday of Carol's funeral dawned cloudy, windy and rainy, which seemed most appropriate to me. The words I had written, words of tribute and hope, came eloquently out of my mouth. I remember feeling nothing at all. I was totally numb. It was not until I put my hand on the casket in the sprinkle of rain at the gravesite that I fell apart. I cried unstoppably for the next few hours up in the church office while the other attendees had lunch down in the fellowship hall. Bob never bothered to check on me.

I was scheduled to pick up the key to the apartment at the seminary later that afternoon. So, pulling myself together, I told my pastor that I was leaving. On the way I stopped to buy a telephone and saw my therapist, whose support I needed urgently. Reaching the apartment quite late, I quickly hooked up the phone and called home. Bonnie answered and assured me that she and her sisters were fine.

I slept very little that night in this strange apartment home between jags of crying from grief, prayers over what was about to happen in my life, and traffic on the freeway, which passed by not far from the building. When I heard the train pass over the railroad bridge with its clumpity-clump as the wheels of each car hit the rails of the bridge, I longed to be able to go along with it, to disappear forever from this mess of a world in which I found myself. I prayed that God would just let me disappear.

By Friday I was back home on the farm. Restless, I went out to the cemetery. I sat near Carol's grave feeling the heat of the morning sun on my back. It was peaceful there. In fact, I felt at peace for the first time that week as I sat there smelling fresh-cut alfalfa and feeling the presence of God wash over me.

Soon I could hear the sound of a tractor on the road. Bob had spotted the car sitting on the grassy, cemetery driveway, and was headed my way. I got up and into the car by the time he arrived. For the first time he said, "Please stay home where you belong," as he brushed his hand gently on the back of my head and neck. I didn't answer. I didn't respond at all.

When he was ready, he opened the car door, climbed back on the tractor and headed home. I turned the car around and headed for the farm as well. There was work to be done as always.

On Sunday I preached and presided at the worship service at church. Bob did not come in from morning chores in time to go along to church. Bonnie was at work. I let the two younger girls sleep. So it was just me in a car loaded for the summer's move that headed out to perform this duty that began the new life into which I was moving professionally. I didn't hurry home, but stayed and visited over coffee.

When I returned, Bob was as angry as a hornet, partly from the stuffy heat, partly out of frustration with the cattle or the milking equipment, but mostly because I had not changed my mind about moving out for the summer. "You can't leave," he yelled! "Who do you think you are?" He picked up a heavy piece of iron from the barn cleaner and began to swing at the car windows. All three girls stood still as statues, watched their father's total loss of control, and worried for me as I blocked him from getting near enough to the car to destroy any part of it. I signaled to Bonnie to call the sheriff's office. She left the scene without question and did so without Bob even noticing. We had talked about the possibility of her needing to take such an action. I had prepared her as best I could, and now the moment had come when she needed to follow my instruction. And she did.

The scene was still in full action when the sheriff's deputy arrived, Bob in his dirty, work jeans, manure-coated shoes, and bare torso. As the deputy tried to calm him down, Bob threw the piece of iron and stood face to face with him screaming at him, yelling something about gladly getting out of here. He stomped over to the deputy's car and climbed in the back seat. The deputy then pulled him out of the squad car, worried that Bob was messing the seat because of the caked mud on his jeans. I was stunned. Bob stomped away, climbed up into the silo, and began throwing down fodder for the cow's evening meal yelling all the while.

Then the deputy walked over to me and said, "There's nothing I can do unless he actually hits *me*!" Walking back to the squad car, the deputy climbed in and left—left me there with a ferocious husband yelling away in the silo.

I stood totally stunned for some moments before sending Bonnie with the two younger girls to a parade I had promised they could attend. I then went into the house to wait—for Bob to come in and for the girls to return. I didn't know what Bob would do to me when he climbed back out of that silo, but I knew that whatever he did, I did not want the girls around to see it. What they thought as they drove away I don't know, and I'm not sure to this day that I want to know. It's a subject we never discussed afterwards.

By the time Bob climbed out of the silo, he had stopped yelling. He returned to the house, went to take a shower, crawled into bed, and turned on the ballgame. I sat quietly in the rocking chair playing the entire scene over and over in my head until the girls came back. Making sure the two older girls were all set for the week, I got Amy into the car and drove away. Bob never came out of the bedroom. I did not see or hear from him until I returned the next Saturday. He was asleep by the time I left with my youngest daughter to begin a new life.

Perhaps I should have been upset by the entire incident—Bob's behavior and the inadequacy of the sheriff's deputy. Certainly the entire scene could have been out of some horror movie. I remember feeling disbelief at the deputy's inability to act. I remember thinking it must be against the law to yell and scream obscenities into a law enforcement officer's face. Certainly there must be some legal protection for a wife and children when a husband displays that kind of dangerous behavior. But I think I was just too tired and depressed to deal with it. It had been a very rough week—Bonnie's graduation, Carol's funeral, opening up the apartment, packing to move, preparing for the Sunday service. I didn't have the strength or energy to fight the battle that presented itself that afternoon. I had to concentrate on getting off the farm without Bob wrecking the car or us.

The Friday following the difficult week of Carol's funeral and the even more frightening ordeal of Sunday noon, Amy and I returned to the farm. Bonnie and Krista had lived through the week, and Bob greeted us happily on our return as if the entire scene the Sunday afternoon before had never occurred. Bonnie's graduation party was planned for that Saturday evening, and it would be held as planned. Bob and I acted as if nothing negative had ever happened between us in our lives. Speaking of false fronts, that night I definitely wore one. I was just glad that Bob was in a good mood so we could host this party without a scene. But then, we never did have a scene in public. Bob always saved his angry episodes for the privacy of our own home or vehicle.

Looking back on that evening now, I simply don't know how I did it—going through all I had the week prior to the move, starting two new classes while also learning to live in a new environment, and also taking care of the details for the party. Maybe keeping myself so busy did not give me time to think or feel—a blessing in disguise.

170

I also continued my therapy throughout. Jan helped me be objective. She helped me identify the disassociative abilities that had helped me survive with Bob on the farm all the years that I did.

By Monday, back at the apartment and busy with classes, I got a call from Bob. "Gloria's dead," Bob's words rang through me. Gloria, Bob's youngest sister, had been battling heart problems for over a year. Just like that, one of the veins near her heart burst, and she was gone. And although I knew he needed me, I also knew I had a heavy load of schoolwork and classes that I dare not miss in a condensed summer session. "I can only come home for the funeral. I'll have to miss the visitation. I have a class that night that I don't dare miss." I returned to the farm after morning class in time for Bob and I to attend the funeral.

I felt like a traitor to both Bob and his family. I felt a strange distancing from them, a disparity between my two homes and my two lives—that of rural farmwife and that of seminary student living in the city. It is little wonder then that I felt a sense of relief as I headed back to the seminary apartment after the funeral lunch in order not to miss the next morning's class. That day I really had no time to mourn. Besides, I don't think I had any feeling left in me to do so. But on Friday during my worship class the dam burst, and I couldn't stop the tears. With the help of my classmates, I was able to release years of emotions and then gather myself together enough to return to the apartment and fall asleep, dead tired of it all.

Amy and I spent the summer, back and forth, to and from the farm on weekends. One week I enrolled Amy in a city school and signed up for an apartment for the fall. I felt terribly guilty for doing both, and I rocked all night curled up in a fetal position in the corner of a futon where I slept that summer, rocked and worried, not about my schoolwork or the seminary life, but about the future of my marriage. Once I realized the abuse, I could not go on living with Bob. I had tried. I prayed to God to help me find a way out. But mostly I prayed for God to let me die. I just wanted to die, the pain and the heartache were so great.

By the time I came home for the local, county fair in August I had worked out a plan. Bonnie would be going off to college in fall. She would live on the college campus. Amy would move with me and start at the new school whether she wanted to or not. But Krista was harder. Not only did she not want to quit the job she had just started, as a sophomore in high school, she did not want to change schools. I had decided to ask a family from church if Krista could live with them while she finished high school. "She can't stay at the farm. If she does, she will be Bob's slave in my place. I can't let that happen," I told these friends on the evening of the county queen coronation in which Bonnie was a participant. "Bob has been beating me up during our entire marriage. I can't stay there any longer. Neither can the girls." I told them the whole, blessed truth about Bob and our marriage.

"We'd love to have her. She'll be just like one of the family," I was assured.

I left their house to attend Bonnie's queen pageant. I had watched the judging the evening before and had cheered Bonnie on. Bob had not come to the judging saying that someone had to stay and get some work done around the farm.

Earlier that summer, when Bonnie had decided to participate in the pageant, she had gotten a letter stating that she needed an escort. It said that in most cases the participant's father served as his daughter's escort. Of course, the coronation was at the same time as evening milking, which caused a problem for Bob. He started making demands of Bonnie. Only if she did such and such for him would he be her escort. The more she did, the more he demanded. And, in the end, she still could not be sure he would rearrange the milking schedule to escort her.

After several days of this, Bonnie was in tears. "Let's ask Grandpa to escort you," I suggested. We would circumvent Bob altogether and take his power away.

"No problem," was his response. "Do I have to wear a suit?"

"Unfortunately, Dad, you do," I responded laughing.

Bonnie was much relieved but still questioned, "What if Dad gets mad?"

"I'll handle your dad," I assured her. Although I could tell that this worried Bonnie, she didn't say anything. I had come to her rescue, and she was used to her father being angry at me.

I suppose I should have been ferocious at Bob for letting his daughter down. I didn't feel that. I simply felt relief that the issue was resolved and the worry over it was out of my mind. Later I felt disgust that he had treated her so badly.

Bob went to town to pick up cattle feed the day of the coronation and had heard that Bonnie had done a very good job during judging. "She has a good chance of winning," he was told.

Although he hadn't said anything to me when I had left to view the pageant, before I knew it, he rushed into the coronation area and sat down beside me on the bench. He acted as if nothing was wrong with the fact that all the other fathers were escorting their daughters, while Bonnie's grandfather was escorting her. He was cheerful and gregarious until Bonnie failed to win. At that moment he got up and said, "What a stupid waste of time this was!" He walked away to go home, saying no word of encouragement to Bonnie. That job was left to me. I felt very ashamed of Bob that evening, and I definitely felt disgusted with him. I think I maybe even felt a little bit of anger. I was beginning to change bit by bit. I had begun taking baby steps which led away from Bob, from the farm, and from a life of abuse.

Prayer

O God,

I wait in the unending darkness
like a chrysalis on a lonely limb.

I am living in the dreadful "in between"
of death and life, of darkness and light,
not coming, not going, just hanging on.

I fight the seeming emptiness
and struggle against required surrender.

Teach me to wait patiently,
while my wings grow strong,
for my time to fly has not yet come.

"Prayer" excerpted from *Little Pieces of Light*, an Illumination Book, by Joyce Rupp, Copyright 1994 by Joyce Rupp, Paulist Press, Inc., New York/Mahwah, N.J. Used with permission. www.paulistpress.com

Thirteen: **Taking Leave**

"Guess what?" I came in joyfully from my history final with my professor to greet Amy. "We're going to get an apartment in which pets are
allowed! Now Whiskers (Amy's farm cat) can move up with us!"

Amy jumped up and down jubilantly on hearing the news. "God answered my prayers!"

What a blessing for both Amy and me that there was a pet apartment
available! Gretchen, Amy's guinea pig could come with us too. The four
of us would live in our small, new home. I arranged for financial aid and
student loans to help pay for apartment rent and utility bills. I also signed
up for classes concurrently doing 400 hours of clinical work required of all
Master of Divinity students seeking to be rostered by the Church.

I had no time for guilt or shame to surface. My mind was occupied with
class work, clinical work, Amy's care, school activities, and the companionship of seminary classmates, who had now become close friends. I was
able to shut out any feelings of discomfort, dread, fear, remorse, or grief
I had regarding my leaving Bob and the farm. Certainly having the girls
away from the farm was a huge relief. I had over the course of the preceding spring, broken free of my responsibilities with cattle chores and farm
work. In fact, when I was home one summer weekend and bales needed
to be unloaded, as I placed the bales on the elevator I experienced both
a feeling of otherness and relief that this task was only very temporary.
What Bob knew of my thoughts or feelings, I have no idea. I certainly
didn't discuss anything of it with him. To do so may have been dangerous.
Sometimes I felt some guilt over having this secret life. I was slowly but
surely shutting him out even if I could not have cognitively acknowledged
that fact. Sometimes I felt elation—a sense of freedom. Mostly I felt totally
numb, like I was going through the motions of living this reality and looking on at all of it strangely from afar.

Amy had become accustomed to living with me at the seminary by the
time summer was over. We had done a little exploring so were beginning
to learn our way around the part of the city surrounding the seminary. She
had met some children living on the seminary grounds, and I went out of
my way in order for Amy to invite friends over and have an enjoyable time
with them, knowing that helping her develop some meaningful friendships
would also help make her transition easier.

By the time late August arrived, Amy, who had protested full force
when I first told her of my plans and the new school, said to me, "Mom, I
want to stay with you. I want to move up to the city with you."

"And the new school–?" I inquired.

"I'm going to go to school here," she replied. It was definitely a relief to have her reassure me with those words.

When September arrived, Amy and I walked the few possessions we had brought with us from the farm or purchased at the local thrift stores across the sidewalk to the apartment I had rented. This wasn't a terribly difficult task. There were a few armfuls and boxes of clothing, a card table, a small bookshelf, a chest of drawers, and two kitchen chairs. Most of our belongings—pictures of the kids, kitchen utensils, and my books from my first year at the seminary I packed in the large box I had been using as my nightstand. Bonnie's friend brought up Amy's bed and bookcase from her bedroom at the farm along with my dining room table. I bought a used but usable sofa and rocking chair and bought a well-used twin mattress and box spring, cast offs from a nearby college. They weren't great, but they were better than the futon on the floor, which I had grown accustomed to over the summer. I went to Wal-mart and bought a television, video player, and computer desk, one of those composite things, which I glued and screwed together myself. Other things like a T.V. stand, lamps, and a few wall decorations, Amy and I accumulated over time.

I left my house with what was in it at the farm, and started over with next to nothing. It was easier that way. We did not have to endure Bob's wrath. I think it was also my way of leaving the past with all its memories behind. I had cremated much of it anyway.

I placed the three eight by ten pictures of the girls on the wall along with a plaque I had picked up at a garage sale, which read, "Those who walk in the sunshine of God's love, gather rainbows along the way." Indeed, I had. Regardless of how difficult and frightening my marriage was at times, I had three beautiful daughters, who were growing and maturing in wonderful ways in spite of the environment in which they had been living. And though Amy and I definitely didn't have much, and when the other two girls came to visit, we had to blow up a vinyl mattress that covered the entire living room floor, it's almost unbelievable how happy we were in our new home.

I'll never forget one of Amy's most significant and insightful comments during those first weeks in our new home. "It's so quiet here–so peaceful." And it was. There was none of the name-calling, swearing, yelling, or physical encounters that we had grown s accustomed to on the farm. We didn't have to walk on eggshells to avoid an almost certain violent, hurtful outbreak. There was instead this empty, almost vacuum-like void. The absence of chaos. We had never experienced that and didn't know what to do with it except sit and listen to the silence. She and I were totally dependent on each other for support.

Yet, leaving two of my daughters behind was heart-wrenching for me. I moved Krista into her new home on Labor Day, the day before she started school. She and I carefully and thoughtfully picked out the clothing and items from her room on the farm that she wanted or needed. For weeks I washed, ironed, and hung her clothing on a makeshift rod in preparation. I purchased a few towels and a washcloth for her along with a jug of laundry detergent. She would be responsible for her own property, which would include washing her own clothes. I assembled a simple desk I had purchased with her consent during the summer. I gave her one of the extra dining room chairs so that she would have a place to sit while studying. Into the box I put a teddy bear, my new phone number, and the carrousel horse music box that played "Somewhere, out there, our love will see us through." She and I moved her stuff without saying much to each other. Bob stayed out on the field and out of our way. I think it was his way of escaping what was actually happening. He didn't find it strange that his own daughter was going to live with another family only five miles from the farm. He didn't feel remorse that she needed to escape her own father to be safe.

After helping Krista arrange her new room, I hugged her and left. I felt as if I were abandoning my child, but I don't remember either of us crying any tears. Perhaps because it was too difficult to feel. We simply turned our respective directions and parted. Later Krista told me, "I thought to myself, how can my mother just dump me off and leave me here." If she had said that, I couldn't have gone.

On Friday, I returned to take Krista to her driver's test. After she passed, I dropped her off at school and went out to the farm to find Bonnie packed for college. To my surprise, Bob was cleaned up and waiting to help with the move. "You're going?" I questioned him.

"Of course. I'm her father, aren't I?" was his response.

We loaded her belongings onto our pickup, which Bob drove to the campus while I followed with the car. After Bonnie moved her belongings into her room, we met her roommate and family. Then Bob and I went to the parents' activities at the student center as if nothing out of the ordinary was going on between us. Following the parents' program, we ate a late lunch in the cafeteria with other parents of college freshmen.

As surprising as it may have seemed under the circumstances, we had a good day. Bob was in one of his good moods. He was really acting like a dad that day for Bonnie and with the other parents. He even bragged to Bonnie's roommate's father, "Yah, my wife is in seminary. She's going to be a pastor." He had always bragged about me in public. Later in private, he would let me know how he really felt. But I knew that wouldn't happen this time. I felt relieved and glad when we parted going our separate ways, him back to the farm and me back to the apartment at the seminary.

Although I found some sense of peace and safety in not having the almost daily encounters with Bob, and Amy and I were happy in our new weekday home, there were often nights when I would rock in the chair beside the window in the living room and stare out into the city-night sky. Listening to Amy's heavy, sleep-filled breathing, I would try to rock away the memories of the past, rock away the tenseness that would rise up in my throat when I thought of all that I had done so far to escape, rock into myself a sense of peace about being away from my two older daughters. The light from the lampposts would shine gently on the shiny pavement below as I would try to take in the reality of my new life. Often the phone would ring and the sound of Bob's voice would come over the answering machine, making me jump when I least expected it. Whatever trepidation I felt about moving away from my home on the farm and my marriage was overridden by the peaceful calmness of our new city home and all the unique possibilities city life held out before us. There was an excitement in it all—the classwork, the new friends, our new apartment, the lights of the city at night, airplanes flying so closely overhead—that was more powerful than my fear and shame over leaving Bob at home on the farm alone.

During that second year in seminary, Amy and I returned home to the farm on the weekends where we remained involved in our church in the local town. On Saturdays I would clean up the mess Bob had made around the house during our absence and wash the weekly laundry. Sometimes I would be disgusted at having to maintain cleanliness and tidiness in two places of residence. Sometimes I felt the disparity of our two lives. Yet Bob and I would sometimes do tasks around the farm he had saved for my return, and I did not balk at his expectations of my responsibilities. If I could find a little time, I would get out my class books in order to keep up with the large amounts of reading that had been assigned. Bob would often get jealous or angry at the amount of time I would need to read and study in preparation for the next week of classes. "What do you do, fool around on the weekday so that you have to bring your work home. Why don't you get your studying done during the week? Are you fooling around on the side?" he would accuse me. But, in reality, I was carrying a very heavy load of classes, and between class attendance and clinical experience, not much time was left for anything but study and life's necessities. So, although it was good to see Krista, who would also come home on the weekends, time on the farm was ever more difficult and tense.

Two weekends before Thanksgiving, Bob blew up. He wanted me to stay until Monday morning. I refused. I did not want to stay the night and sleep with him as sex was what he really wanted. Amy had school early in the morning and did not want to be late. I insisted on leaving, walking around him as he stood in my way. I continued with what I was doing— packing up Amy's and my belongings for the week. Amy was already in the car. As I walked out the door, he gave me a shove, almost sending me headfirst down the white-frost covered, wooden steps of the farmhouse. I gathered myself and proceeded to the car. He picked up a large, mud and ice-covered rock and held it towards me. I was afraid he was going to throw it at the car. Instead he yelled, "I might as well have a rock in the bed instead of you, you bitch! Don't you ever come back!" I started the car and backed away from the house with a very, very sick, sinking feeling in my stomach.

Amy rode with me back to our place at the seminary. Neither one of us said a word. I was choking back my tears, hoping that she would not notice my deep distress. "God, why is all of this happening to me?" I prayed. "Please tell me what to do." I glanced at Amy, her dead expression focused on the windshield, her jaw set tight. I knew the deep hurt she was feeling, and the fear. How could I help her when I couldn't even help myself?

By the time we neared the seminary I recalled that I had a little money in my purse. I looked at my watch. A quarter to nine it read. "Amy, let's see if we can find that snow saucer you have been needing. Then you can go out on the big hill with the other kids tomorrow." Her eyes lit up for the first time since we had departed the farm under such duress. Still feeling sick to my stomach, I mustered up my energy to stop at a store and search for the desired object. We found a snow saucer, a neon pink one, which she liked. Her mood was lifted, and she seemed more calm and ready to face a new week of school. God had answered my prayers, at least in her regard, and the snow saucer helped shift our focus from one life to the other.

I was living two contrasting lives—one filled with the joy of friendship, learning and expansion of horizons, the other filled with fear, mundane drudgery and flares of temper. I know I was not fair to Bonnie in her first year of college. My life was so full, I could hardly be the excited parent for her that I should have been. I even failed to detect that Krista was becoming depressed. I didn't know Bob would come to her workplace and chide or embarrass her. I can look back now and realize the difficulty they went through as I made adjustments to my life. Still I believe what I did in changing my life and theirs will have more important effects in the long run for all of us. I cling to that even now when feelings of guilt creep in and begin to feel overwhelming.

The week following the rock incident I had finals for fall quarter. I had also started attending a group for abused women in addition to my clinical and class work. It was always an evening I looked forward to, both for the company of women who had lived through what I had, and because I could release the emotional burdens weighing me down. I had also done some counseling with a pastoral care professor at the seminary. "Bob's behavior is not okay," he told me. "He has broken his marriage vows by not cherishing, loving, and honoring you." That was slight consolation when, even in his absence, I walked around in fear that he might come after me.

It took all the courage that I had, between sessions of final classes and final tests, to drive downtown to the courthouse and file for an Order of Protection. I had been told that it was the document that I needed in order to have some legal reason for calling the police should Bob unexpectedly show up at my front door. I knew God was with me as I took this very difficult action, because I was so weak and shaky I could never have done it alone. I sat in the waiting area and assessed the other women who were waiting for their turn to do that same thing—single women with faces covered in makeup, women with young children trying to keep them quiet and happy during the wait, women, who looked like a shower and some clean clothing might be a blessing. I felt out of place, like I shouldn't need to be doing what felt to me to be such a degrading thing. Yet here I was, among this small cluster of women seeking safety from the very men who were supposedly in a loving relationship with them. Most of them were young—perhaps no older than Bonnie—with small children in their arms. I felt sorry for them as I waited my turn to be ushered into one of the filing cubicles.

I filled out the paperwork—pages of description of the abusive incidents—and was granted the Order of Protection. I returned to the seminary to my final class in pastoral care as if nothing out of the ordinary was occurring in my life. Yet my mind was completely boggled by the events of the last weekend and what I had just done.

When I was granted the Order of Protection on that lightly snowy, November Tuesday, I had been told that, because it was to be served in a county other than the one I was living in, it would be a few days before my husband would receive it. "Could you make sure that it is not delivered to Bob until Friday?" I had asked the desk attendant. That was only delaying the delivery by one day, and I had a good reason for this request. Krista was turning sixteen that Friday, and I wanted to give her my old '84 Cavalier which was at the farm. She would go out to the farm on the school bus Thursday and get the car under the premise that I had given her permission to use it to take friends out for her birthday. Then she would keep the car at her residence in town.

The sheriff's department brought it on Thursday evening when Krista was still at the farm. Poor Krista had to view the scene of legality for the protection of her mother from her father first hand. At least, even though she had to watch Bob's confused and angry response to the legal document, he did not stop her from driving away with the car as planned. My phone rang off the hook with his queries about and protests against the order. "What is this? Why did you do this? Things weren't that bad between us! Well, last weekend wasn't so good, but it could have been better!" I heard on my answering machine before I turned down the volume. I felt sick, very sick. Needless to say, I did not sleep much that night.

The next day after my Confessions final, even though the weather had turned from a cloudy drizzle to a nasty sleet, I drove out to my hometown to deliver Krista's birthday present and wish her "Sweet Sixteen." I found Krista at a friend's house. The other girls were watching a video. Krista was curled up in the corner of the sofa with her eyes shut. What terrible thing had I done to my daughter? I was ruining her innocent, young life! "No mother should put her daughter through such torment!" I thought. Yet I didn't see that I had any choice in the matter.

I stayed at my parent's farm since I was in charge of making banners for the ecumenical Thanksgiving Service which our church was hosting. With pieces of fabric and glue ready, I was ready to lead a group of ladies in putting the banners together. As we were finishing up, who should come walking through the church door but Bob. There was not much I could do with the other ladies present so I tried to focus on the task at hand and avoid him as much as possible. By the time the ladies left for home, the snow was coming down fiercely, and there was already several inches on the ground. I packed up the assembly materials and headed out the door to my car. Bob followed in pursuit, still begging me, "Come on. Be reasonable. Think this over. You can understand why I acted like I did considering how you were treating me. After all," he said, "I wasn't that bad that you had to go to the sheriff!"

I answered his questions with simple, brief responses, telling him that even his presence here with me was a violation of the Order. Then I got in the car and drove off with him still standing there in the snowstorm hollering at me.

It was snowing very heavily and there were already banks on the road that the car would hit with a thudding sound. But I certainly couldn't go home to Bob and be in danger of being stranded with the girls on the farm in a snowstorm. Besides, I had to preside at my parents' church the next morning. If the weather was going to be horrid, I needed to be as close to the church as possible.

Aside from great anxiety over the entire situation, which was further complicated by the weather, I felt no anger at him. Nor did I feel pity. Instead I was ridden with guilt. Here I was driving away from the husband I had promised to spend my life with. Here I was shirking my wifely responsibilities. After all, I had made a promise. For better or worse were the words I had agreed to. I just didn't know that it could get this bad.

It snowed almost twenty-four inches that night and into the wee, morning hours. By Sunday morning snow had to be cleared from both my parents' driveway and the church parking lot before I could lead worship, a duty I had agreed to many weeks before. My dad was kind enough to take Amy to Sunday School at my home church, while I went to the other one. Although I feared I might see Bob come walking in for the worship service, much to my relief, he did not. The service went wonderfully well, and it was good to see the many people I knew since childhood at this important juncture of my seminary study. My mother and I went home to make Sunday dinner and were soon joined by my dad and Amy.

I did not go back to my home church to see the display of banners I had designed for the Thanksgiving service. I thought it best to remain at a safe distance for those first weeks after the Order of Protection. Instead, on Thanksgiving Eve I headed southeast out of the city to spend Thanksgiving Day at my sister's house with her family. She would be having the family dinner for my parents, sisters, and I the next day. Amy and I rolled out the sofa and spent the night. I felt safe and secure some ninety miles away from Bob, and the warm air of the furnace felt soothing blowing against my skin as I lay awake in the dark of the night. I was able to relax in that feeling of safety in a way I hadn't relaxed in weeks. The next day, following dinner and an afternoon of visiting, I followed my parent's car back to their farm to spend the weekend.

Saturday evening I got a call from Bob. "Would you please just meet with me and the pastor so that we can discuss all this?" he begged. I didn't think it would help to talk. But then again, what could it hurt either? So, although it was in violation of the Order of Protection, we met together with the pastor that evening. Bob more or less begged me to stay, that things would be different. He even cried. I did not cry. I had no tears left to cry. We parted ways that night and each headed our own direction. A feeling of great anxiety that was my constant companion whenever I thought about home and my marriage followed me from that meeting.

During the weeks before Christmas, Bob called me at my apartment several times. Although I should have never answered his calls, I thought that avoiding them would only make matters worse. Besides, his calls were positive. He told me about what was going on at home and in our local town. Although I felt disconnected from it all, I listened without cutting him off. I just wanted to keep some peace between us. Although I could have reported him for violating the Order, I didn't. I came back to my parents' farm on weekends so that Amy could go to Sunday school and I could help with services. Bob would come in and join us in the pew after which we would again go our separate ways. One day, shortly before the holidays, Bob begged, "Won't you please come home for Christmas?" Feeling sorry for him, I gave in to his request.

Bonnie was home at the farm during Christmas break. She had shopped with Bob for a Christmas present for me. She had decorated the house, and Bob had purchased some Christmas goodies in town. "Are you sure you want to do this?" the pastor, with a worried look, asked about my staying the night at the farm, the first night since the rock episode. I would stay at the farm, I had decided. After all, time had passed and all of Bob's and my encounters on the phone and otherwise had been civil. And I wanted more than anything that our family would be together for Christmas. Besides, I was scheduled to preach the Christmas sermon the following day. Being at our own farm would put me closer to my necessary destination.

The evening was a civil one. Bonnie had gone out of her way to clean up the place and decorate it. Bob was as polite as can be, and, for the first time in many years, actually seemed to be in the Christmas mood. I opened my present with my daughters and my husband anxiously look- ing on. The gift was a black skirt and red jacket dress combination. It was the right size and fit perfectly. Although I knew Bonnie had had a hand in choosing it, it was the first Christmas gift I had gotten from Bob since the girls were toddlers. I stayed the night. I slept in the same room and in the same bed as Bob, but I did not succumb to any of his advances. I still did not want him near me in that way.

When the icy cold of January came upon us, I continued to make the weekly commute and once again returned home to our farm on weekends. As for the Order of Protection, well, neither one of us was following it.

But he was the one in trouble legally if anything happened to me during the weekend visits. One might have thought, from the appearance of it all, that we would actually get back together. The weekends were civil. He didn't expect too much of me. He did his work outside. I studied inside while I washed the weekly wash and cleaned up around the house. But, although we slept in the same bed, me always on my edge facing away from him, we did not have sex throughout any of those months. I had totally emotionally left him by then, and try as I might, there was no turning back.

One beautiful evening as I walked alone on the land, I remembered something I'd written in my journal. *"To bid one last farewell, I walked around the farm. How peacefully it breathed on me a breath that brought me harm . . . So in the bidding of farewell, the tears that screamed to be, in grace-filled spaces also spoke in cries to set me free."* (October, 1996)

As the warm breezes of March began to blow the winter away, I knew I was leaving. Although I continued to spend weekends on the farm, I had no feelings, none at all—not anger, or hatred, and certainly not love—for my husband.

When Sunday school ended that May, I no longer returned every weekend to the farm. Amy was beginning to protest the weekly commute and complained that she no longer had anything in common with the kids in her class back home. She asked me one day, "Why can't we be like normal people and stay home on the weekend?" Home for her was now the apartment at the seminary and her involvement in her new school near there. My internship was lined up to begin in the fall, and I was mentally preparing to join a new worshipping community in the city. So, as I took my summer classes that year, our trips to the farm became less and less frequent and were primarily made in order for the girls and me—all my girls—to have a common meeting ground. By the time I started internship, we had pretty much quit making the weekly pilgrimage all together.

I was as glad as Amy to see it end. Going back and forth was physically and mentally exhausting. And when it comes to exhaustion, I had a grand portion of it that summer. Not only was I suffering from an underactive thyroid, which was wearing me down, but just the act of living was taking everything out of me. I was emotionally and mentally worn out from the turmoil of cycling emotions—guilt, fear, shame—constantly swirling around in my head. I was ready for some peace and quiet, a calm schedule, and rest. That summer that is what I did—I rested. I started taking a thyroid medication, read, relaxed, took only two summer courses, and gave my mind, body, and soul the rest they were yearning for. Bonnie and Krista would come up to visit when they could free up some time from friends and their busy work schedules, and I did not worry about them as much. They, as well as Amy and I, had grown accustomed to the way life was for us now. If they had any feelings about the new circumstances, they did not give me any indication that they were displeased with me. They sensed that I needed the rest that staying at the seminary was giving me. They also knew that I had done what I needed to do as far as leaving Bob and the farm goes, and that the four of us would all be better off in the long run because of it.

I spoke to a divorce lawyer, that summer. It was not the first time I had met with him. I had actually consulted with him the summer before I started seminary—to get advice, I had said at the time. At that time I could not and would not have really considered divorce. But it hung out there before me like this huge, uncertain elephant that I wanted to continue to pretend was not in the room.

By the time I had finished my second year of seminary and with the events of the preceding year, I was again feeling a nudge to acquire some legal advice. Certainly having had to obtain an Order of Protection for my own safety, and Bob's history of physical abuse of me gave me every legal reason I needed to end the marriage. But my religious background was still telling me otherwise. Yet I had sought the help of several clergy counselors and had learned in my women's abuse group that divorce is not wrong when one's own safety is at stake. "Does God want 'life' for you, or death?" one of my professors had queried. I went home to deliberate these conflicting views in light of my own disconnection to my marriage, a deliberation that would lie in the background for months as I was busy with my internship and the growing and learning experience which that was for me. There was the question for me always in the back of my mind, "How can someone who is becoming a pastor disobey God's will for marriage by obtaining a divorce?" and, along with it, the ever-nagging reality, "He beats me up. I don't love him."

Continuing therapy helped me get through this time. In late spring of my second year in seminary, I began seeing a different therapist, Dianne, who helped me make major breakthroughs regarding post traumatic stress disorder and my dissasociative abilities. She was the extra support I leaned on to end the marriage and make my final move away from the farm and the life associated with it. With her help I battled the dark angel that had besieged me. I stepped beyond the darkness and found new life.

Although Bob never gave up calling me, sometimes the conversations would take a negative turn. One week our phone conversations were particularly tense. The fall had been a wet one and the harvest difficult. His patience with me had worn thin. "What kind of a wife are you—you won't even come out to help when I need it!" The dairy inspector had come and had not been pleased with the mess in our dairy barn. Bob had been given a week to clean it up. Bob, busy with plowing, did not want to take the time to clean up the mess that had gathered in the barn since the last inspection. It had been my job to clean and prepare the barn for inspections. Now he was in trouble. How could he get the barn, which he had allowed to get filthy dirty, clean and the plowing done as well? Any suggestion I made, like hiring the young man who had helped us on the farm before to come and plow while Bob cleaned, Bob met with an angry retort. He wanted me to come and clean the mess. "After all," he said, "Do you think we have all the money in the world that we can just hire people and have to pay them." I hadn't changed my mind. I was busy with internship. The farm and the barn were no longer a part of my life. Bob had not been supporting us for some months. Why should I go back to clean?

Truthfully, the year had been an up and down one in our distancing relationship. At times Bob would go out of his way to please and placate me. At other times his anger would run away with him and a string of words and names would come spewing forth like lava from a volcano. One weekend when Amy had stayed with him for a visit, he had gotten angry when we met in a parking lot in order for me to pick her up. As we met Bob said that it was still early. "Won't you please come out to the farm for a few hours?" At my refusal Bob suddenly thrust the pickup into reverse while I was standing next to the open passenger door transferring Amy's bag from the truck to the car. He nearly wiped me out on the icy cement.

An incident the following Christmas was just as scary. I allowed him to come up to the apartment to share Christmas with the girls. I told him that we would have dinner at two o'clock. By four o'clock when he had still not arrived, we ate, and I took the girls to have a picture taken together. When he arrived to the apartment, he became angry because we were not there. When we returned, he threw his shoe against the refrigerator door. When I said he should go home, his mood simmered a bit. I was glad for the kids' sake that that was the only unpleasant incident of that Christmas visit.

Should I even have allowed him to come up to my place knowing the Order of Protection was still in force and I might be placing myself in danger? Probably not. But it was still confusing to me. I fluctuated between a cycle of feelings which did not include anger. I didn't know how to say no to him without making him angry. Of course, it wasn't my responsibility to keep the peace. But I was accustomed to that role so it was hard to give up engrained patterns of behavior. Besides, I felt sorry for him having to spend Christmas alone. Sorry enough to put myself in danger? Yes, I guess so. And I continued to think that it was important to the girls for all of us to be together for Christmas. Perhaps I was not thinking clearly. I would certainly agree with that. Yet, I didn't know how to leave the marriage. I didn't understand Bob was responsible for the results of his behavior.

As tough as my marriage was at the time, my internship and my new ministry were wonderful. As time passed I shared the strife in my marriage and the abuse more and more with my supervising pastor, the parish secretary, and the women in my congregation. All of them encouraged me to get out of the marriage and away from the abuse. One of the women, a well-educated, retired teacher, told me, "If you decide to go back, we won't let you!" I listened to what all of these advisors told me, I prayed about my marriage day after day, and I struggled with the decision that I felt I needed to make before I could go out as pastor of my own parish.

There was an incident then that seemed to pull the final thread from the fabric of the marriage. One evening after Bob and I had argued because I wasn't going to the farm when he wanted me to, he actually drove up to the seminary in anger. After an angry call and his threat to come after me, I had called the police. "What should I do when he comes?" I asked them. With an Order of Protection in place, I was advised to call them as soon as he arrived and not to open the door to him. Both Amy and I waited anxiously, nervously, as we knew he was enroute on the hour plus journey from the farm to our apartment.

After what seemed ages, the doorbell rang. I wanted to give him a chance. I did not want to provoke the scene that I felt would follow. And I did not want to get him in trouble with the law. I wanted to warn him that I would call the police if he didn't leave. With the screen door locked, I opened the apartment door with the phone's receiver in my hand. "Go home," I said, trying to sound as confident as I could even though I was trembling from head to foot. "I will call the police if you don't leave now!" I said as I closed the door. He stayed outside ringing the doorbell repeatedly. With Amy anxiously rocking on her bed, finally I opened the door again, and in his view dialed the number. Within seconds there were squad cars and red flashing lights coming from all directions. Seeing them, Bob fled through the stairwell, out the other side and away into the darkness of the night with officers in pursuit.

I locked the apartment door as I had been advised to do and waited, not knowing where he had run, not knowing what was happening. The officers appeared to be searching as Amy and I peaked out between the blinds.

The flashlights and the red, flashing lights were all over the outside area as fellow seminarians looked out wondering what in the world was happening in this otherwise very peaceful place. Knowing Bob was still on the loose, I was afraid that he would return, break down the door, and come after me in anger. Amy and I sat quietly in the dark, seeing the red light from a squad car flash intermittently through the blinds against the living room wall. I peaked out again. The pickup was still parked in the lot near my car. "Oh, dear, will Bob go after and destroy the car?" I wondered.

After a long tenseness, I saw Bob being led by the officers across the parking lot. They were talking to him. Then he got into his pickup and headed up the hill to an adjoining street that would take him back to the freeway which led back to the farm. One of the officers turned back towards my apartment, and soon I heard the doorbell. "Are you alright?" he asked. I assured him that we were shaken but otherwise okay. "We sent Bob home. He's not to return." Then he left his card with the case number and a direct line phone number "in case I needed it."

I was nervous as I looked out of the window into the darkness hoping at least one squad car would remain to guard us through the night. None did. I worried that Bob would drive around the city for a while only to return to the apartment sometime later during the night. I did not fall asleep easily that night. I lay in bed and tried to put the scene of the evening behind me. I was in a state of vigilance for Amy's and my safety. And certainly I was praying that Bob, angry at me, would not seek out the other two girls in retribution. He did not return. When he called some days later, he acted as if the incident had never occurred.

That is what was so confusing about the situation for me. An episode like the one I just described would occur, and a short time later Bob would interact with me as if it never happened, as if life was just normal and everything was great. This type of behavior had occurred time and time again during our marriage. As I've said before, it is called crazy-making behavior, and it is. It keeps a woman constantly off balance so she never knows what to expect next. Because it's so confusing, it keeps the woman from acting consistently for her own safety. Bob certainly did his share of it with me.

On February 14, 1998, I sent the papers to the lawyer filing for a divorce. It was unusually warm on that winter day. The sun had burnt off a morning whitefrost, and the sidewalk was wet as I walked from the car to the post office in the neighborhood near the seminary. By afternoon, the skies had become overcast although the air was mild, and I sat down on one of the benches resting along the sidewalk leading from the campus center to the library. I wrote in my journal, " . . .*so, celebrate this Valentine's Day without me, for the journey only leads 'away'.*" *(February, 1998)*

I did it. I spent Valentine's Day at a workshop, preparing for the summer children's program I was in charge of at my internship site. I was going on with the tasks at hand pushing all feeling beneath the surface. Should I have been angry or disappointed in Bob's behavior, regret the almost twenty-four years I had spent in my marriage? Or should I have been elated and up-lifted that I had finally made the decision and taken the step that so many around me had encouraged me to take? I remember not feeling anything—being totally numb.

About a month later Bob was served with the papers. He immediately came up to my apartment and asked what they were all about. "You can't get a divorce. You're going to be a pastor. Pastor's are supposed to be loving and forgiving." After a few hours of his begging and my refusal to change my mind, he left. Although he still called me occasionally, he did not show up at my doorstep at the seminary until long after the divorce was finalized.

As an identified abuser, the only way Bob could attend the divorce proceedings was if he obtained a lawyer. He did not. So it was only my lawyer and I presenting the case before the judge on that warm, sunny day at the end of May in 1998. Between the cases of traffic violations, under-age drinking, and possession of illegal drugs, the judge heard my divorce case. He reviewed the materials and looked over the Orders for Protection. Within what seemed like minutes, the divorce was granted.

The lawyer spoke as we exited the courtroom door. His words rang deep, *"You've been single now four-and-a-half minutes. How does it feel?' I looked at him, but there was no answer. How does one give answer to what one does not herself understand? . . . and to be single or married at this point seemed immaterial, neither status holding meaning for one who does not know herself. So then, who am I now?"* *(July, 1998)*

Exhaustion was the only emotion I could identify after the entire ordeal. Not sadness, not anger, not guilt, not shame. Exhaustion, pure and simple.

During the summer I was busy with the work of my internship, mothering Amy, and having my other two girls up to stay with us at our seminary apartment occasionally. The heat of the summer moved into the autumn coolness as I moved into the final year of my internship and my final year as a seminary student. This year was be filled with its own joys and challenges as I participated in final interviews and synod assignments in the process of moving toward graduation and ordination. Bob continued to call regularly just to talk or to try to convince me that he had really changed. I traveled back to the farm a time or two to pick up items that were still in the farmhouse. Bob attacked me one last time, that time in front of others behind the church at my dad's funeral. Despite it all, still depressed and very busy learning to deal with my new life, I forged forward, visiting the river or contemplating jumping off a high bridge when despair seemed to get the best of me. Something quite beyond me would hold me back from making the final jump, and I would return to my apartment and my child and go on with life. I had finally taken leave of my marriage. And now I had to learn to live again—live into a future of uncertainty. The butterfly was beginning to find her wings. With God's help, she would finally learn to fly.

To my ex-husband:

Musing Of an Abused Wife

In cries of screaming silence
I dwell in unresolved memories
of undeserved abuse.
Like flashes of frightening light
and crashes of booming thunder
in endless days of "night"
my mind exclaims its terror
in a void.

Was it something I did,
or something I should have done?
Was it my mind in its inadequacy,
or my inability to read yours
that brought you down upon me?

Even cries and pleadings
could not touch
your anger
when wheels of wrath
began to turn.
And I was but the soiled rug
beneath your feet
when stormy waves of violence
spouted from your being.

I could have loved you dearly—
heaven knows I tried to
please you.
I could not bring an earth treasure,
but even angels
could not have loved you more.

I bore your bruises silently
because I couldn't understand
how I had enraged you so.
In shame
I wished to die beneath the sea.

Now
The greatest task of all
stands foreboding in my path.
To forgive—
almost too great a favor
for my human mind to undertake.
To forgive—
Repelling and compelling both.
To forgive, to rid us both of it.
But only to remember
That I may seek help for myself,
That I might pray for help for you,
And that,
In remembering,
It might not happen
Ever again.

(Written in May 1996 in response to "Remebering Jepthah's Daughter",
by Gwen Sayler, Violence, *Lutheran Women Today*,
Augsburg Fortress, Minneapolis, MN, November, 1995, pp. 25-27)

Now I Become Myself

Now I become myself. It's taken
Time, many years and places,
I have been dissolved and shaken,
Worn other people's faces,
Run madly, as if Time were there,
Terribly old, crying a warning,
"Hurry, you will be dead before—
(What? Before you reach the morning?
Or the end of the poem is clear?
Or love safe in the walled city?)
Now to stand still, to be here,
Feel my own weight and density!
The black shadow on the paper
Is my hand, the shadow of a work
As thought shapes the shaper
Falls heavy on the page, is heard.
All fuses now, falls into place
From wish to action, word to silence,
My work, my love, my time, my face
Gathered into one intense
Gesture of growing like a plant.
As slowly a the ripening fruit
Fertile, detached, and always spent,
Falls, but does not exhaust the root,
So all the poem is, can give,
Grows in me to become the song,
Made so and rooted so by love.
Now there is time and Time is young.
O, in this single hour I live
All of myself and do not move.
I, the pursued, who madly ran,
Stand still, stand still, and stop the sun!

Fourteen: **Gentle Unfolding**

It is late afternoon. The summer has drawn to a close, and the tired afternoon sun brushes its strokes of dusty light across my fingers as they work diligently on the keyboard of my computer. I am busy at this task of writing, sitting in the bedroom I turned into my office eighteen months ago. The room is filled with the misty sunlight of autumn and its accompanying warmth. Around me everything is in order—the deep brown, corduroy recliner where Krista's eleven-year-old cat likes to sleep, the side table we bought at a garage sale and topped with multi-colored napkin, the used eggshell lamp, a bookcase with the statue of old man wisdom, perched on top, an etched, wooden rack from which heart-shaped trinkets cast squiggly shadows on the wall. My degrees and certificates hang, neatly framed, above the desk on which my computer rests—degrees and certificates, which are part of my new life, my single life, the simple life in which I now find myself. They are part of this new story of my life.

It has been ten years since I woke up one morning only to see the abuse that dominated twenty plus years of marriage flash through my mind like a lightening storm finally let loose from its clouds. It has been ten years since I began the struggle through the deep depression into which I fell. It has been ten years since God came to me so openly, so blatantly, to call me into this new life in which I find myself. It has been more than five years since I walked out of the courtroom on that late May day as a single woman. It has been five years as well since the law enforcement officers pulled my husband out of the wooded area behind the seminary apartments.

Time has its way of changing the people and the things of life we so often take for granted. I have graduated from seminary. I have been ordained as an official pastor in the denomination of the church, which I now serve. I have been pastor to a congregation in this city for most of the time since my graduation. I'm told that I am good at it, whatever that may mean. I have married and buried, baptized and communed, preached and taught, organized events and led them. I have visited the sick and the shut-ins, counseled people, and prayed with people. It is fulfilling work, and, although I am hesitant to admit it, and at times I feel an inadequacy in my abilities, I am enjoying it. With God's help, I can do this task to which I have been called.

I miss my former job in that I think of my clients and wonder how each of them has progressed since I left eight years ago. I have never gone back to visit since I walked out of the door on my last day as their program coordinator. I think to do so would be too heart-wrenching. I cannot be pulled back into my old life. Often I am reminded of my clients however when I pass a disabled person on the street or overhear the conversation between a direct-care staff person and his or her client in a store. I was called on this past summer to be with a mentally disabled person in the terminal stages of cancer. What a gift my former life was in informing my present responsibilities!

Within the last ten years, I have come to call a number of places home. First there was the seminary apartment to which Amy and I fled for safety and from which Amy and I moved into our new life. It will always hold a special place in both of our hearts.It was from this little apartment that Amy set out bravely on her first day at her new school. It was to this little apartment that Amy brought the results of budding friendships. It was here that I studied and wrote my way into my new career as I made new friends among my fellow classmates. It was here that we celebrated my graduation from seminary.

Next was the apartment in the multi-level, stone, rambler-style four-plex not far from the seminary grounds. Krista moved here to join us following her high school graduation. While we lived here, I received my "call" to the church I now serve. While living in this apartment, I celebrated my ordination. It was here that Amy grew from being a little girl into a teenager starting high school. And while we were here, Krista obtained her first, post-high school degree. This is the apartment home Bonnie would come to visit as she finished her first four years of post-secondary education and began her life as a professional. Both the girls and I did much growing while living in this apartment. Together here, we slowly experienced growth into our new life away from the farm.

Finally, there was the move to the house I purchased on Roma Avenue where I now live. From this house the girls, now young women, have moved forward with their lives. From this house I move forward with my own. I have had more than two years now to make the little house on Roma my own—painting, decorating, collecting needed items from thrift stores. It is a small, one-and-a-half story, wood -frame house that sits neatly some several yards from the street. With trees arching up from behind, it reminds me of a little cottage tucked away in the woods.

The yard is neatly trimmed with morning glories creeping their way up fences and rails. I have laid a border of crescent-shaped brick along the house in places that I have chosen to fill with colored flowers. The tiger lilies and day lilies are direct descendents of the perennials my parents so ardently kept around their farmyard. Others are replicas of the flowers that surrounded my childhood memories—daisies, hollyhocks, tulips, irises, honeysuckle. My father died during my last year of seminary, an event I still feel saddened by, as he did not live to see my graduation or ordination, two events he would not have wanted to miss. And my mother, whose physical disabilities required her to move off of the farm following my father's death, is showing the signs that the years from there to here have laid upon her. The farm of my childhood, and the one to which I sought safety during the most turbulent times of my marriage, is no longer a part of my family's life. I keep in my heart those times when, innocently as a child, my parent's farm held me safely in its care.

Next to this bedroom-turned-office in which I work, is my bedroom, light yellow with white-painted woodwork, bright and inviting. Those items, which are most important to me, are placed throughout this room: Curly, a teddy bear I claimed during my struggle in leaving my marriage; a large, blue, stuffed Eyore, a gift from Amy at a time when I spent many of my days in tears; three eyelet and lace angels, each bearing a bow of the color of my daughters' months of birth; a picture of myself as a three-year-old, dressed in my Sunday best and smiling; graduation pictures of the girls, and a snapshot of my three daughters, now all grown women. Under the pictures I still have the plaque, "Those who walk in the sunshine of God's love gather rainbows all along the way." Indeed, my daughters are rainbows in my life, rainbows which have kept me going in the turbulent struggle of the last ten years.

I still spend a lot of time in my bedroom, just as I spent a lot of time in my little, study-bedroom at the seminary. I find myself often just lying on the bed. I need time to myself these days—time to rest, to let the thoughts of my former life and my present life churn themselves into the proper place in memory; time to re-group in order to go on, in order to meet the new day's challenges as they come. The turmoil of the past has taken its toll on my emotional and physical resources. Sometimes the small CD player, which sits on the shelf beside the bed, provides background music for this churning of memories and thoughts that now seem part of a life that never really belonged to me. Yet, I have these memories. They are part of what has shaped who I am today. They are part of how I do ministry, and of my choices in what is important in life and what is not.

My life on the farm—do I miss it? I think of it often. I think of how pretty the farmyard would look in the summer when the grass was neatly trimmed and the flowers were blooming. I think of the large vegetable garden I so neatly kept when I see farmer's market signs go up around the city. How handy it would be to walk out of my kitchen door and across the lawn to pick some fresh, ripe, juicy sweet corn for supper, or to snack on some crisp, sweet, green, baby peas. I still remember how to process tomatoes or make dill pickles. There are ways in which the farm fed my soul in spite of its incessant, demanding schedule and the accompanying abuse by my husband which occurred there. The farm filled me with nature, fresh air, and space in which to live and breath. I think at times, in the darkness of the night, of the freshly planted windbreak, of nursing the baby trees to life, and of how the breeze would pass through the budding trees and send the grasses swaying. I think of the cool quietness of the empty, corn crib with the rays of sunlight making slanted patterns through its slated sides, the smell of musty, aging corn. I think of the calm sleepiness of the hay barn, where I would lie down on the bales and watch the pigeons walk the rafters, the scent of fresh cut grass and alfalfa wafting through the silent space. I think of how crisp, and shiny, and beautiful my house would look when I had cleaned and polished it from top to bottom in preparation for some special celebration.

Yet the farm is the place where I was punched and kicked, called names and belittled. The farm is the place where I would be forced to hide in a cornfield, or in a cattle bunk, or behind a building, or under a piece of machinery to escape an almost certain attack. There are these memories, these unpleasant and terrifying memories, mixed between the pleasant ones. The thoughts of them cause a certain confusion in my mind. These are the memories that churn alongside the pleasant ones while I lay on my bed and try to make sense of the last thirty years of my life. When I think of these times, I can feel my breathing quicken and my heartbeats grow intense. I hold these memories of the farm in the recesses of my mind like pictures in a scrapbook. I can pull up the pictures of that life or watch them like a video when I catch myself looking inward instead of forward. Sometimes, these memories belong to me. Most often they seem like they belong to someone else, someone who no longer is.

Bob still lives in that farmhouse, running the land which used to be ours. The last time I was out to see it, he had changed little or nothing about its appearance. The decorations I had placed on the wall years before remained. There were pictures of each of the girls at a younger age, like snapshots of a former time, hanging in the dining room. Above them was the photograph of the two of us taken around the time of our fifteenth anniversary. We were neatly dressed and smiling those false smiles that one uses for a professional photographer. The same furniture, my furniture, rested in roughly the same places that I placed it more than a decade ago.

The house had not been cared for. The floors and rugs showed the effects of years of use and wear without being scrubbed or vacuumed. Cobwebs, covered with a thick, dusty film, draped themselves from corners and curtains. Dishes, silverware, pot and pans, and even food items sleep silently in the cupboards just where I placed them so many years ago. The house, a large, square, wood-framed structure, seemed to stand as a monument to a past that now resides like an unreal memory in my mind. Yet, it is the house and a past which resulted in my daughters' births—those persons in my life who transcend the past and bridge it with the present and the future. It is that house and that past which has fed my mind with a wealth of experience, which shapes my todays as I live each day of my life.

It is hard to describe the feeling of how the past and present come together, of what the past ten years of turmoil have been for me. I fell into a black hole and have come out on the other side of it into a completely new and different life. Sometimes the enormous weight of being brainwashed, of living in that state for so many years comes crushing down upon me with a terrible sadness. I feel like twenty plus years of my life are gone—just gone! It is at those times that I entertain thoughts of ending it all, to escape it once and for all.

At times, especially when I was beginning this new life, I just wanted things to be the way they had been before the knowledge of the abuse confronted me. As time went on, however, I came to the conclusion that my life would never be as it was before. I had been awakened, awakened to both the abuse and the possibility that lay before me. I had been awakened to myself, to my own personhood with its accompanying dreams and desires. And, I had been awakened to God's call to me, God's call for me to enter the ordained and formal ministry of the Church.

As I said earlier, I suffer from post-traumatic stress disorder and its accompanying depression. It is a condition which often accompanies soldiers on their return from the danger, violence, and trauma of war. I have learned that when the perpetrator of the violence is someone who is known, trusted, and loved, someone on whom one's life depended, the condition is often more severe and the recovery time longer. The condition affects every moment of every day of my life. I startle easily. I become depressed often for both apparent and unapparent reasons. I have difficulty trusting people, especially those people I want to allow close to me. I have low self-esteem which I try to hide in my professional life but which often shows up insidiously in my private life and relationships. And, yes, even after the passage of ten years and with all of the accomplishments I have attained and the changes I have made during that time, I still sometimes imagine myself jumping over the edge of a bridge, or I find myself pacing the edge of a river. There is not one day that I do not think of the ordeal. It has both affected me and changed me—forever.

I have not had to make this journey into my new life alone. I have had help along the way. This help has come from pastoral counselors, therapists, legal advocacy groups, a women's abuse group and its coordinator, my own sisters, my spiritual director, and new friends who have come into my life. I continue to see my therapists and spiritual director on a regular basis. Help has also come from the members of my congregation, who I think do as much ministering to me as I do with them. I could not have made it without any of these many people, who now fill my life—all people I have met in the last ten years. In my terror, I would have decimated myself long ago without their encouragement and love. I owe them my life.

I could also not have made this journey without God, who remained so faithfully by my side even when I wanted to curse in anger and despair. God would lead me to a Bible passage, to a hymn, to a calm, natural retreat of nature in this large city when I felt most like giving up. Through it I would be restored and strengthened to go on. I have learned to live life in continual prayer these days. God feeds the depths of my heart and soul through constant communication. I owe God my life as well. God has plans for me. I am opening up to the possibilities that are being spread before me.

More than ever in the fifth decade of my life, I have been about the work of finding myself, and it has not been easy. I have had to give up all those definitions of who I was as I gave up the way of life which fed those definitions. I have had to give up ways of living and being in the world in order to move to the new place and be the new person I have become. I have had to define for myself what is important in life and what is not. My values have been challenged in ways I could have never imagined they would. This process is not finished. I suspect it will go on as long as I am alive. And, as it continues, I say that I am surviving domestic abuse. I have not yet survived it. I'm not sure if anyone really totally does.

Do I hate Bob for everything that happened and for all that he did to me? Some women in the abuse group I participated in shared their anger at their partners. I did not. I have felt only a bit of anger related to certain occurrences. I have felt some anger by the fact that Bob was not a good father to his children and that he did not share the duties of parenthood and home life. I have felt some anger as he has interrupted my new life with some inappropriate, short-sighted, or even mean comments. Mostly, I feel a deep sense of pity for him, pity that he seems to be trapped by his limited ways of thinking. I feel sorry for him—that what I call his mistakes have essentially destroyed his life and the life we could have had together. His problem screams for professional help. He cannot see it and does not seek treatment. I still see the up and down, Dr. Jekyl and Mr. Hyde behavior that was such a prominent part of our relationship, although I do not have much contact with him these days.

Do I forgive Bob for what he did? If that forgiveness involves actually saying to him "I forgive you", no. I'm not sure if he has ever said to me that he is sorry for his actions. But I forgive him enough to keep moving forward with my life. I continue to work at building a life for myself that is uplifting and rewarding, a life that is an expression of who I am and my relationship to God. For me, to forgive is to move on and live one's life in the best way one can, letting go of the misfortunes, unfairnesses, and atrocities of the past. That is what I am doing. I have a full life—a nice place to live, a fulfilling career, people—both friends and professionals—who are supportive and surround me with love. I have a very special relationship with God that feeds me and allows me to bring others to faith. What else is life about? The past decade has been a process of definition and redefinition for me.

Yet sometimes, in the midst of all the change and redefinition of the last ten years, I feel like I have been standing still, especially these days as my life moves in a fairly calm, fairly predictable routine. The winds have blown, the branches have fallen, the voices have called for me to return. I, the pursued, who madly ran, stand still even as I become myself.

I am reminded that my life is both mine, and that it's God's. I was created to be free—free to be who I am and who God created me to be. God guides that journey to be sure. God has certainly had God's will with me! Yet, I am free to make choices within the path that God leads me on. I am not someone's servant, an appendage to another person's goals. Like a butterfly can only touch so many flowers in its short life, I can only touch so many people in mine. I can only reach out in so many ways, do so many acts of kindness, preach and teach so much about God's love, and add a bit of sunshine or a rainbow along the way. But God willing, I will do what I can.

As I have been discovering who I am, I have also come to know that God has given me gifts beyond measure—gifts of creativity, intellect, empathy, and compassion. My hope is that through me in some way the world would be changed, one person at a time, moment by moment. I have been given wings to fly. Now I have the responsibility to use them wisely, joyfully. My other hope is that the wisdom and love God imparts through me might give both wings and a song to others who are still in chrysalis that they may take flight and find abundant life. That is my butterfly song. May its melody flow as far as the winds blow and the sun shines.

Appendix I

Courtesy of:
Domestic Abuse Intervention Project
202 East superior Street
Duluth, Minnesota 55802
218-722-2781
used with permission

Suggested Reading

Alsdurf, James and Phyllis. *Battered Into Submission*. Intervarsity Press: Downers Grove, Illinois, 1989.

Hoff, Lee Ann. *Battered Women As Survivors*. Routledge: New York, New York, 1990.

McDill, S.R. and Linda. *Shattered And Broken*. Fleming H. Revell Company: Tarrytown, New York, 1991.

NiCarthy, Ginny. *Getting Free*. The Seal Press: Seattle, Washington, 1986.

Stom, Kay Marshall. *In The Name Of Submission*. Multnomah Press: Portland, Oregon, 1986.

For Clergy:

Adams, Carol J. *Woman Battering*. Fortress Press: Minneapolis, Minnesota, 1994.

Miles, Rev. Al. *Domestic Violence: What Every Pastor Need to Know*. Fortress Press: Minneapolis, Minnesota, 2000.

About the Author

Evelyn Dahlke spent more than twenty years as a teacher and Program Coordinator for a Day Training and Habilitation Program for mentally and physically handicapped adults while co-owning and operating a dairy farm owned by her and her husband. She graduated from Luther Seminary with a Master of Divinity degree in 1999 and currently serves as a rostered pastor in the Evangelical Lutheran Church in America. She has two poems published by the American Library of Poetry, *Butterfly Song* and *Most Precious Gift*. She is also an accomplished artist having done gift design for Augsburg Fortress. She makes her home in Roseville, Minnesota.

Made in the USA
Monee, IL
25 July 2022

10279174R00116